THE ECONOMIC STRUCTURE OF TRUSTS

The Economic Structure of Trusts

M. W. LAU

OXFORD
UNIVERSITY PRESS

OXFORD
UNIVERSITY PRESS

Great Clarendon Street, Oxford, OX2 6DP,
United Kingdom

Oxford University Press is a department of the University of Oxford.
It furthers the University's objective of excellence in research, scholarship,
and education by publishing worldwide. Oxford is a registered trade mark of
Oxford University Press in the UK and in certain other countries

First Edition published in 2011

Published in the United States of America by Oxford University Press
198 Madison Avenue, New York, NY 10016, United States of America

British Library Cataloguing in Publication Data
Data available

Library of Congress Cataloging in Publication Data
Data available

ISBN 978–0–19–960240–7

Preface

This book is based on my PhD dissertation, which began life in the autumn of 2005. Back then, I had very little idea how my dissertation would turn out. In fact, David Hayton, my then supervisor, instructed me at our first working meeting to do some research, write something, and come back in one month's time. Perhaps this was just keeping with British graduate research traditions, or perhaps he knew that something would pique my interest very soon; after all, he did teach me trust law over the years. Nevertheless, I remained clueless, if not slightly demoralized, for a few weeks until I stumbled across John Langbein's article in the *Yale Law Journal*. It was because of Langbein's essay that I spent the next two years responding to his and others' ideas on trusts.

By the time David left King's to become a judge, my project had reached both a milestone and a stumbling block. I had finished writing why the various obligational accounts are wrong; but I had nothing with which to replace them. David asked James Penner, who had just joined from the LSE, to be my new supervisor. James could not have come at a better time. His enthusiasm for property gave me the necessary impetus to offer a property-based account of trusts. It was also James who insisted that I turn my dissertation into a book.

There are two observations that I should make about this book. First, it is as much about trusts as it is about property. The two are so intertwined historically and doctrinally that they are still taught as 'Property I' and 'Property II' in some English law schools. Yet somewhere along the way in legal and economic history, property lost its direction and trusts have been slowly drifting into the orbits of contract and entity. Because of all their ties, I think the only way to rehabilitate the trust is by first restoring property as a coherent concept.

Equally, this is not just a law book. Its title *The Economic Structure of Trusts* neatly captures the fact that it is about trusts, and not trust law. Trust law is very different from trusts, even though understanding the former is a prerequisite to studying the latter. Modern trusts are nothing like the Victorian-esque trusts that form the staple of trust cases and the two might as well be separate subjects. The study of trusts, I think, blends idealistic textbook laws with economics, history, and cynical insights into wealth and human nature. This is why I enjoyed writing this book.

During the last five years, many people have supported me in completing this project and I owe them a lot. David Hayton and James Penner have been great supervisors, but so has Paul Matthews, who was my secondary supervisor throughout my two years at King's. As a practitioner, Paul provided valuable insights to trust practices. Equally instrumental to completing the dissertation is my former wife, Karen Sett Wong; she has probably read the text more than everyone else added together. I was examined by Joshua Getzler, Robert Chambers, and Philip Rawlings. They were tough but fair examiners and the book certainly benefited from their criticisms. For the Delegates of the Oxford University Press to approve the book proposal, I had to secure the endorsement of the three anonymous reviewers; their criticisms and suggestions only made the book better.

Throughout the project, I received help from many people. Frederique Meyer provided trustee practice insights and also motivated me throughout; Michael Goldstein shed light on tax issues. Karen Tang translated some important French text; Carmen Wong, Angie Hung, and Suki Chan assisted me tremendously with proofreading; and Connie Cheung and Eric Cheung commented on the manuscript in its various forms. Last but not least, the staff at Oxford University Press has been very helpful in the last, long mile of this project. Alex Flach and Chris Champion first put my proposal forward whilst Natasha Knight saw to its approval by the Delegates. Lucy Ford and Rob Crossley have been very supportive during the production process.

I have had the tremendous privilege to learn from and work with some of the best trust minds in the world. I have also been supported by many kind individuals along the way. I am very grateful for all of this and I hope that this book will live up to their expectations. All errors and omissions are legally and equitably mine.

M. W. Lau
Stockholm
September 2010

Table of Contents

Table of Cases

Table of Legislation

Introduction

Trusts are ubiquitous among common law jurisdictions and Anglo-Saxon economies. They can be used to structure many aspects of modern socio-economic life: from marriage settlements to divorce settlements; from caring for young children to carrying out the wishes of testators; from securitizing assets to organizing insolvencies; and from investing mutual funds to divesting real estate holdings. In many respects, the trust as a legal institution is as important as the contract or property. Frederic Maitland praises the trust as 'the greatest and most distinctive achievement performed by Englishmen in the field of jurisprudence'.[1]

Lawyers with fond memories of equity mythology from their law school days will recall the medieval origins of the trust. The romantic narrative usually involves a knight embarking on a Crusade, who transfers his land to a trusted friend to hold for and to give to his son in the event of the knight's untimely demise in the Holy Land. When the knight returns victoriously, he finds that his trusted friend has taken over his land. When asked to return the land, his friend refuses and the common law courts reject his case as he made a valid and outright transfer to his friend. The knight pleads with the king's Chancellor, who holds that his friend's conscience has been affected and orders the return of the knight's land—and, as though by magic, the trust was born.

Although this tale may have some historical basis, trusts did not suddenly spring into being but rather evolved through a centuries-old process that continues to this day. They take their basic structure from medieval uses, where a feoffor conveyed land to the feoffee to hold for the benefit of the *cestui que use*. Although often dated back to the fifteenth or sixteenth century, isolated instances of uses can be found as early as the 1320s.[2] Uses for the intergenerational transmission of land arose with the convergence of three

[1] F. W. Maitland, *The Collected Papers of Frederic William Maitland* (Cambridge University Press, Cambridge 1911), volume 3, 272.

[2] J. Biancalana, 'Medieval Uses' in R. Helmholz and R. Zimmermann (eds.) *Itinera Fiduciae: Trust and Treuhand in Historical Perspective* (Duncker & Humblot, Berlin 1998), 113.

practices.[3] The first was the rise of testaments and executors. The second was the practice of granting land to strawmen who would grant the land back. This was done to circumvent common law restrictions on changing the terms of the landholding (for example, converting land from fee simple to fee tail). The third was the practice of making conditional grants, usually to secure the performance of certain activities. Apart from the intergenerational transmission of land, uses were employed very early on to secure debts (1337), to avoid creditors (1376), to evade litigation (1377), and to evade (religious) taxes (1391).[4]

The Statute of Uses of 1535 marks an important milestone in the history of trusts. It sought to abolish uses for fiscal and political reasons but failed because lawyers worked around the Statute and the courts sided with them.[5] In the end, the need to abolish uses came to an end and uses emerged from hiding as trusts. The trust's ongoing evolution can also be marked by other significant milestones, such as its immense popularity in the nineteenth century or the rise of offshore trusts in the latter half of the twentieth century. How we date 'classical' and 'modern' trusts is of historical interest only. More importantly, two aspects of trusts differentiate the classical from the modern ones. The first is the subject-matter of the trust. Most uses and classical trusts concerned land, whence the idea that they were merely sophisticated conveyancing devices. The Law of Property Act 1925 significantly reduced the number of types of legal interests in land and mandated that all other interests must only exist behind trusts. But even before 1925 when more types of legal interests existed, the trust was already performing its role as a creative enabler of co-ownership structures in land. To be sure, medieval uses could be involved with chattels from the outset.[6] Trusts in the sixteenth century also involved money and pieces of gold and silver plate.[7] Nevertheless, the trust of

[3] Ibid. 117. [4] Ibid. 112.

[5] The Statute converted a legal estate held by T for the use of B into one solely held by B. Resonating modern anti-avoidance statutes, it sees through the veil of the use and identifies the beneficial owner as the real owner. To get around the Statute, lawyers devised the use upon a use. This is where a legal estate is held by T1 for the use of T2, who holds it to the use of B. In applying the Statute, the courts executed the use between T1 and T2 but they chose to disregard the use between T2 and B. After execution, T2 still holds the estate for the use of B; the trust as we know it today was born out of the use upon a use. That the use upon a use defeated the Statute is beyond doubt, but some have argued that it existed well before the Statute's introduction. See N. Jones, 'The Use Upon a Use in Equity Revisited' 33 *Cambrian LR* 67 (2002).

[6] R. Helmholz, 'Trusts in the English Ecclesiastical Court 1300–1640' in R. Helmholz and R. Zimmermann (eds.) *Itinera Fiduciae: Trust and Treuhand in Historical Perspective* (Duncker & Humblot, Berlin 1998), 160.

[7] N. Jones, 'Trusts in England after the Statute of Uses: A View from the 16th Century' in R. Helmholz and R. Zimmermann (eds.) *Itinera Fiduciae: Trust and Treuhand in Historical Perspective* (Duncker & Humblot, Berlin 1998), 179.

land, manifested earlier in the form of strict settlements, dominated classical trusts. The change in the dominant subject-matter of trusts came about with the change in the constitution of national wealth. The agrarian economy slowly became industrialized and along with it came new forms of wealth (in bank accounts, bonds, and shares) and a new class of wealthy people—merchants and industrialists—who were as eager as landed families to preserve and transmit their newfound wealth with trusts.

The second aspect that differentiates classical and modern trusts is the nature of trusteeship. In the classical trust, the trustee or feoffee was a name-lender, a human instrument, or mere stooge. To be fair, even stooges had duties to perform beyond lending their names. For example, executors of testamentary trusts often had to give alms to the benefit of the testator's soul; but such duties were one-off in nature. In more sophisticated settlements concerning land, trustees could be asked to take possession of the land if, for example, life tenants were threatened with insolvency. Although not necessarily one-off, such duties were contingent and temporary. One can say that the main function of classical trustees was to distribute assets in ways not allowed at common law.

In the modern trust, however, the trustee is no longer just the mere holder of title to complicated co-ownership arrangements. Trusteeship in modern trusts takes on a significantly more active, if not onerous, character. In fact, it has been suggested that the burdensome and time-consuming nature of trusteeship deterred many and spurred the introduction of trustee remuneration.[8] Modern trusteeship is active in two significant respects. First, with assets mainly held in the form of cash, bonds, and shares, the trustee actively manages a fund of money and seeks to maximize its value for beneficiaries. The main exception to this is trusts in land for beneficiary occupiers, as they are not considered by law to be held for investment purposes.[9] Second, the changing nature of the subject-matter of trusts also means that distribution is subject to management and influenced by tax and other considerations. Trusts of land were predominantly for beneficiary occupiers, and there was not much distribution to speak of other than the trustee conveying to subsequent beneficiaries. This was only reflected in late twentieth-century legislation, when the imperative nature of the trustee's duty to sell the land was removed.[10] But where funds of investments are concerned, more flexibility with distributions is possible.

[8] C. Stebbings, *The Private Trustee in Victorian England* (Cambridge Studies in English Legal History, Cambridge University Press, New York 2001), 30–4.

[9] See *Re Power's WT* [1947] Ch 52; Trustee Act 2000, s 3(3); and generally Trusts of Land and Appointment of Trustees Act 1996.

[10] Trusts of Land and Appointment of Trustees Act 1996, s 4(1).

To put trusteeship in perspective, trustees did not have a default and broad power of investment until recently, with the Trustee Act 2000.[11] But the practice of trustee investing goes back much earlier. Even the important case of *Speight v Gaunt* is not particularly historic.[12] The law on trustee investments was already developing more than one and a half centuries before *Speight*; the case of *Bromfield v Wytherley*[13] decided—wrongly, with hindsight—that where a trustee of money places it out in funds, or on other security, he is entitled to retain the profit because he also bore the risk. The same can be said of trustee management of distributions. Charitable trusts have always involved trustee discretion and are almost as old as the ecclesiastical courts that recognized them. Trusts to protect vulnerable people—through a primitive form of accumulation and maintenance—were also recognized very early on.[14] But despite the existence of trustee discretion over distribution amounts and timings, the discretionary beneficiary class was either very narrow, or in the case of many trusts, there were no such discretions at all.

Genuine discretion on distribution was intended from quite early on, but judicial willingness to give effect thereto arrived quite late. Initially, purported trustee discretions were overruled. For example, in *Warburton v Warburton,*[15] a testator appointed his two daughters as executors and directed them to distribute a sum of £400 and also the residue of his personal estate among themselves, and their brothers and sisters, according to their needs and necessities, as they in their discretion think fit. However, the court intervened and distributed a double share to the eldest son and heir, deeming him a 'necessitous person'. The court has oscillated among various positions throughout history, from the outright overriding of the trustee's discretion to blindly following the equitable principle that equity is equality,[16] and sometimes taking the middle ground by ordering the trustee to submit a distribution proposal.[17] Intertwined with the issue of the court's willingness to intervene in trustee discretions is the certainty of objects principle.[18]

11 Trustee Act 2000, s 3.

12 The case concerned trustees placing money with a broker who turned out to be fraudulent. As the trustee's actions were in accordance with standard business practices at the time, he was held not to be liable. (1883–84) LR 9 App. Cas. 1.

13 (1718) Prec Ch 505, 24 ER 227.

14 See generally N. Jones, *supra* note 7, 184.

15 (1702) 4 Bro. P. C. 1, 2 ER 1.

16 *Kemp v Kemp* (1801) 5 Ves. 849, 21 ER 617.

17 *Supple v Lowson* (1773) Amb. 729, 27 ER 471; *Bennett v Honywood* (1772) Amb. 708, 27 ER 459; *Brunsden v Woolredge* (1765) Amb. 507, 27 ER 327.

18 *IRC v Broadway Cottages Trust* [1955] Ch 20; *McPhail v Doulton* [1971] AC 424. In England, discretionary trusts are valid so long as the trustee can ascertain whether an object is or is not a

Nevertheless, despite judicial intervention over trustee discretions, trustees sought to actively manage distribution as early as the eighteenth century.

The combination of trustee discretion in investment and distribution—epitomized by the discretionary trust of an investment fund—blossomed in the nineteenth century, probably due to the confluence of two socio-economic developments. The industrial revolution was at its peak and large amounts of intangible wealth were being created, and the introduction of estate duty during this period made discretionary trusts—with no fixed beneficiaries for tax purposes—attractive, if not imperative, to the new rich.[19] The trust remained popular and experienced another boom after the Second World War with the rise of offshore jurisdictions. By the end of the twentieth century, the modern trust had taken shape as the discretionary trust of a fluctuating investment fund, requiring the active management of the trustee, whose role had been transformed from mere stooge into 'manager' in every possible sense. Of course, this stereotyping needs to be qualified: at the other extreme, bare trusts and nomineeships of land resembling medieval uses still exist today and continue to be useful for structuring simple co-ownerships of land. The evolution of the trust has not yet run its full course—this is most evident in the development of exotic offshore trusts.[20]

In modern times, trusts perform two functions. They allow specialization whereby the trustee and his delegates actively manage the trust assets, and they are chosen to manage because they have special expertise or are in a special position to do so. The second function is asset holding and distribution. Trusts allow for the temporal distribution of assets beyond the mortal limits of individuals, and, through discretionary distribution powers, also allow for the adaptation of distribution needs to changing conditions. Two other functions are often identified with trusts: tax avoidance, or even evasion, and achieving privacy. The former is arguably just a subset of the asset holding and distribution functions. More importantly, tax and fiscal benefits are essentially a gift of the state that can be removed at its whim, and

member of the class. This is so even if the trustee cannot draw up a complete list of beneficiaries and objects. In the United States, see Restatement (Third) of Trusts, §46 Reporter's Notes on comment d.

[19] Estate duty was introduced in 1889 (52 Vict. c. 7) and was the culmination of many other death-related duties such as the probate duty, the legacy duty, the succession duty, and the account stamp duty. When it was first introduced, estate duty was charged at the rate of £1 for every full sum of £100 (ie 1%). See generally A. W. Norman, *A digest of the death duties: with numerous examples illustrating their incidence, a copious index, and an appendix of the Customs and Inland Revenue Acts, 1880, 1881, 1888, 1889, the Mortmain and Charitable Uses Acts, 1888, 1891, and the Intestates' Estates Act, 1890* (W. Clowes, London 1892).

[20] The modern development of offshore trust products resonates with the uncontrolled growth of exotic financial instruments; and they are done in the name of market completion, ie there is something suitable for everyone.

are not intrinsically built into trusts. The latter is also a common function, but again, this is more a result of the state's light touch regulation and lack of reporting requirements than the inherent design of trusts.

Asset protection is often cited as an essential function of trusts, but this is a misunderstood feature. By virtue of the trustee's duty to segregate trust and personal assets and the trustee's lack of equitable title to trust assets, trusts do have some built-in asset protection. But this is better understood as a necessary corollary to the separation of ownership and control of assets, as the functions of specialization and asset holding and distribution cannot be performed if the claim to the asset is itself at risk. Although certain commercial transactions employ trusts primarily for the 'purpose' of asset protection (for example, a ring-fenced special purpose vehicle), such trusts are in essence just performing the holding and distribution functions. Asset protection is better understood as a means to an end—of specialization and asset holding and distribution—rather than an end itself.

Trust practices and functions have evolved, but how has trust law fared? The trust's continued success is clearly a testament to the ability of trust law to adapt and evolve. Closer inspection, however, reveals that trust law significantly lags behind trusts. This can be illustrated by the law's treatment of the rule against perpetuities. In the early years, the courts were happy to give effect to settlors' intentions, even if this tied up land for an extended period. In fact, some argue that the 'rule against perpetuities' is better labelled as the 'rule of perpetuities': judicial developments sterilized the policy issue of alienation into one of technical compliance—the timely vesting of future interests. As a commentator observes, 'recourse to the analogy with strict settlements in fixing the perpetuity period as a life in being plus the minority of the remainder-man paved the way for liberalisation of the rule to allow for any life or lives in being to be chosen and a period of twenty one years "in gross"...'.[21]

Crucially, however, 'a step of more fundamental significance was the extension of the rule regarding the remoteness of vesting from its original context within land law to settlements of personalty alone or mixed personalty and realty. This step was in fact taken in 1727, without apparent consideration of the fact that different policy issues are at stake'.[22] Furthermore, 'retention of the same underlying rule to govern both [realty and personalty] situations represents a significant and not wholly satisfactory

[21] M. R. Chesterman, 'Family Settlements on Trust: Landowners and the Rising Bourgeoisie' in G. R. Rubin and D. Sugarman (eds.) *Law, Economy and Society, 1750–1914: Essays in the History of English Law* (Professional Books, Abingdon 1984), 140.

[22] Ibid. 141.

legacy from the land law surrounding the emergence and acceptance of strict settlements to the trust law of the present day'.

The transplant of land law doctrines into trust law was not in itself sufficient to fill the analytical and legal gap created by trusts of investment funds. The phenomenon of trustees investing in funds of fluctuating assets with no intention to 'hold' them *in specie* but only to maximize their value required the development of genuinely new rules.[23] The development of the rule in *Saunders v Vautier*—from an originally narrow and specific one (the sole *sui juris* legatee of a testamentary disposition can take the legacy immediately) into a broad and general one (allowing all *sui juris* trust beneficiaries, regardless of the nature of their interests, to consent to trust termination)—reflects the changing nature of trusts and trusteeship.[24] As to trustee investments, existing ecclesiastical laws on executorships were also transplanted. But even then, trust law could not kick the old habit—the distinction between income and capital in trust law is also derived from land law.[25]

These doctrinal imperfections aside, the trust continues to be a spectacular success. But something is still amiss. The application of land law doctrines to trust relationships involving non-land assets does not sit well analytically. It may provide comfort to modern investment trust 'life tenants' that their interests are as solid and property-like as those of an eighteenth-century life tenant of a house. However, in light of modern portfolio theory that emphasizes total returns,[26] life tenancy in a fund does not really signal anything more than the temporal duration of the life tenant's claim.[27] How much the modern life tenant actually receives depends on the trustee's distribution and reinvestment rate, which is not fixed (although the trustee must be even-handed with all beneficiaries).

Another analytical problem posed by modern trusts and the retention of land law doctrines is the nature of the interests of discretionary objects. Because most trust interests are mapped out along common law property

[23] Ibid. 150–1.

[24] That is, tying up financial assets is not as strategically important (to wealthy families) as tying up land; therefore, the courts are less inclined to give effect to dynastic trusts of financial assets.

[25] M. R. Chesterman, *supra* note 21, 163.

[26] Modern portfolio theory seeks to maximize the risk/return trade off of any portfolio by emphasizing diversification and reducing the correlation between different investments within the same portfolio. The total return approach seeks to maximize the value of the fund for all beneficiaries by transcending the traditional dichotomy between capital appreciation and income. Although it is theoretically sound, the actual practice of total return is hampered by transaction costs and tax considerations.

[27] Although the life tenant will continue to receive income, the trustee is often empowered to reclassify and reallocate capital if, say, the capital gains significantly outweigh the income gains, causing an imbalance.

interests (for example, an equitable life tenant is just like a pre-1925 legal life tenant), there is the instinctive desire to find a common law property counterpart for the interest of discretionary objects—but there is none. The nature of such interests is so radically different from other equitable interests that to identify such interests in familiar terms (for example, applying the rule in *Saunders v Vautier*), we have to resort to viewing them as a group. Put simply, the land law doctrines and vocabulary that exist in trust law today and the Blackstonian conception of absolute property that such doctrines and vocabulary support do not fit modern trusts in terms of trusteeship or trust subject-matter. The problems that this ill-fitting relationship engenders are very subtle, but present significant analytical challenges.

There may be specific issues such as the inaptness of investment rules and the dislocation of discretionary beneficial interests. But, more fundamentally, modern trusts of investment funds defy our legal and economic understandings of property and ownership. When trusts concerned only land and other tangible things, beneficial interests could be considered informal rights of ownership, shadowing the common law in letter as well as in spirit; there was no fundamental problem with the legal analysis of beneficial interests. Bare trusts and nomineeships are conceptually no more difficult than, say, bailments or powers of attorney. Trust investments consisting of income and capital gains simply flowed to life tenants and remaindermen respectively. There was also no fundamental problem with any economic analysis—before and after 1925, the main economic function of trusts was to enable ownership interests and structures that were otherwise not allowed at common law. In other words, the trust can be seen as equity's response to an overly restrictive *numerus clausus* at common law.[28]

Modern trusts of investment funds challenge our legal understanding of property and ownership like never before because the beneficial interest, along with the assets involved, becomes intangible. In classical trusts, beneficiaries have a direct and strong relationship with the trust assets, hence the idea that they are the beneficial 'owners'. But with a pool of investment funds whose assets fluctuate, the beneficiaries' relationship with the trust assets is significantly weakened, if not completely severed. This offends our traditional understanding of property and ownership. From an economic perspective, the modern trust of investments is also in need of rationalization. The idea that the trust addresses the *numerus clausus* principle, although still valid

[28] *Numerus clausus* means 'closed number' and refers to the idea there can only exist a limited number of types of property interests. This rule has been rationalized as conserving information-processing costs. See T. W. Merrill and H. E. Smith, 'Optimal Standardization in the Law of Property: The Numerus Clausus Principle' 110 *Yale L. J.* 1 (2000).

in land and other tangible contexts, is significantly weakened. Financial assets—being the predominant asset class in investment funds—answer to no *numerus clausus* principle.[29] If the trust is no longer only about enabling co-ownership interests that are otherwise not allowed, then what is its economic function?

Just as land law loses its influence and meaning on trust law, something else is happening. For reasons of ideology and jurisdictional competition, alternative conceptions of trusts have emerged and the trust idea is rapidly changing. In the United States, trust law is influenced at every level by contractarian and entity approaches. From the country's leading trust scholars arguing that the trust is a contract or an entity to individual states legislating for entity-trusts based on maximum freedom of contract, these approaches—loosely termed 'obligational' for their emphasis on the personal obligations of trustees and third parties—dominate.

In offshore jurisdictions, trust law is being rewritten to suit the desires of settlors, who ultimately bring trust business to these island statelets. The centre of gravity that traditionally lies in between the trustee and the beneficiary significantly shifts towards the settlor. As Langbein would describe it, the trust becomes a deal between the settlor and the trustee. This seemingly innocuous shift, dubbed the 'trust deal syndrome' in this book, has profound implications. As the settlor's expectations and sense of entitlement grow, trust terms and practices will reflect the settlor and trustee's 'trust deal'. This ultimately translates into settlor-centric, if sometimes settlor-exclusive, trust laws, which, coincidentally, can draw support from obligational accounts of trusts. In doing so, very little regard is being paid to the conceptual coherence of the trust, let alone the practical consequences of such legislative handiwork.

On many counts, the obligational approach is just wrong. Apart from maximizing individual autonomy, neither doctrine nor policy informs the obligational approach. In fact, the beauty of this approach is that it breaks the trust idea down into mere personal rights and duties between the principal parties. Without any fixed framework, any conception of trusts can be created and rationalized. Also, implicit in the obligational approach is the rejection of the proprietary approach, which has worked relatively well for several centuries. The obligational approach is incorrect because it overlooks the property doctrines and policies that are so crucial to trusts as a functioning legal institution. Such an approach can only explain and rationalize areas of trust law that its proponents favour. A key omission of the obligational approach is

[29] Mainstream investments such as shares and bonds still conform to certain standard forms for regulatory and marketability reasons.

the nature of the beneficial interest, which can only be understood on property terms.

Beneficiaries are frequently referred to as residual claimants to the trust fund and its assets; even obligational accounts recognize this. But this is a gross simplification of their entitlement. Not only are beneficiaries residual claimants who take after trust creditors, each and every one of them is a residual claimant who may take after the others' claims. This is true whether we are describing a trust with a life tenant and a remainderman or a discretionary trust with multiple members in the object class. It is the proprietary niceties of beneficial interests that are key to understanding trusts, it is also these niceties that obligational accounts choose to overlook.

To their credit, the obligational accounts can certainly describe discrete areas of trust law, such as the generally default nature of trustee duties. But to project trust law as a general body of law through the lens of obligational accounts is to distort the legal reality. As a result of this distortion, the 'trust law' described in obligational accounts is either selective aspects of law that lend support to such accounts or, worse, merely the 'trust law' that such accounts want to see.

For example, apart from trustee duties, the vast majority of trust law consists of mandatory rules, where the default/mandatory rule model of contracts has little to contribute. Equally, the asset-partitioning attributes of trusts, on closer examination, consist of porous and patchy liability protection that will only frighten business organizers. Yet it is based on these features that obligational accounts assert that trusts are contracts or entities. And by projecting this distorted view of trusts a little further, one would arrive at their normative assessments that settlors should have standing to enforce their trust contracts or that trusts should get the legal personalities they deserve. Put simply, they are neither compatible nor coherent with the cases and statutes that we call trust law.

Further encroachment by the obligational accounts will have significant practical consequences. The kinds of trusts that the obligational accounts support have the potential to mislead creditors and counterparties and are also economically inefficient. Trusts that allow settlors to part with their beneficial interests but retain significant powers can mislead in both directions (that is, creditors mistakenly thinking that the settlor still retains an interest or that the settlor has disposed of his interest). Trusts that promote the perpetual tying up of wealth will lock up capital that could otherwise be used in risky, yet socially useful activities. Trusts that effectively disable the enforcement mechanisms of beneficiaries—the only incentivized enforcers in the trust relationship—encourage imprudent asset management, if not outright fraud.

The goal of this book is to argue that the obligational approach is wrong and that trusts are best understood from the perspective of property. That the obligational approach consists of contract and entity accounts of trusts is clear. The proprietary approach, however, lacks a proper definition and, where definitions can be found, they lack coherence. The legal idea of property that William Blackstone defended—tangible things protected by the right to physically exclude others from them—is now anachronistic. The predominance of intangible wealth in modern society means that almost anything of value and protected by the state can be considered property; this has led scholars to decry the disintegration of property.[30] Equally, the economic idea of property has contributed to the decline of the proprietary approach to trusts. This is because economists treat property rights as mere bilateral rights over the use of resources—they are contractual rights in all but name. In this way, economists are accessories to the obligational approach. For these reasons, it is not surprising to witness the decline of the proprietary approach and the rise of the obligational approach as the easy way out.

In the last decade, however, there is an evident revival of the idea of property. Philosophers, lawyers, and economists have written extensively about property and the policies and doctrines that it serves, seeking to understand property as an integrated and coherent concept. Drawing on these ideas, this book advocates a proprietary approach to trusts that can not only explain key aspects of trust law but also defend them on economic grounds.

The proprietary approach makes two central claims. The first claim explains that trusts exist as a functional extension of property. The institution of property incentivizes economic activities and helps coordinate the efficient use of resources, but it has limits. Where property stops, trusts extend its functions. The second claim is that trusts operate as a derivative form of property. This only works when trust laws exist to govern trustee behaviour, to define and delineate the beneficial interest, and to maintain a high degree of freedom to alienate it. Within this framework, the key criticism against the obligational approach is that it affords too much flexibility in these critical areas of trusts, to the point that this derivative form of property breaks down.

The proprietary approach is not merely an intellectual response to contractarian and entity accounts of trust. It is offered because the obligational approach is not only wrong, but is also being taken seriously in practice. To the extent that the Restatement (Third) of Trusts is heavily influenced by leading obligational scholars and silently endorses the idea that trusts are

[30] T. C. Grey, 'The Disintegration of Property' in J. R. Pennock and J. W. Chapman (eds.) *Property* (New York University Press, New York 1980).

entities, the obligational approach has already captured mainstream legal thinking in the United States. On the practical side, individual states have legislated for abolishing the rule against perpetuities and creating entity-trusts. This mirrors similar legislative development in offshore jurisdictions, which have been designing ever-friendlier trusts for settlors. Getting trusts right is important at the conceptual level if the trust is to remain as an independent legal institution and, more importantly, at the practical level if we want to mitigate the harmful effects obligational trusts can create. Abolishing the rule against perpetuities, creating non-charitable purpose trusts, diminishing the rights of beneficiaries, and stripping away trustee duties are harmful because they encourage trust assets, or the wealth they represent, to be inefficiently used or abused. If promoting efficient use of resources is one of the many goals of the law, then the proprietary approach should be taken seriously and trust developments should be reassessed.

The difficulty of undertaking this enterprise is compounded by the fact that there are many different kinds of trusts. That *Black's Law Dictionary* lists over 160 different types of trusts is testament to the institution's success and proliferation. The problem posed by this diversity is that any argument for or against the various accounts of trusts will have exceptions. An obvious example is that the beneficiary of a bare trust has real and direct equitable ownership of the trust asset, whereas this cannot be further from the truth for objects of discretionary trusts. This book will refer to and discuss all kinds of trusts, including bare trusts, discretionary trusts, business trusts, revocable trusts, and spendthrift trusts. But its main focus is modern donative trusts. These trusts are characterized by their gratuitous nature in that the settlor dictates the trust terms and beneficiaries have virtually no bargaining power at the time of settlement. Equally important is the reliance of such trusts on the trustee's exercise of his discretionary powers of investment and distributions. And as a result of the trustee's power to invest, an additional dimension of property—the fund concept—is embodied in these trusts.

This book focuses on modern donative trusts for three reasons. First, the law of trusts—as taught in law schools across the common law world—is primarily about donative trusts. Students may come across charitable trusts, pension trusts, or business trusts in their classes, but what they learn is the law of donative trusts. Second, donative trusts involve the greatest separation of ownership and control and their assets fluctuate from time to time as a fund. This makes them the most difficult kind of trusts to reconcile with our understandings of property and poses the greatest intellectual challenge. Third, the contractarian accounts of trusts are based on modern donative trusts. Hence, to refute these accounts and argue why the proprietary approach is the correct one, it is important to compare similar kinds of trusts.

Unless otherwise stated, the trusts referred to in this book are modern donative trusts.

This book is organized into three main parts. Part I deals with accounts of trusts as contracts. Chapter 1 discusses John Langbein's account of the trust as a tripartite contract. This is the original work of the obligational approach and represents the most extreme form of the obligational conception of trusts. Langbein's work is driven solely by his desire to see greater flexibility in trust terms and the settlor gaining standing to enforce the trust. For this, he frames a contract-based account of trusts where the settlor strikes a trust deal with the trustee over the management of trust assets. Not only is his account descriptively inaccurate and analytically flawed, it also completely ignores the nature of the beneficial interest and the conflict the beneficiary would have with the settlor if the latter were granted standing to enforce the trust. However, Langbein's account sheds light on the trust deal syndrome that exists worldwide, especially in the offshore jurisdictions. In this sense, Langbein is right to call the trust a deal between the settlor and the trustee over how trust assets should be managed and distributed.

Chapter 2 discusses Robert Sitkoff's agency costs theory of trust law, which is another contractarian account but infused with more sophisticated corporate law and economics analyses. The agency costs theory of trust law makes two claims: that the trust is a nexus of contracts (like a corporation) and that trust law seeks to reduce agency costs. These two claims mirror those found in Michael Jensen and William Meckling's agency costs theory of the firm, upon which Sitkoff's ideas are based. The nexus of contracts idea is untenable because the trust at best resembles a tripartite contract and one requires stretched imagination to conjure up a multitude of contractual parties within the trust. But Sitkoff's insistence on the nexus of contracts idea is unnecessary as there is some independent merit to the idea that trust law reduces agency costs. Most obviously, the trustee's duties of care and loyalty are unequivocally agency cost reduction devices. However, other duties and relationships that Sitkoff frames as agency ones are dubious. For example, Sitkoff labels the tension between the settlor and the trustee as to whether the latter will continue to implement the wishes of the former once he is dead as 'temporal agency cost'. This tension is less an agency cost problem than a simple conflict of interest between the settlor and the beneficiary. Other trust duties and rules, such as the duty of impartiality, are better understood as addressing conflicts of interests between various parties rather than being agency cost reduction devices. Sitkoff appears to implicitly acknowledge this but this calls into question how much of trust law—apart from the duties of care and loyalty—is really about reducing agency costs. Finally, an unintended consequence of the agency costs theory of trust law is that it accidentally lends credence to the idea that the trust is an asset-partitioned agency. This observation extends Langbein's trust deal syndrome where the more controlling the settlor becomes, the more the relationship resembles an agency, albeit one with asset-protection features.

Part II evaluates the idea that trusts are firms and there are two strands to this idea. Chapter 3 looks at the argument that the trust is a legal firm, in other words, a legal entity. This is the view espoused by, among others, Henry Hansmann, Ugo Mattei, and Reinier Kraakman. Their argument is that because the trust has asset-partitioning features—just like the corporation—it is a *de facto* legal entity. While it is true that the trust has asset-partitioning features, they are a lot weaker and more porous than those found in corporations. This lack of ironclad asset-partitioning is probably why most businesses are organized as corporations rather than trusts. Also, legal personality is not a prerequisite to asset-partitioning. As Joshua Getzler and Michael Macnair argue, the judiciary achieved a high degree of asset-partitioning long before the state allowed general incorporation. This chapter also questions two commonly held beliefs: that the trust is a key player in commerce and that civilian lawyers can only conceive of trusts as entities. On the former, trusts merely have a supportive role to commerce and proponents of the trust-as-entity idea over-emphasize its importance. On the latter, although conceiving the trust as an entity is the easiest way out as entities are universally recognized, there are other functioning civilian legal concepts that the trust could map along. After all, trusts are not and need not be legal entities.

Chapter 4 serves as a rejoinder to the first three chapters by testing if trusts are economic firms. Whether it is the tripartite contract, the nexus of contracts, or the legal entity account of trusts, these theories either are transplantations of economic theories of the firm or at least rely heavily on their ideas. For such interdisciplinary transplant of ideas to work, there must be substantial similarity between trusts and economic firms. Therefore, it is important to test the link between the two. To do this, leading economic theories of the firm can be applied against trusts. These theories explain why firms exist and, if trusts are firms, should also be able to explain why trusts exist. After applying three of the leading theories in the field, the chapter reaches the conclusion that the existence of trusts cannot be explained by theories of the firm. In other words, trusts are not firms. The reason is obvious: trusts do not generally produce goods and services—they hold and manage assets. As trusts do not produce goods and services, two key features of firms—the transfer of partly finished products or services between participants of the firm and the endgame of selling them to the open market—do not exist. Since trusts lack the touchstones of firms, it is no wonder that the theories struggle to explain their existence.

Chapter 5 concludes Part II by answering the question: since trusts are neither entities nor firms, how can their commercial utility be explained? To do this, the trust is compared with the corporation. The trust's perceived weaknesses—being its lack of legal personality and transfer of goods and services within it—are actually its strengths. The duties and potential liabilities of trustees encourage trusts to conduct risk-averse activities that involve open market transactions. In this way, the market pricing mechanism supplements the trustee's comparatively limited knowledge and skills (the trustee is usually alone, whereas the corporation may have hundreds or thousands of people). Whether it is cause or effect, trusts are at their best when they are used to hold property.

Part III is all about understanding trusts as property. Chapter 6 traces the historical decline of property and trusts as coherent concepts. Property in law declined during the twentieth century and prior to that, the Blackstonian idea of property—with its emphasis on man's relationship with things protected by the right to exclude—captured people's minds for centuries. This changed as wealth increasingly took on intangible forms and scholars such as Wesley Hohfeld atomized *in rem* rights so that they are indistinguishable from *in personam* rights. As a result, almost any transferable rights of value are recognized as property. Blackstonian property, which was most suitable to land and tangible things, has become an anachronism. Attempts to reformulate Blackstonian property, by reinterpreting the thingness and exclusionary requirements, are commendable but do not succeed analytically. Even worse, economists' understanding of property never got off to a right start. From the very beginning with Ronald Coase's seminal article, economists' idea of property rights consist of bilateral use rights over resources; they are indistinguishable from contract or tort rights. Coase's work is so influential that it has dominated the law and economics field for several decades. It has only been recently that scholars such as Thomas Merrill and Henry Smith have revived conceptualist views of property. With the legal and economic understandings of property in tatters, it should come as no surprise that trusts cannot find a stable proprietary base. Scholars such as Austin Scott and James Penner have tried unsuccessfully to defend proprietary conceptions of the beneficial interest that are strictly based on the *in rem* right to exclude. The end result is that property is no longer a credible foundation for trusts and in its place are the obligational approaches. The ascendancy of the obligational approaches can be found everywhere: in non-charitable purpose trusts, in trust laws allowing settlors to retain extensive powers, in trustee exemption clauses, and, sadly, even in leading United States Uniform Acts and Restatements of the Law.

Chapter 7 charts the conceptualist revival of legal and economic property, which has only occurred in the last decade or so. On the legal side, it is now accepted that the exclusion requirement is no longer sacrosanct, but separability remains a key criterion when defining property. Property scholars have also gone one step further by rationalizing property in a fund as a distinct legal concept. Although there are conceptual disagreements between proponents of property in a fund, the idea goes a long way to explain the fluctuating nature of trust assets and the beneficial interest. On the economic side, Merrill and Smith have revived the traditional *in rem* conception of property and justified it on economic grounds of conserving information-processing costs. More importantly, the right to exclude is seen as a useful, low-cost proxy to govern resource use. Only with these refined understandings of legal and economic property in place can a proprietary approach to trusts be considered.

Chapter 8 lays out the economic rationale and organization behind trusts. The rationale behind trusts is that they extend the functions of property. The functions of property are twofold: it incentivizes economic activities and it coordinates the efficient use of resources whilst conserving on information-processing costs. But there are limits to property's ability to deliver on these functions and where property stops, trusts extend them. Most importantly, the coordination function of property relies on the right to exclude as a rough proxy, or baseline, for access to and use of a resource. The exclusion strategy is binary and blunt in nature, in that either an owner grants someone access to a resource or he denies him of it. The opposite end of this strategy spectrum is governance, which uses specific rules and terms (such as contract or tort) to control more precisely the use of resources. The trade off between the two strategies is that exclusion is cheaper but imprecise and governance is costly but customizable.

The trust is a rarely seen exclusion and governance paradox, where it uses governance rules to achieve effective exclusion. This exclusion effect is felt by the trustee and third parties in the sense that they are economically and physically excluded from the trust assets. The beneficiary effectively gains a right to exclude through the myriad rights and powers against the trustee and outsiders. This use of governance rules to achieve an exclusion strategy is reflected in the legal and beneficial title split. The two titles are not competing against each other; the latter is simply a derivative of the former. The beneficial interest is an interest in a fund, which is made up of trust assets that change from time to time. It is often said that the *bona fide* purchaser exception is the Achilles' heel of the beneficial interest. But properly understood, this is its strength because it enables the beneficiary to have an interest in a fluctuating fund and not just in static property.

Trust law is organized at two levels: it is both asset-centric and wealth-centric. By asset-centric, trust law—especially trustee duties—ensures that trust assets are well managed and productively used or invested. At this level, trust law serves to protect trust assets rather than the beneficiaries. It is at the wealth-centric level that trust law protects the economic interests of the beneficiary. For example, trustee damages are restored to the trust fund and not to the beneficiary. This affirms the idea that the beneficiary's interest is in the fund and not directly in the assets. The *bona fide* purchaser exception seeks to ensure that when transactions are made and assets are exchanged—even in breach of trust—the trustee obtains good value for the asset and thereby preserves the value of the fund. At the same time, the rule against perpetuities and the rule in *Saunders v Vautier* serve as a bridge for the beneficiary to transition from intangible wealth to tangible things. This is necessary because much that trusts are a functional extension of property, they are temporary and second-best. Trusts must eventually terminate.

Chapter 9 applies this new understanding of trusts and defines the boundaries of the trust concept. Further understanding the nature of the beneficial interest as a residual claim and the organization of trust law are key to identifying the proper limits of trusts. The residual claim idea is a very useful tool for understanding beneficial interests, especially when it comes to objects of discretionary trusts. The residual claim idea and the asset- and wealth-centric natures of trust law enable us to understand why some modern trust developments are bad. Excessively generous trustee exemption clauses, non-charitable purpose and perpetual trusts, and settlor retention of wide powers have all been criticized for violating the trust concept and stretching it too far; but so far these criticisms have been piecemeal and sporadic. Using the residual claim idea and other tools developed in this book, the property-based understanding of trusts provides a coherent argument against these novel trust developments.

In all, this book sets out to achieve two things. The first is to introduce and defend a property-based economic account of trusts. This account stands in stark contrast to the contractarian and entity ones that are prevalent in contemporary academic literature. The second is to influence legal scholarship on and developments of trusts. Given the state of trust law in the onshore and offshore worlds, these are rather challenging goals. But these are worthy goals because the contract and entity accounts are analytically wrong and the harmful consequences of novel trust developments will not become apparent for decades to come.

PART I
TRUSTS AS CONTRACTS
The Failings of Corporate Law and Economics

Part I examines two contractarian accounts that conceive of the trust differently. John Langbein's account conceives of the trust as a tripartite contract and Robert Sitkoff's account describes the trust as a nexus of contracts. Whereas Langbein emphasizes the predominantly default nature of trust rules, Sitkoff highlights the agency costs reduction role of these rules. Their accounts are clearly different and they complement each other in some respects, yet they do not succeed as theories of trusts. There is a reason for this failing: both accounts took corporate law and economics theories and forcefully transplanted them onto trusts without paying due regard to the trust's unique attributes.

Why was this mistake made twice? There are two reasons. The first reason is that with the decline of property as a coherent concept, scholars can hardly draw inspiration from property theories or ideas to explain trusts. As a result, they look to the trust's closest living relative, the corporation. Corporate law and economics is a rich and developed field with countless theories covering everything from the constitution of firms to director duties to shareholder rights. Since trusts and corporations are close cousins, it makes a lot of sense to apply corporate theories to trusts. The second reason is that corporate law and economics is predominantly libertarian in nature, as its proponents advocate for maximum flexibility and individual autonomy. This suits the ideology and agenda of scholars like Langbein, who wish to see a much more permissive and flexible trust law regime. But they are ultimately unsuccessful because the corporate theories are ill-fitting to begin with and unique trust attributes and doctrines reject them.

1

The Trust Deal and the Rhetoric of Contracts

Introduction

In 1996, an article by John Langbein in the *Yale Law Journal* started the obligational approach to trusts.[1] Despite its descriptive inaccuracies and conceptual flaws, 'The Contractarian Basis of the Law of Trusts' has pervasive reach in the common law world and all other law and economics accounts of trusts trace their intellectual lineage to it. Of course the contractarian account has its detractors, but their criticisms are topical and not sufficiently comprehensive. This chapter offers a thorough examination of Langbein's contractarian account. Although he relies on the forceful rhetoric of contracts, Langbein undermines his premise throughout the article. In the beginning, he claims that 'trusts are contracts'[2]; but towards the end he concedes that 'the trust is a hybrid of contract and property'.[3] Sandwiched between these two claims are countless concessions to and compromises with property doctrines whenever contract ones fail to explain certain trusts features. Trustee duties may look like contract terms, but ultimately trusts are not contracts.

Trusts should not be understood as contracts, even if only metaphorically, as there are too many anatomical differences between the two legal concepts. More importantly, trusts and contracts have very different philosophical foundations. Most trust rules are actually mandatory rules and most contract rules are default rules. It is easy to fall for the contract illusion when one only considers trustee duties (which are often default in nature) in isolation and

[1] J. H. Langbein, 'The Contractarian Basis of the Law of Trusts' 105 *Yale L. J.* 625 (1995), hereafter *Contractarian.* Langbein may have kick-started the obligational approach to trusts, but he is certainly not the first to analyse trusts in economic terms. See A. I. Ogus, 'The Trust as Governance Structure' 36 *U. Toronto L. J.* 186 (1986).

[2] Ibid. 627.

[3] Ibid. 669.

when one mistakenly believes that consent equates to contract. This leads to Langbein's incorrect assertion that the 'trust deal' between the settlor and the trustee is at the heart of trust law.

Although his account is flawed, Langbein's use of contractarian analysis and his normative arguments neatly capture the mindset of contemporary trust practitioners and their clients. This mindset, dubbed 'the trust deal syndrome', is closely associated with settlors' insecurity over trustees and their desire to retain control. This is why the trust can be considered as a 'deal' between the settlor and the trustee and not a relationship between the trustee and the beneficiary over trust assets. The contractarian approach encourages the trust deal syndrome with its doctrines that maximize flexibility, personal autonomy, and control.

This chapter is organized as follows. First, it lays out the contractarian account and its normative agenda. Second, it critically explains the account's flaws and weaknesses. Third, drawing on Langbein's emphasis on the 'trust deal', it discusses the trust deal syndrome and how it is influencing modern trust developments. Finally, it questions the merits of one of Langbein's normative claims: allowing settlor standing to enforce the trust.

The Trust Deal

Langbein's approach to trusts is simple and effective: he describes the trust as a tripartite relational contract and applies contractarian principles of corporate law and economics to it. It is simple because corporate law and economics have been studied for decades and many rules and principles have been developed.[4] It is effective because the corporation is a direct descendant of the trust and many corporate law and economics ideas appear to be applicable to the trust. In Langbein's account, the trust is a tripartite relational contract between the settlor, the trustee, and the beneficiaries. A contract is a relational one when important terms cannot be reduced to well-defined obligations.[5] Most relational contracts are long in duration, for example: long-term supply contracts, franchise agreements, and even marriage.[6] The role of contract law is merely to provide default terms—this reduces transaction costs because the contracting parties only need to state the terms that they want to depart from the default position.

[4] See the leading text in this field, F. H. Easterbrook and D. R. Fischel, *The Economic Structure of Corporate Law* (Harvard University Press, Cambridge 1991).

[5] C. J. Goetz and R. E. Scott, 'Principles of Relational Contracting' 67 *Va. L. Rev.* 1089 (1981).

[6] E. S. Scott and R. E. Scott, 'Marriage as Relational Contract' 84 *Va. L. Rev.* 1225 (1998).

According to Langbein, the trust is 'a deal, a bargain, about how the trust assets are to be managed and distributed'.[7] Crucially, this deal between the settlor and the trustee 'is functionally indistinguishable from the modern third-party-beneficiary contract. Trusts are contracts'.[8] By claiming that trusts are contracts, Langbein analyses trusts in contract terms. This analysis begins the moment the parties call their deal a trust. He says, '... by calling their deal a trust, the parties automatically incorporate an extensive body of default terms that have proven highly suitable for implementing deals of this type. The contractarian account views the parties as choosing this default regime for their particular deal, except to the extent they modify it'.[9] The generally default nature of trust law has been further developed by Langbein in other articles.[10]

Langbein applies corporate law's philosophy of default terms to trust law: the state should provide an off-the-rack set of rules that parties are most likely to adopt or, where necessary, modify. Mandatory rules should be kept at a bare minimum as it is not the state's business to govern consensual dealings that are neither illegal nor contrary to public policy. To this extent, Langbein's account of trust advocates a minimalist regulatory role of the state and argues for terms expressly agreed by the trust parties to be given maximum effect.

Another important consequence of treating trusts as relational contracts is the role of good faith in fiduciary duties. Langbein adopts Frank Easterbrook and Daniel Fischel's analysis of corporate fiduciary duties, which states that 'when the task is complex, when efforts will span a substantial time... a detailed contract would be silly. When one party hires the other's knowledge and expertise, there is not much they can write down. Instead of specific undertakings, the agent [the manager in corporations, the trustee in the law of trusts] assumes a duty of loyalty in pursuit of the objective and a duty of care [prudence in the law of trusts] in performance... The process is contractual—because both principal and agent enter this understanding for gain... [A] "fiduciary" relation is a contractual one characterized by unusually high costs of specification and monitoring. The duty of loyalty replaces detailed contractual terms....'.[11] More importantly, he agrees with

[7] *Contractarian, supra* note 1, 627.

[8] Ibid. 627.

[9] Ibid. 660.

[10] See J. H. Langbein, 'Mandatory Rules in the Law of Trusts' 98 *Nw. U. L. Rev.* 1105 (2004); J. H. Langbein, 'Questioning the Trust Law Duty of Loyalty: Sole Interest or Best Interest?' 114 *Yale L. J.* 929 (2005).

[11] F. H. Easterbrook and D. R. Fischel, 'Contract and Fiduciary Duty' 36 *J. L. & Econ.* 425 (1993), 426–7, Langbein's emphasis.

Easterbrook and Fischel, who say 'the concept of the duty of good faith, like the concept of fiduciary duty, is a stab at approximating the terms the parties would have negotiated had they foreseen the circumstances that have given rise to their dispute'.[12] For trusts, fiduciary duties serve as intention-implementing, gap-filling, default terms in the trust-contract between the settlor and the trustee. When a dispute arises, it is up to the court to conduct relational interpretation to 'discover' the terms that the parties would hypothetically have agreed to had the dispute been foreseen.

Continuing along the idea of hypothetical bargaining, Langbein argues that the prophylactic duty of loyalty ought to be relaxed if doing so would be consistent with the parties' intentions.[13] Using the well-known *Boardman v Phipps* case as an example, he argues that had the principal known about the potential for him to profit from the fiduciary's self-dealing, he would have allowed the deal.[14] Therefore, the application and enforcement of the duty of loyalty ought to vary according to the circumstances. Another important implication that Langbein argues is that settlors should have enforcement standing by default. This is a natural consequence of the idea that a trust is a tripartite contract but he strengthens his case by asking 'what was the intention of the parties to the trust deal respecting this point [?] . . . when such an intention-seeking standard is applied . . . the parties are routinely assumed to have intended enforcement by the promisee (settlor) as well as the beneficiary'.[15]

So much for trustee terms and settlor standing and their contractarian justifications. But when it comes to the proprietary features of trusts, Langbein does not offer substantive arguments as to why they are contract-like and not property-like. He does make note of the debate between Frederic Maitland and Austin Scott on whether the beneficial interest operates *in personam* or *in rem* and, unsurprisingly, supports Maitland's *in personam* position. In addition to explaining the law's historical resistance against characterizing the trust as a contract, he discusses the proprietary aspects of trusts only in passing. On the ring-fenced nature of trust assets, he simply says 'the handling of trustee insolvency is the feature of the modern trust that resonates

[12] Ibid. 438, fn 28.

[13] *Contractarian, supra* note 1, 665–7; Langbein has recently elaborated on this issue. See *supra* note 10.

[14] The case concerned a family solicitor to a trust that held a minority share in a company. The solicitor and one of the beneficiaries purchased a majority share in the company, with the acquiescence of the trustees, who decided against the investment opportunity. The solicitor and the beneficiary realized a large profit but the court held that the solicitor breached his duty of loyalty and must account for his profits, even though he could be generously remunerated for his services. [1967] 2 AC 46.

[15] *Contractarian, supra* note 1, 664.

most strongly in the property tradition'.[16] On the binding nature of the beneficial interest on third parties, he argues that 'the Chancellor's decree embodies a judgement about how far to impinge on outsiders to the trust deal between settlor and trustee in order to vindicate the deal. The policies that are being balanced do not turn on understanding the beneficiary's interest as property rather than contract'.[17] Towards the end of his account, he does concede that the property-like features of trusts require explanation. He achieves that in one stroke by asserting that 'the traditional, property-based account is easy to reconcile with the contractarian account: Trust is a hybrid of contract and property, and acknowledging contractarian elements does not require disregarding property components whose convenience abides'.[18]

Trusts are not Contracts

No contract or trust law textbook is known to entertain seriously the trust-as-contract idea and this tells us that, at best, it is a minority view of the law. But this has not stopped the contractarian account of trusts from gaining popularity and wielding academic and practical influence; so much that leading trust and equity academics considered and rejected it at a conference on trust law.[19] They did so primarily by pointing out the anatomical differences between trusts and contracts and they can be summarized here:

1. The settlor has no standing to sue the trustee in case of a breach of trust. This would not be the case with a breach of contract.
2. The settlor is able to act as trustee himself by a self-declaration of trust. One cannot contract with oneself through any means.
3. The beneficiary of a trust acquires a set of rights far greater than that of any beneficiary of a third party contract. In particular, the trust beneficiary's rights can bind external third parties.
4. The death of a trustee does not automatically terminate a trust; a reappointment of trustee will ensure the trust's continuity. In the case of a contract, the death of a contracting party usually terminates the contract.
5. A major breach of trust will not terminate the trust, which would be the case with a contract.

[16] Ibid. 667.
[17] Ibid. 648.
[18] Ibid. 669.
[19] D. J. Hayton, 'Overview' in P. Birks and A. Pretto (eds.) *Breach of Trust* (Hart Publishing, Oxford 2002), 379.

6. In the case of a breach of trust, the trustee is liable to restore the trust fund rather than compensate the beneficiary directly; the opposite is true with a contract. Also, unlike contracts, restorative rather than expectation damages are the norm for trusts.
7. The courts have an inherent special jurisdiction to advise a trustee on his powers and can even modify the terms of a trust. With contracts, courts will normally not interfere unless there is a dispute.[20]

Langbein's account only addresses some of these points, none of which is particularly satisfactory:

1. He normatively argues for the reversal of the no settlor standing rule because he says it is the parties' likely intention to allow for settlor standing.
2. He excludes self-declarations of trusts from his main account and deals with it in an appendix.[21]
3. He states that the beneficiary's ability to bind third parties is not necessarily proprietary in nature.
4. He rationalizes the court's inherent special jurisdiction as being part of the procedural regime that allows trust deals to be implemented.

So when trusts and contracts are compared side-by-side, it is clear that they are distinct legal concepts. Trusts are not contracts.

But this should not be the end of the enquiry; it is only the beginning. Suppose that one gives the benefit of the doubt and assumes that Langbein's tripartite relational contract is only an analogy. In that case, his inconsistent positions on whether trusts are contracts can be explained: trusts may analogously be contracts; but in reality it exhibits characteristics of contract and property. Can this be the case?

The Illusion of the Contract Analogy

The contract analogy may be a useful one. The advantage that analogies and metaphors have is they only need to approximate the subject-matter; factual inconsistencies can arguably be overlooked if the analytical benefits are strong enough. But it is wrong to analyse trusts analogously as contracts. The

[20] Ibid. 379–83. See also D. J. Hayton, 'The Trust in European Commercial Life' in J. Lowry and L. Mistelis (eds.) *Commercial Law: Perspectives and Practice* (LexisNexis Butterworths, London 2006).

[21] *Contractarian*, *supra* note 1, 627–8.

contract in Langbein's analogy is not just any contract; it is the Easterbrook and Fischel kind. Langbein subscribes to Easterbrook and Fischel's idea of the corporate contract, which minimizes mandatory rules and maximizes the role of default rules. Specifically, they claim that (a) default rules are rules that the parties would have wanted; but (b) by definition they are waivable so that parties can use specifically desired terms; and (c) the duty of good faith triggers the hypothetical bargaining process.[22] Trusts that follow such contractarian philosophies are almost a contradiction in terms.

On the first claim, whether or not default rules actually fulfil their role of supplying terms that the contracting parties would have wanted, the importance of their role is exaggerated. Default rules are merely the logical consequence of incomplete contracts: if the contract terms are silent on a particular matter and a dispute arises, the adjudicated or legislated result is deemed the default term. The contractarian narrative that default terms are what the majority of parties would have wanted and are designed to save transaction costs is just that, a narrative. As to whether default rules are actually what most parties would have wanted, it is difficult to provide an empirical answer. However, Alan Schwartz and Robert Scott point out that good default rules are hard to come by.[23] To be effective, default rules must (a) apply in very few possible states of the world; (b) be relatively simple in form; (c) be efficient in a highly heterogeneous set of circumstances; and (d) not rely on information that courts cannot conveniently recover.[24]

In the case of trust law, Langbein claims that the vast majority of trust law is default law. What he actually means is that trust law provides default terms to empower the trustee, to regulate his exercise of powers, and to provide for compensation.[25] If one adopts a narrow view that trust law is all about regulating the trustee, then Langbein's claim is correct. But in actual fact, most of trust law—be it statute law or case law—are mandatory rules. One must include within the body of trust law mandatory rules such as the beneficiary principle, the rule against perpetuities, the requirements of administrative workability, and the duty to segregate trust assets. These rules are the bread and butter of trust law; but they rarely come up in the trust deal between the settlor and the trustee precisely because they are non-negotiable.

In areas of trust law that are not mandatory, trust law is actually silent. For example, there is no default material purpose for why a trust exists (an

[22] F. H. Easterbrook and D. R. Fischel, 'The Corporate Contract' 89 *Colum. L. Rev.* 1416 (1989), 1444–8; F. H. Easterbrook and D. R. Fischel, *supra* note 11, 438.

[23] A. Schwartz and R. E. Scott, 'Contract Theory and the Limits of Contract Law' 113 *Yale L. J.* 541 (2003).

[24] Ibid. 547.

[25] *Contractarian, supra* note 1, 660.

important point when applying the *Claflin* rule)[26] and there is no default criterion for selecting objects for distribution. This is clearly because there is no lowest common denominator for trust uses and, applying Schwartz and Scott's criteria, no default rule operating in these areas of trust law can be remotely efficient for all trust situations.

So long as the mandatory rules are respected, most areas of trust law are not governed by default rules. To be sure, almost all contracts and agreements are incomplete. Yet there is no need for default terms on trust purposes or distribution criteria because disputes cannot arise in these areas of trust law. So long as the trust purpose and distribution criteria respect other mandatory rules such as public policy and administrative workability, the settlor's choices are unimpeachable. There is no need for default terms in these areas because it is whatever the settlor decides. Just as we do not generally distinguish between mandatory and default rules for property law, the same can be said about trust law. Property law demarcates the boundaries of property and ownership but does not suggest how owners should use their assets; we do not speak of residing in one's home as the default use of a house. Beyond mandatory trust rules, the minute details of how the trust operates are not governed by default rules; they are subject to 'freedom of trust'.[27]

Surely, when it comes to the trustee's powers and duties, the statutes and case law have much to say but to a large extent they can be overridden by the trust instrument. Therefore, notwithstanding the above arguments, trust law does contain some default rules and this is where they are found. But there are reasons why default rules have developed in trust law. One reason is the historical transformation of the role of the trustee. As the modern trustee becomes more active in the management of the trust assets, he needs explicit powers to perform his duties and also corresponding duties to keep him in check; he also needs to be compensated for his increased workload. As Langbein observes, United States trust law, especially those concerning the trustee's duties of investments, is largely shaped by the trust industry to reflect contemporary needs.[28] In both the United States and England, laws relating to the trustee's powers and duties have been codified in the last half-century.

A more important reason is that without default trustee rules, trusts are simply not workable. Even the most upright and diligent trustee cannot perform if he does not know what is expected of him; there must be some

[26] See text accompanying footnote 22 in Chapter 2.

[27] J. E. Penner, 'Exemptions' in P. Birks and A. Pretto (eds.) *Breach of Trust* (Hart, Oxford 2002), 250.

[28] See generally, J. H. Langbein, 'Why Did Trust Law Become Statute Law in the United States?' 58 *Ala. L. Rev.* 1069 (2007).

form of guidance for him. The waivability of these default rules does not have much to do with enabling the haggling settlor and trustee to reach their unique trust deal. Rather, they should be understood as being waivable because the settlor can choose how the trust asset is managed (in the same way that he can specify the trust's purpose and beneficiary class) and such default terms simply stand in for the sake of trust workability.

Certain trustee duties are not waivable, for example the duty to act in good faith. But instead of just explaining the simple non-waivability of this duty, Easterbrook and Fischel use it to introduce something completely different: the hypothetical bargaining process, which takes the 'what the parties would have wanted' spirit of default rules one giant step further. For them, the duty of good faith operates when a dispute arises and the contract is silent on the matter, courts would use it as an excuse and retrospectively look at the relationship and determine what the parties would have wanted had they foreseen the circumstances leading to the dispute. Surely if the parties want the court to 'discover' the terms that they would have agreed upon had they foreseen the circumstances leading to the dispute, they could explicitly address that with a 'hypothetical bargaining' clause rather than hope for it to happen with a good faith clause.

Another flaw of the hypothetical bargaining process is that the parties sometimes get a lot more than what they bargained for. On this point, it is instructive to review Deborah DeMott's criticism of contractarian metaphors.[29] Courts have actually recognized the hypothetical bargain mechanism that fiduciary duties imply.[30] But she distinguishes between courts finding implied-in-fact contractual clauses and recognizing a fiduciary relationship. With the former, courts will always imply a clause that is consistent with the express terms. With the finding of fiduciary duties, however, the courts are willing to override express terms.[31] DeMott believes that fiduciary duties possess superimposing attributes that mere contractual terms do not.

[29] D. A. DeMott, 'Beyond Metaphor: An Analysis of Fiduciary Obligation' *Duke L. J.* 878 (1988), hereafter *Beyond Metaphor.*

[30] See *Jordan v Duff and Phelps, Inc.*, 815 F.2d 429 (7th Cir. 1987).This case was decided by a panel of judges that included Frank Easterbrook (representing the majority) and Richard Posner (dissenting).

[31] DeMott cites the case of *Pillois*, involving an agency contract where the principal expressly had an unfettered discretion to determine the agent's compensation; the court held that there was an implied good faith requirement and that the agent was entitled to market rate remuneration. Here, implied-in-fact or hypothetically bargained terms have the effect of overriding expressly agreed terms. Even the prevention of opportunistic behaviour, often cited as a reason for the good faith requirement, fails to explain this case, as the contract here explicitly allowed the principal to engage in opportunistic behaviour himself. *Beyond Metaphor, supra* note 29, 893.

Hypothetical bargains and default rules aside, the single biggest failure of the contract model is its inability to explain the law. The contractarian approach is a rhetoric-rich ideology that seeks to promote individual autonomy and freedom. Its *modus operandi* is to muddle up consent with contracts and Langbein's contractarian approach to trusts is precisely doing that. At first glance, almost all private activities or relationships involving two or more parties can be reduced to contracts. But contractarians deliberately confuse contracts with consent. Consent is an easily understood concept, and is core in all activities or relationships that attract the contractarians' interest, including contract law itself. Contract law, in contrast, is a simple and narrow body of law that enables the formalization of most consensual agreements.

As DeMott reminds us, contract law is a 'richly textured body of law whose constructs cannot simply be transported into other legal contexts'.[32] This is rightly demonstrated in the difficulties of calling trusts contracts. Because contract law is the epitome of individual autonomy (at least in the private law context), it is being abused as a lowest common denominator in attempting to explain all consensual activities or relationships. In advocating for maximum freedom and autonomy, contractarians would garner more support if they characterized companies or trusts as consensual agreements, rather than insisting on contract law and the narrow and technical doctrines and terminologies it carries. It is precisely these narrow and technical terms that make contractarian analysis too simple and unable to explain the real world. Trust law is not merely a specialized branch of contract law with special features, which do not obviate the basic contractual analysis. The inability of basic contractual analysis to explain the vast majority of the trust's proprietary features cannot simply be ignored. One can only find an explanation in state-sanctioned property law. But, to contractarians, the introduction of property law overly complicates the analysis and irreparably violates their idea of contractual freedom and flexibility.

The Trust Deal Syndrome

The contractarian account of trusts is wrong in many regards, but it has got one thing right: it candidly captures the mindset of the trust industry and its clients—that the trust is a management contract between the settlor and the trustee. Langbein observes that trusts have evolved from medieval land conveyancing devices managed by socially upright gentlemen into platforms

[32] Ibid. 888.

for managing financial assets by professional service providers. By definition, the settlor is the one who bargains with the trustee and agrees to the trust terms. So, rightly or wrongly, the centre of gravity lies between the settlor and the trustee. The beneficiaries—even if they are the ones holding the beneficial interest—are secondary in the trust deal. There is also another reason why contractarian accounts place so much emphasis on the deal between the settlor and the trustee. Since it is already established law that beneficiaries have beneficial interests over trust assets, the property-like features of trusts may not be of great interest to academics and practitioners. The deal between the settlor and the trustee thus becomes the focus.

In addition, modern trusts are often characterized by several features that make the contract analogy useful:

1. The settlor's transfer of assets to strangers, sometimes in faraway lands.
2. The boilerplate nature of most trust deeds, even after they take into account the settlor and beneficiaries' unique circumstances.
3. The professional trustee's charging of a fee for its services.
4. The central role settlors play in trust creation and, sometimes, operation.

Objectively speaking, transferring title and control of property to a stranger—but not for his benefit—is a very unnatural act and requires more than just a leap of faith. It requires a contract, or rather, an enforceable agreement that could give the settlor peace of mind. This agreement is often the only connection the settlor has with what was formerly his asset so it should be drafted as extensively as possible, specifying what should and should not be done with the asset. This contributes to the boilerplate nature of trust deeds and provides a crucial security blanket to settlors.

The flipside to the desire for security and comfort through enforceable terms is the settlor's sense of entitlement. This sense of entitlement comes from the fact that the trustee is earning a fee that is normally deducted from the trust assets, which—but for the trust—belong to the settlor. To this end, a settlor would consider that the trustee is providing a service to him rather than to the beneficiary. As such, the 'trust deal' that Langbein claims is very real in many settlors' minds.

But the trust deal—a naturally occurring condition—turns into a malignant syndrome when settlors, encouraged by trustees and lax jurisdictions, go too far with it. Trust deal syndrome occurs when the trust relationship becomes one that is almost exclusively between the settlor and the trustee, to the virtual exclusion of the beneficiary. Of course, unless the settlor is the sole beneficiary, it will never occur on paper as beneficiaries will be involved. But when settlors retain too many powers or beneficiaries are completely sidelined, trust deal syndrome occurs. Offshore trusts or trusts that are used exclusively to avoid tax and shield assets are most prone to the trust deal syndrome.

Settlors of onshore trusts may be given the benefit of the doubt that they simply want a skilled professional corporate trustee to look after assets for the beneficiaries. On the other hand, settlors of offshore trusts are often driven by other additional considerations such as tax and privacy. The use of the trust's form purely as part of an asset-holding structure often diminishes the gift-giving and beneficial-interest-relinquishing motivations, and it certainly increases the settlor's sense of entitlement that the trustee is providing a service to him. To the settlor, the offshore trustee who is holding assets for his beneficiaries is no different from the accountants, lawyers, and other advisors; they are all just service providers. This trend is fanned by offshore jurisdictions' competition for trust business. To attract the trust business of settlors, they have produced trust laws that cater to almost all their wishes. The most tangible result is a variety of trust laws that allow settlors to retain substantial powers, which would not be possible under traditional trust doctrines.[33] A sympathetic interpretation of this would be that settlors are insecure and wary of what trustees thousands of miles away would do to the trust assets, which ironically are often located onshore. But the mirror image of this insecurity is the settlor's desire to retain control. In fact, the contract illustration starts to look weak and is arguably replaced by agency-in-law, as will be discussed in the next chapter.

To United States practitioners and users of trusts, these remarks are not that radical as some trusts there are indeed cognitively treated as contracts or even as the settlor's personal property. In terms of maximizing settlor control and minimizing beneficiary's rights, the American revocable trust simply puts even the most exotic Cayman Island STAR trust to shame.[34] Settlors of revocable trusts can revoke the trust at any time and it requires the trustee to obey the instructions of the settlor, even if they are contrary to the terms of

[33] For example, s 3(1) of the Bahamian Trustee Act 1998 provides that a trust shall not be invalidated by reason of the settlor reserving to himself powers, among other things, to revoke the trust; to appoint trust property; to amend the trust; to appoint or remove trustees, beneficiaries, and protectors; to require his consent to any act or abstention of trustees. Similar laws can be found in the various Caribbean jurisdictions.

[34] The STAR trust is the Cayman Islands' non-charitable purpose trust. In addition to non-charitable purposes, they can also be settled for human beneficiaries but with their enforcement rights and powers all removed and assigned to an enforcer. Cayman Islands law also validates settlors' retention of powers, including the power to revoke the trust. See Cayman Islands Trusts (Amendment) (Immediate Effect and Reserved Powers) Law 1998.

the trust or the trustee's fiduciary duties. Furthermore, the rights of the beneficiaries are exercisable by and subject to the control of the settlor.[35]

Most non-United States lawyers would consider such a trust to be a testamentary trust or a bare trust with a power of appointment; yet it is a valid *inter vivos* trust. The difference in opinion is primarily driven by tax considerations. In the United States, settlors do not use revocable trusts as a means to avoid taxes. Rather, a revocable trust provides a good alternative to the probate system, with greater privacy and efficiency. Since there is no need to give due regard to greater tax liabilities, settlors can drop the pretence and treat assets of revocable trust as theirs. There is a lesser need for comfort, security, and entitlement as all of these are actually enshrined in the law and the settlor is at the centre of the trustee's attention. Cognitively, at least, the trust deal between the settlor and the trustee is real.

The Conceptual Uncertainties of Granting the Settlor Standing to Enforce

One of Langbein's key normative arguments is the creation of a default rule to give the settlor standing to enforce the trust. Langbein's main reason is that the settlor and the trustee probably intended such an arrangement and, by extension, contracting parties ought to have standing to enforce contracts. This idea of allowing settlor standing can be considered independently, regardless of the merits of the contractarian approach. The juridical basis for allowing settlor standing can indeed be found; but once it is established, it is not easy to reconcile with the position of the beneficiaries. In other words, it is not a workable proposition.

The idea of allowing settlor standing is just one of many aspects of enabling the settlor to participate in the trust. As discussed above, the most extreme form of settlor participation is the revocable trust in the United States. Offshore jurisdictions have also legislated for special trusts that enable settlors to be almost as omnipotent as their American counterparts. To do this, offshore legislations specifically (a) allow settlors to reserve a list of significant powers without invalidating the trust; (b) also allow non-beneficiaries to enforce the terms of the trust, often in lieu of the actual beneficiaries.[36]

[35] Restatement (Third) of Trusts, §74.

[36] See *supra* note 33 and also Cayman Islands Trusts Law (2001 Revision), s 100.

Langbein's idea of allowing the settlor to enforce the trust by default does not fall neatly into either category. Standing to enforce is qualitatively different from powers typically retained by settlors, such as those on investments and distributions. These powers enable settlors expressly to take an active role, whereas allowing standing only enables the settlor to seek recourse against the trustee for breaches of trust. Also, special offshore trusts do not confer enforcement rights to beneficiaries by default. Langbein's idea envisions the settlor's standing to enforce coexisting with that of the beneficiaries.[37]

Although standing to enforce has not been legislated in any major jurisdiction and is qualitatively different from other modes of settlor participation, it is a comparably tame idea. Yet, this tame idea gives rise to perhaps more conceptual problems than any other ones. When the settlor retains powers such as those on investments or appointment, there is no uncertainty as to the allocation of functions and powers. Similarly, when a third party is designated as the enforcer in lieu of a beneficiary, it is clear to the trustee to whom he is accountable. Never mind the nature and validity of such trusts; the allocation of rights and duties is crystal clear.

But in the case of granting the settlor standing to enforce—alongside the beneficiaries—it quickly becomes unclear as to who should prevail. If a trustee breaches his duty of care and the settlor is not pleased but the beneficiaries deem the breach to be acceptable, can the trustee still be sued? One can compare the situation with a corporate derivative suit and argue that the settlor can indeed sue; but what if the beneficiaries actually consented to the breach? In addition to granting the settlor standing to enforce, such a default trust law must also address these potential settlor-beneficiary conflicts. In line with the contractarian spirit, Langbein would probably argue that the settlor should prevail if there were disagreement with the beneficiaries over enforcement. However, this would render the beneficiaries' position quite awkward—not as weak as beneficiaries of revocable trusts but definitely not on par with beneficiaries as we know them. On the other hand, if the law states that beneficiaries should prevail, the settlor's standing to enforce is meaningfully watered down. If both the settlor and the beneficiaries are aware of the breach and the latter do nothing about it, it is probable that they do not want to enforce and if the settlor chooses to do so, he would be vetoed anyway. Until such conceptual niceties are addressed, this idea cannot be seriously considered, let alone be implemented.

37 *Contractarian*, *supra* note 1, 664. This position is in line with that of third party beneficiary contracts. See Restatement (Second) of Contracts, §305.

Conclusion

Trusts are clearly not contracts. The two legal institutions have significantly different features and doctrines such that it is a mistake to equate the two. The application of the contract analogy and the use of corporate law and economics to analyse trusts are also misleading and draw the wrong conclusion. Yet the rhetoric of contracts is so appealing that Langbein's account continues to capture the minds of academics and lawyers. One reason for this is that the property aspects of trusts are no longer being contested in courts or in law schools; the boundaries of beneficial interests and other proprietary features have been sufficiently demarcated. Therefore, that leaves the *in personam* relationships between the three principal parties to be developed. This is best done through the lens of contracts because when the *in personam* rights and duties of the trust parties are considered in isolation, trusts superficially resemble contracts and contract doctrines offer maximum freedom and autonomy. What Langbein's account offers is a genuine and candid reflection of the state of trust practices. The trust deal syndrome is real and hundreds of thousands of settlors worldwide are probably experiencing it.

2

Agency Costs and the Nexus of Contracts

Introduction

Langbein's contractarian account may not be an accurate reflection of trusts, but it has created an intellectual void that needed to be filled. He is correct insofar that certain aspects of trust law are indeed default rules, but he has not said much about the content of these default terms. Robert Sitkoff assumes this role and explains the agency costs rationale behind various trust rules.[1] When applied properly, agency costs theory is an immensely powerful tool for lawyers and economists alike. Almost any relationship that involves multiple parties with divergent interests can be analysed with it.[2] At first sight, trusts—with three principal parties who have separate interests and goals—appear to be fertile grounds for applying agency costs theory.

In doing so, Sitkoff makes an important departure from Langbein's ideas. He considers the trust not to be a tripartite contract, but a nexus of contracts. This is due to the different conceptual origins of Sitkoff's and Langbein's ideas. Sitkoff turned to the agency costs tradition that Jensen and Meckling (J&M) established[3] whereas Langbein's account of trusts can trace its lineage to Easterbrook and Fischel's work on corporate law. However, Sitkoff's adoption of J&M's work is a double-edged sword. On the one hand, agency

[1] R. H. Sitkoff, 'An Agency Costs Theory of Trust Law' 89 *Cornell L. Rev.* 621 (2004), hereafter *Agency Costs.*

[2] Though the two concepts have significant overlaps, it is important to distinguish agency in economics and agency in law. In economics, Jensen and Meckling define an agency relationship as a contract under which one or more persons engage another person to perform some service on their behalf which involves delegating some decision-making authority to the agent. In law, agency is a relationship where a person has express or implied authority to act on behalf of another, and consents so to act. The key difference between the two agency concepts is that in economics, an element of delegation is presumed; whereas this need not be the case in law. Most of Sitkoff's analysis of trust law involves applying theories of agency in economics.

[3] M. C. Jensen and W. H. Meckling, 'Theory of the Firm: Managerial Behavior, Agency Costs and Ownership Structure' 3 *J. Finan. Econ.* 305 (1976), hereafter *Agency Costs and Ownership Structure.*

costs analysis of trust rules is far more insightful and richer than the contractarian rhetoric on which Langbein relies. On the other hand, Sitkoff unconditionally adopts J&M's idea that the corporation is a nexus of contracts and imposes it on trusts. This is not necessary as certain trust rules can be explained on agency costs grounds without having to agree that a trust is a nexus of contracts. In fact, Sitkoff created an unnecessary distraction to his analysis of trust rules with the nexus of contracts idea. Not only are many of the relationships within the trust nexus not contractarian, the nexus itself, strictly speaking, does not exist.

In his analysis, Sitkoff also stretches agency costs theory too far. The trustee's duties of care and loyalty are classic ways to reduce agency costs, but this has already been documented by Robert Cooter and Bradley Freedman (in the context of corporate fiduciary duties) almost two decades earlier. Other trust rules that Sitkoff analyses are not agency costs problems *per se.* Instead, they can be considered as rules (sometimes arbitrarily imposed) that resolve mere conflicts of interests; the *Claflin* rule or the duty of impartiality simply do not meet the technical definitions of agency costs. But no matter how one characterizes trust problems, the asymmetric nature of the relationship between the settlor and the beneficiary—where the former dictates all the trust terms and trustee duties and the latter has no bargaining power whatsoever—means that regulating trustee behaviour cannot be resolved with the straightforward application of agency costs theory. Furthermore, Sitkoff has not acknowledged that in a trust relationship, other non-legal mechanisms are at play to reduce agency costs and trustee misbehaviour in general. The law is not the be all and end all of agency costs reduction in trusts.

Finally, 'agency costs theory' is an unfortunate label in a world already suffering from the trust deal syndrome. In the most extreme forms of trust deal syndrome, the trustee acts on the whims of the dominating settlor whilst the beneficiary disappears into the background. Such a relationship appears less a trust than an agency, one between the settlor and the trustee. Of course, Sitkoff's theory was not developed with such trusts in mind, but it surely gives apologists of settlor-centric trusts intellectual credence.

This chapter is organized as follows. First, it introduces and then debunks Sitkoff's nexus of contracts conception of trusts. Second, it reviews his agency costs analysis of trust law and highlights its faulty application and characterization of agency theory. Third, it argues that trust law as an agency cost reduction mechanism is inadequate and non-legal factors must also be considered. Finally, it implicates the agency costs account of trusts in fuelling the perception that the trust is just an asset-partitioned agency.

The Nexus of Contracts Fallacy

It is ironic that J&M's work, one of the most cited articles on theories of the firm, is actually not a theory of the firm.[4] Theories of the firm seek to explain why firms exist, but J&M's ideas presuppose the existence of firms and simply offer additional insights on their capital structure and the resulting agency costs implications. Two ideas in J&M's article capture the imagination of Sitkoff and other law and economics scholars. The first is that the firm is a nexus of contracts and the second is the existence of agency costs. The nexus of contracts idea was only mentioned in passing by J&M and was not a prerequisite to their study. Yet it is now a standard law and economics construct of the firm. Agency costs—although prominently discussed in their article to support their findings on capital structures—has now been elevated to star status. These ideas form the premise of Sitkoff's account of trusts.

According to J&M, 'most organizations are simply *legal fictions* which serve as a nexus for a set of contracting relationship among individuals' and 'it makes little or no sense to try to distinguish those things which are "inside" the firm (or any other organization) from those things that are "outside" of it.'[5] As a result, 'there is in a very real sense only a multitude of complex relationships (that is, contracts) between the legal fiction (the firm) and the owners of labor, material and capital inputs and the consumers of output.'[6] The beauty of this contractarian view of the firm is in its simplicity. As Robert Flannigan observes, 'at its level of generality, it cannot be challenged . . . that is because it is true in a trite sense.'[7] But he continues, 'that tells us nothing about the nexus point itself—the point of conscious coordination of control rights (as opposed to their mere acquisition) into actual production.'[8]

[4] Chapter 4 offers a complete examination of these economic theories of the firm in relation to the trust.

[5] *Agency Costs and Ownership Structure*, *supra* note 3, 310–11. What is inside or outside the firm refers to the dichotomy that exists between open markets and closed organizations. A food supplier to a restaurant is outside the restaurant-firm as the former does not belong to the latter and they transact in the open market. A waiter would be considered inside the firm as he is an employee and acts on his manager's orders for a fixed salary.

[6] Ibid. 311. J&M's contention is that since all relationships inside or outside firms are governed by contracts, there is no point carrying on this distinction; the firm is just a contractual counterparty against all those who interact with it.

[7] R. Flannigan. 'The Economics of Fiduciary Accountability' 32 *Del. J. Corp. L.* 393 (2007), hereafter *Fiduciary Accountability*, 405.

[8] Ibid. 405.

Critically, 'it amounts to a reassertion of the neoclassical black-box view of the firm, where nothing inside the firm is important.'[9]

Despite this, Sitkoff adopts the nexus of contracts idea and applies it to the trust. He conceives of the trust 'as a *de facto* entity that serves as the organizing construct for an aggregation of contractarian relationships'.[10] This, he says, 'is analogous to the Jensen and Meckling nexus of contracts model of the firm'.[11] According to him, the following contractarian relationships can be found in the prototypical trust:

1. Settlor and Trustee;
2. Trustee and the Beneficiaries;
3. Settlor and the Beneficiaries;
4. Trustee and Trustee's creditors;
5. Beneficiaries and Beneficiaries' creditors;
6. Settlor and Settlor's creditors;
7. Settlor and the Trust Protcctor;
8. Beneficiaries and the Trust Protector;
9. Trustee and Trustee's agents; and
10. Trustee's delegates and the Beneficiaries

Sitkoff recognizes that the dominant relationships are those between the settlor and the trustee and between the trustee and the beneficiaries. If these are the dominant relationships, is the trust not just a tripartite contract rather than a nexus of contracts? This would depend on the quality and strength of the other contractarian relationships that Sitkoff identifies as part of the nexus of contracts.

On closer examination, however, these other contractarian relationships are inessential to the trust. For example, take the creditors of the settlor, the trustee, and the beneficiaries: their relationships with the trust are not governed by contractarian principles or contract law. The settlor's creditors can claw back trust assets according to laws on insolvency; the trustee's creditors cannot reach trust assets according to the laws of trusts; and the beneficiaries' creditors can reach trust assets according to laws of property. In none of these cases can one find an implied or express contract between the trust parties and their respective creditors. Contracts simply do not govern the relationships between trust parties and their creditors.

[9] Ibid. 405.
[10] *Agency Costs, supra* note 1, 639.
[11] Ibid. 639.

It is also inappropriate to characterize the relationship between the settlor and the beneficiaries as contractarian.[12] The settlor is not likely to have contracted—legally or metaphorically—with the beneficiaries over the trust. What would the terms of such a contract be? In consideration for the settlor's settling of the trust, would the beneficiaries have undertaken to accept trust asset distributions? There is clearly no such contract. Admittedly, there are conflicts and tensions between the settlor and the beneficiaries, but characterizing the relationship as contractarian does not aid the analysis at all. Sitkoff acknowledges this defect but continues to argue that the nexus of contracts model is useful for analysing agency costs in trusts.

As to the trustee's agents and delegates, introducing them into the nexus of contracts is also problematic. It is true that such parties are popular features of modern trusts, but to consider them to be an integral part of the trust raises the question of where does one demarcate the boundaries of trusts? To paraphrase J&M, what counts as inside and outside the trust? Sitkoff disclaims contractarian nihilism and believes that organizations should have boundaries, but only as far as asset-partitioning is concerned.[13] If the trustee's agents and delegates are part of the nexus of contracts, why not other parties who supply the trustee with non-trust services that enables him to carry out his duties?

A trustee may be under a duty to invest and to present trust accounts but, if he chooses to do so, he can delegate these duties to investment managers and accountants. At the same time, a trustee may need legal advice from time to time and he will certainly hire a lawyer for this; surely the lawyer should be part of this web of contractarian relationship on par with the investment manager. The only difference between the investment manager and the lawyer is that the former is recognized by law as a delegate and the latter is not (presumably there is no need to, as a right-minded trustee would only seek legal advice from a lawyer). The same can be said for investment consultants that a trustee may hire to evaluate the investment manager's performance. In fact, any third party performing functions that the trustee is supposed to perform can in theory be part of this nexus of contractarian relationships.

[12] This is true with donative trusts, which is the subject-matter of Sitkoff's analysis. But even in a trust settled in pursuance of a commercial deal, the relationship between the settlor and the beneficiary is not that much different from that in a donative trust. The commercial beneficiary may have a greater say in the drafting of the trust instrument; but unless he is given special powers and rights within the trust, the trustee will simply manage the trust according to the trust instrument, just like any donative trust.

[13] *Agency Costs*, *supra* note 1, 672.

If one stretches this logic further, anyone who provides any service—including plumbers, computer technicians, photocopier repairmen—that furthers the trustee's performance of his role can be part of this nexus. If this sounds ridiculous, then that is because it is: the nexus of contracts idea is over-encompassing. How does one demarcate what is inside and what is outside the firm? The parties that are central to the firm are part of the nexus of contracts and, crucially, they contract directly with the firm. As a legally fictitious person, the corporate entity is the contractual counterparty with the firm's creditors, suppliers, customers, and employees. Herein lies the most serious deficiency of the trust as nexus of contracts idea: there is no central counterparty in the trust; there may be contracts, but there is certainly no nexus.

This leads to the another criticism of Sitkoff's use of the nexus of contracts idea. The idea itself lacks intellectual substance and to use it only as an analogy—as Sitkoff has done here—is unproductive. Sitkoff's conception of the trust as a nexus of contractarian relationships is no more useful than one saying that a person is a nexus of contractarian relationships between his friends, family, employer, creditors, and debtors. There may be a set of intertwined and complex relationships, but that is just stating the obvious. As Flannigan says, the nexus of contracts idea 'appears to amount to little more than a label for the banality that coordination involves connection'.[14]

Despite the criticisms of the nexus of contracts idea, one should not be detracted from analysing firms or trusts through the lens of agency costs. Sitkoff appears to believe that the nexus of contracts model is an intellectual prerequisite to agency costs analysis, which is probably why he goes to great lengths to include tenuous contractarian relationships like that between the settlor and the beneficiaries in the model. Conflicts of interest exist in trusts and they need to be addressed, regardless of whether the trust is a tripartite contract, a nexus of contracts, or something else.

Reducing Agency Costs . . .

Sitkoff's agency costs analysis is more important than his conception of trusts. The trust can be characterized as a web of complex relationships with intense conflicts of interest and it is difficult to challenge the notion that a key purpose of trust law is to manage these conflicts.

[14] *Fiduciary Accountability, supra* note 7, 406.

Like many law and economics scholars before him, Sitkoff follows J&M's definition of agency costs. Agency costs exist because people pursue different interests and objectives. A homeowner (principal) may hire an architect (agent) to perform architectural services. But the homeowner faces several problems: the architect knows more about architecture than the homeowner and it is difficult for the latter to assess the former's quality of work. The homeowner may want to maximize the design and quality of his house but the architect may not share this goal. He may simply want to maximize his fee income (by inflating his billable hours or by working at a leisurely pace) or he may want to maximize the creative and architectural value of his work (at the homeowner's costs, in terms of beautiful but impractical designs, unnecessarily expensive building materials, etc.). These problems are agency problems.

Sitkoff notes that agency costs only exist with incomplete contracts where one party has discretion and unobservable decision-making authority that affects the wealth of another party.[15] Incomplete contracts exist whenever all possible terms and contingencies cannot be explicitly stated, which is the case for virtually all contracts. In the architect example, the contract between him and the homeowner may only speak of the general scope of works and the outline of the project. It is very difficult for the homeowner to spell out how the architect will work and impossible for him to list out all contingencies. Continuing with the example, the architect has a high degree of discretion and unobservable decision-making authority because he alone designs and implements the project; and clearly this affects the wealth and welfare of the homeowner. The bottom line is that unless incentives are perfectly aligned an agent will never act in the best interest of a principal.

Agency costs are not unilateral as both parties will suffer losses in different ways. First, the principal will incur costs when he tries to monitor the agent's behaviour to prevent the agent's shirking and misbehaviour. Second, the agent will incur costs if he is asked to take steps to guarantee the principal that certain actions will not occur or, if they do occur, that the principal will be compensated. Third, the principal also incurs losses if the agent ultimately shirks or misbehaves. These losses are respectively known as monitoring expenditure, bonding expenditure, and residual loss; agency costs are the sum total of all three.[16] Agency costs will inevitably exist in all trusts and it is the function of trust law, especially trustee duties, to mitigate them. Sitkoff explains how different trust rules address agency costs that exist in different relationships within the trust.

[15] *Agency Costs, supra* note 1, 636.
[16] *Agency Costs and Ownership Structure, supra* note 3, 308.

The duty of loyalty and its prophylactic nature are a classic response to the agency costs that arise from the trustee-beneficiary relationship. A trustee would only engage in self-dealing if it benefits him; but benefits may not accrue to the beneficiaries at all. In the normal course of things, a principal can monitor the agent's behaviour and assess whether the self-dealing is beneficial or not. In a trust, however, beneficiaries are often unsuitable to perform the monitoring role, as 'they [may be] unborn, incapacitated, or simply irresponsible'.[17] The duty of loyalty and fiduciary duties generally serve as a substitute for beneficiary monitoring.[18] Furthermore, the prophylactic nature of rules such as the duty of loyalty acts as a deterrent against trustee misbehaviour.

The duty of care also seeks to address the agency costs that arise from the trustee's indifference and lack of incentives to manage the trust assets properly. By imposing liabilities for failing to meet the duty of care, trustees are incentivized to exercise proper care rather than shirk. Sitkoff notes that the level of duty of care in trust law is tailored for prototypical beneficiaries.[19] Because their wealth may be concentrated in the trust assets, beneficiaries are likely to be risk averse and trust investments should also reflect this conservatism. This is manifested through the prudent investor rule in United States and English trust laws.[20]

Sitkoff also discusses the duty of impartiality and the *Claflin* rule. He argues that the duty of impartiality seeks to address the inherent tension between different classes of beneficiaries (a life tenant and a remainderman, for example).[21] This duty requires the trustee to be even-handed and deal with different classes of beneficiaries fairly, especially when it comes to trust investments and distribution. On the *Claflin* rule, Sitkoff claims that it addresses a rather unique type of agency cost, namely temporal agency costs. This is used to describe the trustee's dilemma of whether to adhere to the beneficiaries' wishes or the settlor's instructions once the settlor is dead. Sitkoff notes that the *Claflin* rule requires the settlor's wishes to take precedence over those of the beneficiaries, at least in the context of termination and modification.[22]

17 *Agency Costs, supra* note 1, 680.

18 D. Fischel and J. H. Langbein, 'ERISA's Fundamental Contradiction: The Exclusive Benefit Rule' 55 *U. Chi. L. Rev.* 1105 (1988), 1114.

19 *Agency Costs, supra* note 1, 654–7.

20 See Restatement (Third) of Trusts, §90 and also D. J. Hayton, P. Matthews, and C. Mitchell, (eds.) *Underhill and Hayton The Law Relating to Trusts and Trustees* (17th edn. LexisNexis Butterworths, London 2006), art. 52.3; the prudent man rule in the English case *Re Whiteley* (1886) 33 Ch. D. 347 has now been superseded by the Trustee Act 2000.

21 *Agency Costs, supra* note 1, 650–2.

22 Ibid. 657–63. The *Claflin* rule is the antithesis of the rule in *Saunders v Vautier*. The latter provides that all beneficiaries of full age and capacity can jointly terminate the trust whereas the

The primacy of the settlor's wishes also manifests itself through spendthrift trusts. Put simply, spendthrift trusts automatically place trust assets out of reach of the beneficiaries' creditors. Beneficiaries can neither sell their equitable interests nor use them to settle debts. Sitkoff observes that spendthrift trusts reduce the trustee's managerial discretion (and potential agency costs) but also deprive beneficiaries of the ability to sell their interest (exiting the relationship is also considered a mechanism to reduce agency costs).[23] Sitkoff also looks at equitable tracing, an important area of trust law that Langbein's account fails to explain. Whereas Langbein's tripartite contract model cannot be extended to cover non-contractual third parties, Sitkoff claims that his conceptualization of trusts offers that possibility. He says 'by including those who deal with the trustee in the relevant set or nexus of relationships, the rule of equitable tracing appears to reflect the parties' presumed intent in light of the comparative advantage of the outsider to bear the agency costs associated with this particular potential breach by the trustee'.[24] His argument implies that the third party recipient agrees to be the monitor of a potential breach of trust in the transaction.

... or Just Managing Conflicts of Interests?

To some extent, Sitkoff has filled the intellectual void created by Langbein. The tripartite contract account of trusts does not tell us much about the content of trust law and Sitkoff's analysis has illuminated some of the rationale behind various trust rules. However, Sitkoff's agency costs analysis cannot accurately account for all the trust rules that he discusses. Many of the problems identified under the agency costs banner are not actually agency problems. They are merely tensions resulting from conflicts of interest between the various parties, which means that the agency cost model is not always appropriate. Despite being a vast improvement from Langbein's account, that of Sitkoff is also incomplete because it does not offer a good explanation of the nature of the beneficial interest and other property-like features of trusts. Sitkoff rationalizes the trustee's duties of care and loyalty as solutions to classic agency problems. This is not in doubt and has been

former only allows termination if the trust no longer serves a material purpose of the settlor. *Claflin v Claflin* (1889) 149 Mass. 19, 20 N.E. 454. See P. Matthews, 'The Comparative Importance of the Rule in *Saunders v Vautier*' 122 *LQR* 266 (2006).

[23] *Agency Costs, supra* note 1, 675; see also A. O. Hirschmann, *Exit, Voice, and Loyalty: Responses to Decline in Firms, Organizations, and States* (Harvard University Press, Cambridge 1972).

[24] *Agency Costs, supra* note 1, 673.

argued previously by Cooter and Freedman in their research on the corporate duties of care and loyalty.[25] Other duties and rules, however, do not comfortably fit into Sitkoff's framework of agency costs.

The duty of impartiality requires the trustee to treat all beneficiaries equally, irrespective of the nature of their interests. If this duty addresses an agency problem, then the nature of the agency relationship is unclear. Is it an agency relationship between the trustee and each beneficiary? That is, each individual beneficiary may query whether the trustee will make decisions that will maximize his interests. The problem with this characterization is that there are no agency costs as traditionally understood. As Sitkoff explains in his introduction to the economics of agency, trustees may act opportunistically when the trust suffers from information asymmetry, enabling the trustee to either shirk or profit illegitimately from his office. Trust rules mitigate agency costs by changing the trustee's incentives. However, even without the duty of impartiality, the trustee's preference for one beneficiary over another does not enable him to shirk or profit from his decision: he is still required to invest and distribute trust assets. Short of a bribe from an opportunistic beneficiary, the trustee has no economic incentives to prefer one beneficiary over another. In other words, the trustee by default should be beneficiary-neutral. The only other possible characterization of the agency relationship that the duty of impartiality is trying to address is one between the various beneficiaries. This reflects the zero-sum nature of competing beneficial interests but the idea fails on the fact that beneficiaries do not have powers to affect investment and distribution outcomes. A much better idea is to recognize that the duty of impartiality does not address agency problems at all. Rather, the duty of impartiality is the law's response to a simple conflict of competing beneficial interests.[26]

Another rule that supposedly solves agency costs is the *Claflin* rule. Sitkoff attaches the label 'temporal agency problem' to this rule because, broadly speaking, it concerns whether the trustee will follow the settlor's wishes after his death. Again, it is interesting to ask whether one should characterize this problem as an agency one and, if so, who are the parties? Even with the *Claflin* rule, after the settlor's death, all the beneficiaries can request and the trustee can indeed consent to trust termination and no court or representative of the settlor can object to this. So the rule does nothing to stop the trustee from frustrating the settlor's intentions. To be sure, the rule does not

[25] R. Cooter and B. J. Freedman, 'The Fiduciary Relationship: Its Economic Character and Legal Consequences' 66 *N. Y. U. L. Rev.* 1045 (1991).

[26] There exists research on agencies involving multiple principals; but as will be seen below, the theories on common agency are not useful to trusts.

allow the trustee to deviate unilaterally from the settlor's intentions: he will need the consent of all beneficiaries, and vice versa.

But if the rule is meant to provide comfort to the settlor that the trustee will not yield to the wishes of the beneficiaries, it is an ineffective one. The rule does not change the trustee's incentives to adhere to or to deviate from the settlor's intentions; it simply stipulates the conditions for legally doing so. In fact, when it comes to incentives, the (paid) trustee ought naturally to favour continuation of the trust. This is because to terminate the trust is to deprive the trustee of his office and his remuneration. Therefore, all else being equal, the trustee should naturally be incentivized against trust termination. The other possible framing of this agency relationship is one between the settlor and the beneficiaries. But, again, there is no agency-like or contractarian relationship between the settlor and the beneficiaries. What exists is a simple conflict of interest or, perhaps, conflict of preferences. The *Claflin* rule does give priority to the settlor's preferences, but it is not cast in iron. Either the trustee can consent to trust termination or modification or, failing that, the court can provide the consent if it thinks that the trust is no longer serving any material purpose. At best, the *Claflin* rule is a poor response to a problem awkwardly described as an agency one.

The Inadequacies of Trust Law as an Agency Cost Reduction Mechanism

In Sitkoff's account, the duties of care and loyalty address agency problems by substituting for beneficiary monitoring. As discussed earlier, this standalone explanation of fiduciary duties is supported by other law and economics scholars and is not in doubt. However, much that Sitkoff highlights the various agency problems in a trust relationship, his mere offering of trust law as the solution to these problems is inadequate from an economic perspective. As far as incentives are concerned, the only one offered to the trustee in Sitkoff's account is the prospect of being sued for breaching trust law. In practice, trustees are not only motivated by the trust instrument and trust law. Although the stick is important, the carrot is much more appreciated. A more comprehensive understanding of the trust parties' incentives can only be gained by studying beyond black letter law. Non-legal factors such as trustee remuneration, altruism, and social norms encourage trustees to undertake trusteeship and settlors to settle trusts.

To begin with, very few people are willing to act unconditionally as trustee and risk all the legal liabilities that the office entails. For professional and paid trustees, the monetary remuneration is arguably the most important motivation for undertaking trusteeship. Modern professional trustees are remunerated on either a fixed or variable basis, or both. The fixed component could simply be a predetermined lump sum amount or a percentage of the value of trust assets under management. The variable component is often an hourly rate for the time spent by trustees—just like lawyers. Such fees operate as the core incentive for trustees to accept and continue with the trust office, whereas the strong arm of trust law seeks to ensure compliance. A professional trustee can be adequately incentivized by fees alone without trust law, but not vice versa. Without the fees, a professional trustee will not be willing to accept the office and be subject to the regime of trust law. On the other hand, with adequate fees, a professional trustee *might* just duly perform his duties even without a trust law regime. Therefore, trustee remuneration should be seen as an integral part of the incentives package that reduces the agency costs in the trust relationship.

However, neither trustee remuneration nor trust law offers high-powered incentives for the trustee. High-powered incentives are essentially performance-based rewards, such as employee bonuses based on sales or profits individually achieved. In the case of trusts, the remuneration only motivates the trustee to accept the office and stay on whilst the law only imposes liability when the trustee's performance is substandard. With such an incentive structure, it is difficult to motivate the trustee to perform beyond the legal standard. But on the other hand, what might performing beyond the legal standard entail? Without perfect information, it is impossible for the settlor or the beneficiary to ascertain whether the trustee has expended effort beyond what is required in performing his duties of investment and distribution and whether the end result is a direct consequence of those efforts. There is simply a dearth of objective information that would enable high-powered incentives in trusts.

The unavailability of high-powered incentives leads to a rather disconcerting conclusion: what the settlor and the beneficiary gain from the trustee is universally fixed (his performance that meets legal standards) but what the trustee monetarily gains is subject to change and negotiation. If the settlor and the beneficiary price the trustee's service incorrectly and over-generously remunerate him, the trustee pockets the excess. Whether trust services are priced correctly can be the subject of an interesting empirical study, but the common use of blunt proxies such as value of trust assets under management or time spent does not indicate particular sophistication or ample forethought. At the risk of denigrating professional trustees, the nature of their activities and their compensation structure entails a degree of rent-seeking.

So much for incentivizing professional paid trustees—how are volunteer trustees motivated? Like their professional, paid counterparts, volunteer trustees cannot only be motivated by the threat of legal sanctions—they also need carrots in addition to sticks. Instead of tangible monetary rewards, volunteer trustees are often motivated by intangible ones. Volunteer trustees may be motivated by altruism, which Richard Posner defines as 'the condition in which the welfare of one person is a positive function of the welfare of another'.[27] Volunteer trustees may simply feel good when the welfares of the beneficiaries they look after increase and this alone is enough to motivate them to accept trusteeship.

Along these lines, a more sophisticated explanation of what motivates trustees is offered by Eric Rasmusen who likens central bankers to trustees rather than agents of the state.[28] He contends that in addition to the meagre salary central bankers receive, they are motivated by policy, pride, place, and power. Policy refers to the trustee's desire to see particular policies in place, usually because of his political or moral principles; pride refers to the trustee's reputation for competence; place refers to the trustee's liking of his job and the tangible and intangible benefits that comes with it; power refers to the end itself, not the means to influence policy.[29]

Although these factors are discussed with central bankers in mind, they are applicable to legal trusts. With policy, trustees who can exercise discretion may make investment and distribution decisions that are consistent with his personal preferences (choosing a hardworking beneficiary over a spendthrift, for example). Pride and a reputation for competence can also motivate trustees, but there is also an external dimension to this, which will be discussed shortly. With place and power, only trustees of larger and better known trusts would be materially motivated by such factors as there is not much stature and power to be gained from managing run-of-the-mill testamentary trusts and estates.

Whether through altruism or one of Rasmusen's four P's, volunteer trustees can reap intangible rewards from trusteeship. More importantly, these rewards are primarily for the trustee's internal consumption. Apart from sharing with others his altruistic trusteeship vibes, these rewards have no effect on third parties. The main exception to this would be what Rasmusen calls pride (and, to some extent, place). In his account, pride involves maintaining a reputation for competence. Although one can feel

[27] R. A. Posner, *Economic Analysis of Law* (6th edn. Aspen Publishers, New York 2003), 147.

[28] E. Rasmusen, 'A Theory of Trustees, and Other Thoughts', 1998, <http://papers.ssrn.com/sol3/papers.cfm?abstract_id=84388>, last accessed 7 January 2010.

[29] Ibid. 8–10.

good about doing a good job as a trustee and keep this feeling to oneself, one can also externalize this good reputation for personal gains.

Because trusteeship is associated with highly regarded social norms such as honesty, loyalty, diligence, and care, these norms will generally attach to a trustee who complies with the trust. In other words, a trustee—especially one of a well-known trust—will have his reputation enhanced by virtue of his office. To borrow Eric Posner's ideas on law and social norms, undertaking trusteeship can be considered as a costly and observable action or, in his words, a 'signal'.[30] This signal serves the purpose of telling others that the signaller is a cooperator. According to Posner, cooperators tend to fulfil promises and are more willing to forego short-term gains for long-term benefits; cooperators have lower discount rates and their adherence to social norms advertises this fact.

In the case of a volunteer trustee, the signal of a lower discount rate he gains from the office of trusteeship can be applied to his personal dealings. Business associates may perceive an individual who is a member of the board of trustees of a major charity as having a lower default risk and hence are more willing to deal with him than others. Signalling is all the more important for professional trustees because low discount rates directly affect their trust business prospects. To state the obvious, a professional trustee with a widely perceived reputation for integrity and competence is more likely to retain existing businesses and capture new ones than a trustee without such a reputation. However, this argument is weakened by the fact that trustee accomplishments or failures are not frequently aired in public. At a basic level, signalling can be achieved by the mere fact that one is a trustee, but the quality of such a signal is low because, at best, it only offers a presumption that the individual is associated with trustee-like norms. Actual trustee actions—that confirm or rebut these presumptions—would provide a much better signal but in the privacy-obsessed world of private trusts, such signals being made public is exceedingly rare.

Just as there are various non-legal motivations that affect trustee behaviour, the settlor's incentives are also shaped by factors beyond trust law. Some would argue that, true to its historical origins, the trust is a trusting relationship. Tamar Frankel is a proponent of encouraging trusting relationships in the financial and business world. She argues that equitable trusts are 'based on legally enforceable trusting'.[31] The role of the law is to offer incentives for parties to enter into trusting relationships and to protect the

[30] E. A. Posner, *Law and Social Norms* (Harvard University Press, Cambridge 2000).

[31] T. Frankel, 'Trusting and Non-Trusting: Comparing Benefits, Cost and Risk', 1999, <http://papers.ssrn.com/sol3/papers.cfm?abstract_id=214588>, last accessed 7 January 2010, footnote 21.

entrustor against the fiduciary's abuse of power.[32] Others argue that 'legally enforceable trusting' is an oxymoron. According to Oliver Williamson, what is popularly known as trusting is really just stone cold calculations and balancing of risks.[33] Williamson classifies trusting into three types: calculative trust, personal trust, and institutional trust.[34]

Williamson defines calculativeness as a situation where the parties (1) are aware of the range of possible outcomes and their associated probabilities; (2) take cost-effective actions to mitigate hazards and enhance benefits; (3) proceed with the transaction only if expected net gains can be projected; and (4) select their respective counterparties with the largest projectable net gain.[35] An example of calculative trust is where a lender lends money to a borrower because the lender knows that the borrower is trustworthy and is a man of integrity. The idea that the lender trusts the borrower is just the sum total of the lender's knowledge of the borrower and his estimation of the likelihood of repayment.[36] According to Williamson, no trust is involved and calculative trust is simply a contradiction in terms. Personal trust, in contrast, is a unique phenomenon. Williamson concedes that certain relationships or transactions are better off with calculativeness suppressed, but only after claiming that the decision to suppress calculativeness is in itself calculative.[37] In a loving relationship, for example, continuous calculation, or 'metering', does more harm than good to the parties. Personal trust exists where there is (1) the absence of monitoring; (2) favourable or forgiving predilections; and (3) discreteness.[38]

Frankel's legally enforceable trusting is certainly not Williamson's personal trust, for legal enforcement would only occur as a result of successful monitoring, which should not exist with personal trust. In any case, the possibility of legal enforcement significantly increases the likelihood of trustee compliance to the point that a settlor or beneficiary would not need personal trusting. Therefore, the settlor-trustee-beneficiary relationship would be one of calculative trust as the rights and duties are all set out in

[32] T. Frankel, 'Fiduciary Law' 71 *Cal. L. R.* 795 (1983), 799.

[33] O. E. Williamson, 'Calculativeness, Trust and Economic Organization' 36 *J. L. & Econ.* 453 (1993), hereafter *Calculativeness.*

[34] Even this classification of trusts is just a simplified starting point. Trusts and breaches thereof often overlap in categories. A victim's relationship with a fraudster can begin as calculative trust before evolving into personal trust, giving the fraudster the opportunity to defraud. After all, it is confidence on which con men rely.

[35] *Calculativeness, supra* note 33, 467.

[36] Ibid. 467–71.

[37] Ibid. 479.

[38] 'Discreteness' exists when one considers a breach (of personal trust) independently and not in relation to previous breaches; to consider previous breaches is to be calculative. Ibid. 482–4.

law. But there is also a middle ground that arguably accommodates the ideas of Sitkoff and Frankel. There is institutional trust, which is achieved through the environment in which the transaction or relationship is based.[39] Societal culture, politics, regulation, professionalization, networks, and corporate culture can all foster an environment of trust. For example, certain religions promulgate trustworthy norms (like the Religious Society of Friends, or Quakers); the rule of law offers protection of rights; certain professions are known to live up to high quality norms; and corporate cultures foster cohesive behavioural pattern. While these environmental factors appear to foster 'natural' trust, Williamson argues, again, that they merely change the calculus. Put differently, coercive legal measures, non-legal sanctions, and social norms together affect the probability that a promise is kept. In the case of the settlor, his decision to entrust the trust assets to the trustee in the first place is probably motivated by a combination of the existence of trust law, the trustee's reputation and business prospects, and existing social norms that lead people to frown upon negligence and dishonesty. Therefore, like the trustee, the settlor is motivated by a package of legal and non-legal incentives.

The beneficiary's position has so far been omitted from this discussion, and for good reason. The beneficiary is not in a position to dictate the trust terms or choose the trustee. At best, he can disclaim his interest if he is so unsatisfied with the trust terms and his beneficial interest. The two dominant relationships that Sitkoff identifies are those between the trustee and the settlor and between the trustee and the beneficiary. Superficially, this tripartite relationship resembles common agency, where an agent acts for more than one principal. Economic theories of common agency have been developed to supplement the works of J&M and others.[40] To some extent, a trust is considered to be an intrinsic common agency, where an individual is naturally endowed with the right to make a particular decision affecting other parties, who may in turn attempt to influence his decisions. Political decision-making affecting different interest groups exemplifies intrinsic common agency.

In the case of a trust, the trustee would be considered as endowed with the right to make decisions affecting the interests of either the different members of the beneficiary class (for example, income/capital distribution decisions) or the beneficiary and the settlor (for example, whether to terminate or modify the trust). Under the common agency analysis, the trustee as agent would be acting on behalf of the settlor and the various beneficiaries, the multiple principals. But apart from this interesting characterization, the theories of

[39] Ibid. 475–9.

[40] B. D. Bernheim and M. D. Whinston, 'Common Agency' 54 *Econometrica* 923 (1986).

common agency do not have much to offer to the analysis of trusts in the agency costs context.

This is because the key assumption in the works of common agency theory is that multiple principals simultaneously and non-cooperatively announce incentive schemes for a common agent.[41] Although the settlor of a trust can be considered as a principal who can offer incentives to the agent, the same cannot be said about the beneficiaries. The nature of the trust relationship is asymmetric in that the beneficiaries, as donees of the settlor's gift, have no incentive schemes to offer to the trustee. Perhaps the beneficiaries can agree with the trustee to terminate and resettle the trust on new terms with higher trustee fees. But apart from this extreme example, beneficiaries cannot really compete with the settlor in a common agency situation. It is the settlor who initially sets out the trust terms and in the normal course of things, the beneficiaries cannot incentivize the trustee to deviate from such terms. The same can be said about different classes of beneficiaries, such as life tenants, remaindermen, and discretionary objects—none of them individually is in a position to terminate and resettle the trust on better terms. The inapplicability of theories of common agency points the trust back to the tripartite contract model.

Going Full Circle from Bare Trusts to Discretionary Trusts and Back?

Just as Langbein's contractarian account epitomizes the trust deal syndrome, an unintended consequence of Sitkoff's account is that it fuels the perception that trusts are not *de facto* entities, as he argues them to be, but *de facto* asset-partitioned agencies.[42] Sitkoff does not actually make such a claim, but several features of his account do encourage this idea. This also leads to another interesting question: is there a market for asset-partitioned agencies?

Apart from superficially sharing the 'agency' label, the agency costs theory of trusts resonates with the asset-partitioned agency idea in many important ways. To understand why this is the case, one must go back to J&M's definitions of a firm and an agency. According to them, the firm is a nexus of contracts and each pair of contractual relationship can be analysed as

[41] Ibid. 925.

[42] This refers to a fictitious legal concept consisting of a special legal agency relationship where any asset that forms part of this relationship is protected by asset-partitioning rules. The closest living legal species would probably be Chinese trusts, which are essentially ring-fenced contracts. See L. Ho, *Trust Law in China* (Sweet & Maxwell Asia, Hong Kong 2003).

discrete principal-agent problems. An agency involves a principal engaging an agent to perform some service on his behalf which involves delegating some decision-making authority to the agent.[43]

Drawing on the nexus of contracts idea, Sitkoff argues that the trust is a *de facto* entity that represents a nexus of contractarian relationships. However, he does not explain how these contractarian relationships fit into the economic definition of agency. As argued earlier in this chapter, most of the contractarian relationships are, strictly speaking, not of the principal-agent type, so they cannot easily be reconciled with the definition of agency. But the dominant relationships (settlor-trustee and beneficiary-trustee) do correspond to J&M's agency definition: the trustee is performing a service on the settlor's behalf which involves delegating some decision-making authority to him. This good match is testament to the generality of J&M's definition of agency. Most service-oriented transactions between two or more parties fall under the economic definition of agency, whether they are legally characterized as agency, employment, trust, or contract. One cannot criticize J&M for this generality because their insightful analysis of agency costs is applicable to any relationship that fits their definition of agency.

Sitkoff does not need to distinguish the trust from agency in law because the difference is clear from the outset; but he should have qualified the dominant relationships from agency in economics. In characterizing the settlor-trustee and beneficiary-trustee relationships as agency problems, Sitkoff should have said that unlike principals of normal agencies, settlors and beneficiaries of prototypical trusts do not retain much control over how trustees behave.[44] The trustee may be performing a service on behalf of the settlor or the beneficiary, but not under their continuous orders; as long as his actions are above board and unimpeachable, the trustee is relatively independent.[45] Of course, certain trusts do retain this agent-like control element. Trustees of bare trusts and United States revocable trusts do hold assets to the order of settlors. But the discretionary managerial trusts that Langbein and Sitkoff describe are not of this nature: they envisage trusts where trustees are genuinely empowered to make investment and distribution decisions.

[43] *Agency Costs and Ownership Structure*, *supra* note 3, 308.

[44] Sitkoff does discuss the settlor's lack of standing, but only to explain the agency costs that this arrangement produces. Sitkoff should have noted that unlike principals of agencies (in law or in economics), settlors or beneficiaries do not have the power to revoke trustees' 'agency authority' at will. This is a significant qualitative difference between trusts and agencies.

[45] This important distinction is first noted by Eric Rasmusen, who argues that the agency model is not apt for analysing the behaviour of independent central banks. Instead, he proposes a trusteeship model to understand the motivations of central bank leaders. See E. Rasmusen, *supra* note 28.

Recognizing this difference would not detract the agency costs analyses of, say, the trustee's duties of loyalty and care, but Sitkoff's silence on this matter encourages the perception that an agency relationship exists, if not in fact then at least in spirit.

Another feature of Sitkoff's account that furthers the asset-partitioned agency idea is his neglect of the trust's proprietary attributes. On the trust's asset-partitioning feature, Sitkoff simply incorporates the ideas of Hansmann, Kraakman, and Mattei into his *de facto* entity conception of trusts[46]. As for the beneficial interest, Sitkoff discusses the fact that beneficiaries are residual claimants and that equitable tracing can be justified by the idea that external parties are part of the contractarian nexus who have agreed to monitor for breaches of trust. But at no point does Sitkoff reconcile these proprietary attributes with his application of agency costs theory; in other words, they were sidelined. Must Sitkoff talk about proprietary attributes when applying agency costs theory? Probably not, because J&M's theory is not based on property and doing so would neither support nor detract agency costs analysis of trust law. But by ignoring all of the trust's proprietary niceties, it reinforces the idea that the trust is simply an asset-management service contract between the settlor and the trustee.

None of this would matter if all of those who are involved with trusts appreciate the differences between trust and agency; but not everyone does. Offshore jurisdictions and practitioners encourage settlors who experience the trust deal syndrome to use the trust as a kind of asset-partitioned agency. At a casual level, settlors experiencing the trust deal syndrome want enforceability and certainty, hence the 'contractification' of trusts. But they also desire more than just the cold comfort that the trust is an enforceable asset-management contract. They want contracts with 'smart terms' that will guide trustees towards proper performance. Viewed from the lens of agency costs, default trust law provides many of these terms and enhances the utility of the trust deal for the settlor. In this respect, Langbein's work sets out the template of the trust deal and Sitkoff's account extends it by filling in the key terms of the deal.

But when viewed in conjunction with the use of revocable trusts and offshore legislations enabling settlors to retain significant powers, the trust deal is transformed from a mere contract into an asset-partitioned agency. Why? Trusts with settlors retaining powers of investments and distribution appear agency-like because, on one hand, the trustee could be seen as acting under the continuous orders of the settlor. On the other hand, a settlor's

[46] See *Agency Costs, supra* note 1, 631–3.

retention of powers to remove or appoint trustees or to revoke the trust puts him on par with the principal of an agency: he now has the ability to remove at will the agent's authority to act on his behalf. So nowadays a settlor can engage a trustee to act on his behalf whilst retaining the abilities to provide continuous orders and to remove the trustee's authority at will. One must ask, how is this functionally different from an agency?

Of course, the key functional difference between an agency and such a trust is that the trust has some asset-partitioning features. If that is the key difference, why would settlors choose trusts rather than agencies to organize their affairs? Because they want to relinquish their beneficial interest, or at least appear to have done so. There are many good reasons for choosing trusts over agencies. For example, a trust continues long after a settlor is dead and because trusts inevitably involve assets, the trustee's legal title empowers him to manage the trust asset more effectively than could any agent: an agent cannot have a stronger apparent authority than holding legal title to the assets. In addition to these factors, there are other important reasons to choose trusts over agencies. Exogenous considerations such as tax and insolvency laws motivate settlors to undertake the chore of relinquishing their legal and beneficial interests, so as to avoid undesirable present or future liabilities.[47] After all, the much cherished asset-partitioning features of trusts only come into existence because the settlor has settled a trust and has parted with the beneficial interest. As a way to attract more trust and allied businesses, offshore jurisdictions offer settlors the ability to retain key powers to compensate them for parting their legal and beneficial interests in trust assets. By doing so, they allow settlors to achieve the asset-partitioning effects of trusts whilst retaining agency-like relationships with trustees—in other words, asset-partitioned agency relationships.

Of course, not every offshore trust settlor has tax and creditor avoidance in mind, but with the multitude of trust products on offer nowadays, such aspirations are much easier to realize than ever before.[48] As to the earlier question of whether there is a market for asset-partitioned agencies as a distinct legal concept, the answer is probably to the negative. This is so for the simple reason that by being identified as the 'principal' in such an agency,

[47] When asked what are trusts used for, members of the Society of Trust and Estate Practitioners responded that they use trusts for tax mitigation 25% of the time and asset protection 20% of the time. The remaining 55% is divided between estate planning, confidentiality, and providing employee benefit trusts. See Society of Trust and Estate Practitioners, *STEP Survey 2004*, 2004. Copy with Author.

[48] The use of trusts is only one of many factors in avoiding tax and creditor liabilities. Nowadays, strict anti-money laundering and tax disclosure rules reduce the effectiveness of using offshore jurisdictions for such purposes.

a settlor or beneficiary would lose most of the tax and insolvency benefits that come with relinquishing his legal and beneficial interests in the trust assets in the first place.[49] To be sure, Sitkoff's agency costs theory of trust law does not advocate the idea of the trust as an asset-partitioned agency and not all trusts—offshore or otherwise—behave as such. However, the unintended consequence of Sitkoff's work is that apologists of settlor-centric trusts can draw support from it.

As this book's introduction highlighted, trusts began life as medieval uses and they were functionally similar to bare trusts. As social, economic, and historical circumstances changed, the trustee became empowered with investment and distribution decision-making. The trustee's empowerment is epitomized by the modern discretionary trust, which maintains its popularity today. But the rise of exotic offshore trusts is turning the clock backward. What we have witnessed in the last few decades is no less than an intellectual regression. In his essay, Paul Matthews notes that the doctrinal nature of trusts has gone from obligations to property and back again; in practice, it appears to be the reverse: we have gone from bare trusts to discretionary trusts and back again.[50]

Conclusion

Sitkoff's agency costs theory of trust law is the first attempt to transplant economic theories of the firm comprehensively onto trusts. It is comprehensive because it was transplanted as a package consisting of a nexus of contracts conception of trusts and also an agency costs analysis of trust rules. But much that it is a laudable attempt, it is unsuccessful on many counts. The trust may appear superficially like a tripartite contract, but it does not even remotely resemble a nexus of contracts. With the exception of the duties of care and loyalty, agency costs analyses of other trust rules are dubious as they are better understood as resolving mere conflicts of interests. What is more, the incorrect application of agency costs theory to trusts can be seen as fuelling the extreme form of the trust deal syndrome, the asset-partitioned agency.

These flaws highlight the inherent risks of inter-disciplinary transplant of ideas. A lot of the times, theories and ideas from one field can be helpful to

[49] Of course, trusts do not only serve private wealth-management clients; they are also widely used for commercial transactions.

[50] P. Matthews, 'From Obligations to Property, and Back Again? The Future of the Non-Charitable Purpose Trust' in D. J. Hayton (ed.) *Extending the Boundaries of Trusts and Similar Ring-Fenced Funds* (Kluwer Law International, London 2002).

understanding another. But very rarely can these ideas in their entirety be lifted up and redeployed in a different discipline successfully. More often, parts of these ideas can be borrowed and used fruitfully, but to take an all or nothing approach is asking for disappointment. One cannot expect a grand theory of trust law coming straight off the shelf of another discipline.

PART II
TRUSTS AS FIRMS
The Firm-like Qualities of a Non-Firm

The term 'firm' means different things to different people. A lawyer would consider his employer a firm, as a sole proprietor would his business. One thing the law firm and the proprietorship have in common is that both are real businesses. We do not often call an offshore corporation that merely holds an asset a 'firm'; we can call it that but a 'shell company' or 'holding vehicle' seems to convey the meaning a lot more naturally. In this book, 'firm' means a legal entity or an economic organization because both have been implicated with trusts. Scholars of organizational law argue that trusts are legal entities whilst in the previous part Langbein and Sitkoff describe trusts using theories of economic organizations. There is something firm-like about trusts.

Part II dismisses the idea that trusts are legal entities or economic organizations, as traditionally understood. The same methodological mistake outlined in the previous part is also made by proponents of the 'trusts as firms' idea: they draw on attributes of trusts that are superficially or partly similar to firms, and they assert that trusts are firms. This is especially true among scholars who argue that trusts are legal entities. As for economic organizations, no one has actually claimed that trusts are such creatures. But this is strongly implied by Langbein and Sitkoff's unconditional and unquestioned reliance on theories of the firm. The ideas that trusts are legal entities or economic firms are wrong.

These mistaken views can be attributed to the confusion over form and function. Just as corporations can be used to organize real businesses that produce goods and services, they can equally be used as shell companies to do nothing more than hold assets. The same can be said for trusts as they can equally hold assets or, if one really insists, organize a real business. Therefore, one must go beyond casual observations and examine the trust's unique legal and economic attributes in order to discover its true function.

3

Trusts as Entities

Introduction

Although Langbein and Sitkoff rely on corporate law and economics theories, they do not actually claim that the trust is a legal entity. Instead, this idea has been taken up by Henry Hansmann, Reinier Kraakman, and Ugo Mattei ('HKM'). In their various writings on entities and organizational law, they argue that the trust is a *de facto* legal entity.[1] This reification of the trust transforms it from a two-dimensional contractarian concept into a three-dimensional one and is a giant leap within the loosely-defined 'obligational approach'. This chapter examines the claim that the trust is a legal entity.

For many years, the literature on legal entities has focused on the limited liability protection that they provide to owners and managers. Recently, the attention has shifted from limited liability's 'owner-shielding' attribute to the idea of 'entity-shielding'. This is the idea that organizational law protects the entity by preventing the personal creditors of owners or managers from attaching their liabilities to the firm or even liquidating it to satisfy those claims, thereby enabling the firm to continue as a going concern even if individual owners and managers become insolvent.

HKM contend that entity-shielding is the essential role of organizational law and this argument has been extended to the trust. They note that the asset-partitioning features of trusts are not easily replicable, if at all, with mere contracts. It is trite law that the personal creditors of the trustee cannot claim trust assets to satisfy his personal obligations; this asset-partitioning feature of trust law is not controversial. However, in highlighting this proprietary aspect of trusts, they also make the claim that it is a *de facto* legal entity. In addition

[1] H. Hansmann and U. Mattei, 'Trust Law in the United States. A Basic Study of Its Special Contributions' 46 *Am. J. Comp. L.* 133 (1998), hereafter *Trust Law in the United States*; H. Hansmann and U. Mattei, 'The Functions of Trust Law: A Comparative Legal and Economic Analysis' 73 *N. Y. U. L. Rev.* 434 (1998), hereafter *The Functions of Trust Law*; H. Hansmann and R. Kraakman, 'The Essential Role of Organizational Law' 110 *Yale L. J.* 387 (2000), hereafter *Essential Role.*

to possessing asset-partitioning attributes, trusts often compete with corporations as the vehicle of choice in commercial transactions. HKM also draw on this to further support their idea that the trust is a legal entity.

HKM are certainly not alone in arguing that the trust is a legal entity. Some civil law scholars conceive of the trust as a separate patrimony with legal personality in order to fit it comfortably into their legal systems. Conceiving of the trust as a legal entity has two significant advantages. First, it makes it a lot easier to understand for civilian lawyers. Second, it 'fortifies' the trust and provides normative justifications for strengthening its owner- and entity-shielding attributes to a level on par with that of corporations.

In summary, it appears that granting the trust legal personality can be justified by its inherent asset-partitioning features and also by the ease of understanding for civilian scholars. The common law trust is generally not considered to have legal personality, so the question really is: should the trust be given one?

This chapter argues that trusts are not *de facto* legal entities, that they do not need to be granted legal personality, and that the legal entity view is not necessary for civilian reception of the trust. Trusts do exhibit asset-partitioning attributes, but it is weak and materially different from entities that offer ironclad shielding. The trustee is hardly shielded by the trust and, when he is at fault, is always financially responsible for debts and torts incurred by the trust. With a real entity, corporate directors enjoy a much higher level of comfort and security. Equally, beneficiaries can sometimes be liable for trust obligations; but the same would almost never happen with corporate shareholders. Another reason why asset-partitioning need not equate to legal personality is history. Judge-made laws have created asset-partitioning organizational laws long before general incorporation was made available. Historically speaking, asset-partitioning existed without legal personality.

But most importantly, the quality of the relationship between a beneficiary and the trust asset is different from that between an entity-member and the entity's assets. The former is a lot more direct and strong whereas the latter is intermediated by a fictitious legal person.[2] As for civilian conceptions of trusts, the legal entity approach is the most pragmatic one if we want the trust concept to be exported worldwide. But existing civilian understandings of obligations, property, and patrimonies are sufficient to provide a conceptual

[2] For sure, different trusts will have different relationships between beneficiaries and trust assets. A bare trust beneficiary has a much more direct relationship with the trust asset than an object of a discretionary trust. In any case, the beneficiary's relationship with trust assets is intermediated by his interest in the trust fund. See Chapters 8 and 9.

basis for trusts, without needing to resort to legal entities. Trusts are not legal entities and need not be understood as such.

This chapter is organized as follows. First, it outlines HKM's asset-partitioning and *de facto* entity views of the trust. Second, it demonstrates that the trust, at best, exhibits weak and porous asset-partitioning features. Third, borrowing from legal history and the commercial use of trusts, it shows that the common law trust does not need legal personality to fulfil its existing functions. Fourth, it highlights a key difference between trusts and entities: that beneficiaries have a much stronger and more direct relationship with trust assets than members of entities. Fifth, it debunks the idea that trusts play a very active role in finance and commerce. Finally, it examines civilian conceptions of trusts and argues that trusts need not be understood as entities in the civil law world.

Creditors, Liabilities, and Asset-Partitioning

HKM's conception of the trust stems from its essential functions and contributions. In agreeing with Langbein, they note that trust law provides the parties with a body of default rules and they do not deny the transaction cost savings these rules provide. However, they state that this function of trust law is not irreplaceable by specialized bodies of contract and agency laws. On the other hand, the creditor and proprietary consequences created by trusts and trust law are not easily replicable by contract and agency laws.

HKM introduce the idea of asset-partitioning and distinguish between defensive and affirmative asset-partitioning. Defensive asset-partitioning shields the owners of an organization from its creditors—this is commonly manifested through the limited liability of shareholders. Affirmative asset-partitioning shields the organization from its owners' personal creditors, thereby protecting the organization as a going concern.[3] In both cases, the respective creditors of the organization and its owners are excluded from cross-claiming assets to satisfy debts and obligations. HKM argue that while defensive asset-partitioning is popularly perceived as the highlight of legal entities, it is affirmative asset-partitioning that is the crowning achievement of organizational law. They also observe that it is costly to replicate asset-partitioning with mere contract and agency laws. To replicate asset-partitioning imperfectly, the organization and its owners must insert into all contracts they

[3] In the case of a corporation, the most that creditors of owners can do is to take ownership of their shares. Even then, unless they have enough voting control, creditors cannot force the corporation to liquidate its assets; they merely have a claim to a share of the corporation's cash flow.

enter into clauses that limit their counterparties' claims. Even then, it is difficult to limit the claims of unforeseen tort claimants.

Trust-like asset-partitioning attributes can be achieved with contract and agency laws only at a prohibitively high cost. They say that 'the most important contribution of the law of trusts is that it facilitates the partitioning of assets into bundles that can conveniently be pledged separately to different classes of creditors. Of particular importance in this respect is the use of trust law to shield trust assets from claims of the trustee's personal creditors'.[4] They argue that trust laws 'makes the trustee, vis-à-vis creditors with whom he contracts, two distinct legal persons: a natural person contracting on behalf of himself, and an artificial person acting on behalf of the beneficiaries'.[5] This observation is reinforced by the fact that a trustee can contract with third parties in his capacity as trustee and thereby limiting his liability to the trust assets available.[6] Defensive asset-partitioning can also be observed in the trust as beneficiaries are generally not liable for debts and obligations incurred by the trustee.

Since the trustee's personal creditors cannot claim trust assets and trust creditors cannot claim beyond trust assets, HKM argue that a high degree of affirmative asset-partitioning is achieved with the trust. Furthermore, defensive asset-partitioning is achieved as the trustee's creditors cannot claim against beneficiaries. As the trust features both types of asset-partitioning, it is just like a legal entity. HKM claim that 'while it is sometimes said that the common-law trust lacks legal personality, in our view it is, on the contrary, quite clearly a legal entity, and trust law is consequently a form of organizational law'.[7]

Treating the trust as a legal entity is not a new idea. Scholars, practitioners, and users of trusts often speak of 'the trust', just as they would refer to 'the company'. But this is arguably done so out of convenience. It is much easier to say that an asset is owned by 'the trust', rather than 'the trustee on trust for the beneficiaries'. Until HKM's works appeared in recent years, the 'trust as entity' idea remained as a matter of linguistic anomaly in the common law world.

HKM also draw on the commercial use of trusts to support the idea that it is a *de facto* legal entity.[8] They note that in terms of asset value, the commercial use of trusts completely overshadows private use.[9] Trusts have become a common

4 *The Functions of Trust Law, supra* note 1, 438.

5 *Essential Role, supra* note 1, 416.

6 *The Functions of Trust Law, supra* note 1, 459—60; see also D. J. Hayton, P. Matthews, and C. Mitchell. (eds.) *Underhill and Hayton The Law Relating to Trusts and Trustees* (17th edn. LexisNexis Butterworths, London 2006), hereafter *Underhill & Hayton*, art 83.5. For the equivalent rule in the United States, see Restatement (Second) of Trusts, §263.

7 *Essential Role, supra* note 1, 416.

8 *The Functions of Trust Law, supra* note 1, 466—9.

9 *Trust Law in the United States, supra* note 1, 133.

feature in pension funds, mutual funds, and asset securitization. Trusts are the favoured vehicle in these examples precisely because of their asset-partitioning attributes. HKM also query the blurring distinction between the trust and the corporation and they do this by examining business trusts.

Put simply, business trusts are trusts where trustees carry out a business for beneficiaries, who provide the capital for investment. In the early days, there were significant uncertainties surrounding the status of business trusts and their participants. They were often characterized as partnerships rather than corporations. Modern state statutes have overridden common law problems of entity recognition and limited liability for beneficiaries. To consolidate these developments, the National Conference of Commissioners on Uniform State Law is now drafting the Uniform Statutory Trust Entity Act. Under this Act, a statutory trust is a *de jure* legal entity and neither the trustee nor the beneficiaries is liable for the trust's debts and obligations.[10] Being very much like corporations, modern business trusts are used for various purposes. The most notable ones are using it to structure a mutual fund or to hold real estate, which could otherwise be achieved with a corporation. In discussing the Delaware business trust statute, on which the Uniform Statutory Trust Entity Act is based, Hansmann and Mattei say that '[it] is effectively a generic corporation statute'.[11] With the existence of such entities, they question what the differences between such trusts and corporations are and why do parties choose one over the other.

The Essential but Insufficient Role of Asset-Partitioning in Trust Law

The arguments for considering trusts as entities are as follows: trusts exhibit asset-partitioning features, just like real legal entities. Modern commercial practices employ trusts and corporations almost interchangeably in many forms of transactions—reinforcing the trust's entity-like image. While these arguments have functional appeal, each of them is, to a large extent, flawed.

Outside the United States, common law trusts are not considered to be legal entities as conventionally understood.[12] *Black's Law Dictionary* defines an entity as 'an organization . . . that has a legal identity apart from its members or owners'.[13] If legal personality is deemed to be a prerequisite to a legal entity, then trusts fall short on this technical requirement. But a better

[10] Uniform Statutory Trust Entity Act (Tentative Draft 2009), §302 and 304.

[11] *The Functions of Trust Law*, *supra* note 1, 475.

[12] See *Underhill & Hayton*, *supra* note 6, art 1.1 (3).

[13] 'Entity' in *Black's Law Dictionary* (9th edn. 2009).

question to ask is whether an entity must have legal personality. Unincorporated associations, such as clubs and societies, do not have legal personalities but are often treated as legal entities. They are treated as such not because they can independently enter into legal relations or hold property, but because it is convenient to consider them as juridical or accounting units. A married couple's relationship is referred to as 'the marriage'. 'It' often has asset-partitioning attributes and can even enjoy tax breaks, but 'the marriage' can neither enter into legal relations nor hold property. Just like 'the marriage', 'the trust' remains as a very convenient linguistic and administrative shorthand.

In the United States, the position is different and the trust is considered implicitly as a legal entity. Until the end of the twentieth century, the United States followed the English position and trustees were personally liable for contractual and tort obligations. For example, case law holds that a plaintiff must sue the trustee in his personal capacity and cannot sue him in his entity-like fiduciary capacity.[14] Towards the end of the twentieth century, however, scholars and practitioners began systematically to encroach on the common law position. Through drafting influential documents such as the Uniform Trust Code (UTC) and the Restatement of the Law, they have overridden centuries-old case law and imposed quasi-legal personality on the trust. In the UTC, §1010(c) overrides the common law position on suing the trustee in his personal capacity, giving the trust more entity-like attributes. As far as being sued is concerned, the trust under the UTC has its own legal identity. In fact, §103 goes as far as defining 'persons' as to include trusts and other legal and commercial entities. The UTC arguably introduced the entity-trust through the back door. The Restatement (Third) on Trusts relies significantly on case law so it cannot simply brush aside established precedents. Instead, it does not disclaim the idea that the trust is a legal entity and the Reporter's comment discusses extensively the emerging trends toward recognizing the trust as an entity.[15] Even with all these recent changes, the trust in the United States still does not enjoy all the powers or privileges of its corporate cousins. In other words, the trust is not a full-blooded legal entity. But given the divergence between the United States and the rest of the common law world in conceiving the trust as an entity and given the fluid meaning of the entity concept, we should be less concerned with whether the trust is a legal entity and more concerned with whether the trust ought to be considered as such.

[14] See for example *Smith v. Chambers*, 117 W. Va. 204.

[15] See Restatement (Third) of Trusts, §2 comment a. The Restatement (Second) of Trusts gives a historical and untainted view of the common law position in the United States.

Since the asset-partitioning attributes are the hallmark of entities, what is one to make of these attributes in the trust? There is a high degree of asset-partitioning when an asset is held on trust. However, whether one is considering affirmative or defensive asset-partitioning, the trust is a lot weaker and more porous than the corporation. With affirmative asset-partitioning, it is true that the personal creditors of trustees cannot claim trust assets; but this feature is over-emphasized by HKM at the expense of the position of the beneficiaries' personal creditors.

Beneficiaries with a fixed interest retain beneficial ownership of the trust asset and their creditors can step into their shoes to claim the trust asset or, if they do not wholly own it, seek its partition. In the case of objects of discretionary trusts or beneficiaries of spendthrift trusts, it is true that their personal creditors usually cannot claim the trust asset. But then again, trusts that appear like entities and fit for commercial applications would typically not have discretionary objects or spendthrift clauses. They would instead have units or shares, where their holders' entitlements are unambiguously defined. As a result, common law trusts generally have weak affirmative asset-partitioning attributes.

The trustee's limited liability with trust creditors is often cited as an entity-like attribute. However, the trustee's limited liability with trust creditors is a product of contract law and not trust law. By entering into obligations 'as trustee for X and not otherwise', the counterparty acknowledges and accepts that the trustee's liability is limited to the trust assets. Crucially, this requires the counterparty's consent and is not part and parcel of trust law. This stands in contrast to the trustee's personal creditors who cannot claim trust assets whether they consent to this arrangement or not. Nothing actually stops a trustee from contracting with third parties in his own name and without the liability limitation; he would just be a very generous and selfless trustee. In the case of a corporation, a director who enters into a contract in his personal capacity will be treated as acting for himself and not the corporation;[16] there is no functional symmetry here between the trust and the corporation.

In the case of unforeseen tort creditors, the positions in England and the United States are superficially different but practically the same. In England, the trustee is personally and unlimitedly liable to such creditors.[17] This is logical because the trustee holds the legal title to the trust asset and should naturally be in the same position as other absolute owners as far as the burdens

[16] Of course, directors and other fiduciaries are subject to the no-profit rule, which can render their personal contracts (or at least their benefits) the corporation's.

[17] See *Underhill & Hayton*, *supra* note 6, art 41.5. For the equivalent rule, see Restatement (Second) of Trusts, §261.

of ownership are concerned. The harshness of this rule is somewhat mitigated by the trustee's right to indemnity and creditors can subrogate the trustee's reimbursement claims. The caveat to this is that the trustee (and his creditors by subrogation) can only seek indemnity if the trustee is not at fault. If the trustee is deemed to be at fault, after setting off his liable share of the claim, there may not be a positive indemnity value on which the trustee can rely.

In the United States, HKM state that the trustee's liability is automatically limited to the value of the trust assets.[18] But this seemingly trustee-friendly and entity-like position is illusory. In both the Restatement and the UTC, the trustee will actually be liable for torts if he is personally at fault.[19] In essence, both English and United States trustees remain *financially* liable for torts if they are at fault. The key difference is that an English creditor risks having a worthless indemnification subrogation claim whereas an American creditor can sue the trustee in his fiduciary capacity; the American trustee's fault is his own problem, not that of his tort creditors.[20]

As a general rule for corporations, directors do not enter into contracts or hold assets in their own names and cannot be sued personally for obligations of or torts committed by the corporation. The immediate protection afforded by the corporation is much greater than that provided by the trust. Obviously, directors can be sued by shareholders for negligence for the very same acts that gave rise to corporate liability, but at least creditors will not have to deal with uncertain issues such as indemnification and subrogation.

The trust is also considerably more porous than the corporation when it comes to defensive asset-partitioning. Where the beneficiary of an English bare trust (for example, of shares) is of full age and capacity, the trustee is entitled to be indemnified for expenses incurred and he can claim against the beneficiary personally.[21] With burdens and expenses that arise merely because of the trustee's ownership of or holding of title to assets, such as capital calls and land taxes, the trustee's entitlement to indemnity is automatic. With other expenses, the beneficiary's consent is required. The reasoning behind this seemingly harsh rule is that since the beneficiary enjoys

[18] *The Functions of Trust Law, supra* note 1, 460.

[19] Restatement (Second) of Trusts, §265; Uniform Trust Code §1010 (b).

[20] The UK Trust Law Committee proposes that creditors' right of subrogation should be modified so that the trustee's fault cannot be used to set off the indemnity claim, thereby giving trustee creditors an almost direct claim against the trust fund. See Trust Law Committee. 'Rights of Creditors Against Trustees and Trust Funds—Report', 1999, <http://www.kcl.ac.uk/content/1/c6/01/11/90/TLCCredRightsReport140499_1.pdf>, last accessed 15 June 2010, art 10.3.

[21] *Hardoon v Belilios* (1901) AC 118. This case concerned a nomineeship where the trustee faced a capital call for shares he held on bare trust for the beneficiary. The court held that the beneficiary must indemnify the trustee.

all the benefits of the trust asset, he should also bear the burdens. This rule does not apply to trusts involving beneficiaries that are unborn or lack capacity as they are not in a position to disclaim their beneficial interests and the burdens that come along with them.

This is the English position. The liability of an identical beneficiary in a United States trust is less clear. In the decades after *Hardoon v Belilios* was decided, the majority of American scholars took the view that the rule applied, especially to business trusts.[22] In modern times, a definitive view cannot easily be found. The Restatement (Second) of Trusts provides conflicting opinions on this point. In the Reporter's comments to §249 dealing with 'Indemnity from the Beneficiary Personally', he mentions *Hardoon v Belilios* in passing but also observes that a beneficiary is not personally liable to indemnify the trustee. But in §277 dealing with the 'Liability of Beneficiary as Title Holder', he clearly states that where a trustee holds shares and his only duty is to convey them as directed by the beneficiary, the beneficiary would be liable to assessments directly with third parties. §709 of the UTC states the trustee's right to reimbursement of expenses but is generally silent on the question of indemnity from the beneficiary.

Two reasons suggest that the rule in *Hardoon* is still good law in the United States. The first is that it is a historical position that does not appear to have been overridden by recent cases or texts. The second is that the rule is largely based on the principle that the beneficiary can voluntarily consent to indemnifying the trustee. The fact that the beneficiary in this case chose not to disclaim his interest gave rise to an implied consent of indemnification.[23] Therefore, in modern times, judicial interpretation of non-statutory trust law should yield the same result as a century ago.

In an analogous case of a limited liability corporation with a sole shareholder, the same result would not happen. Creditors seeking to claim money for capital calls or land taxes will struggle to claim beyond the corporation itself.[24] The

[22] See H. F. Stone, 'A Theory of Liability of Trust Estates for the Contracts and Torts of the Trustee' 22 *Colum. L. Rev.* 527 (1922); A. W. Scott , 'Book Review' 31 *Yale L. J.* 455 (1922); A. W. Scott, 'Liabilities Incurred in the Administration of Trusts' 28 *Harv. L. Rev.* 725 (1915); and R. S. Stevens, 'Limited Liability in Business Trusts' 7 *C.L.Q.* 116 (1921). The main dissenting voice of the times was John Sears, who advocated the efficacy of the trust as a business vehicle; J. H. Sears, *Trust Estates as Business Companies* (Vernon Law Book Company, Kansas City 1921).

[23] A. Oosterhoff states that United States beneficiaries are not liable to indemnify trustees unless they consent to do so and he cites the leading text *Scott on Trusts*. However, the proposition that Oosterhoff relies on (indemnity only with the beneficiary's consent) is precisely the one that gives rise to judicially implied consent that the *Hardoon* case concluded. A. H. Oosterhoff, 'Indemnification of Trustees: The Rule in *Hardoon v. Belilios*' 4 *Estates and Trusts Quarterly* 180 (1977).

[24] Unless the corporation has a high net asset value, creditors and other counterparties will of course demand additional guarantees and indemnities from directors and shareholders.

corporation is considered the owner of the asset and is solely responsible for all the liabilities that arise out of the asset. It is true that corporate veils can be pierced and shareholders can be found liable for a corporation's liabilities, but veil piercing only succeeds where there are highly unusual circumstances.[25] The mere fact that an individual is the sole shareholder—or even also its sole director—is not enough to establish his liability; whereas being a beneficiary of a bare trust will suffice.

All of the trust's asset-partitioning weaknesses put it at a disadvantage for conducting business. However, another danger lurks when the non-statutory trust is used for business or trading. Non-statutory business trusts have repeatedly been classified as partnerships.[26] The main factor for classifying business trusts as partnerships is the degree of beneficiary control. When beneficiaries have too much power to dictate how the trustee conducts his affairs, the beneficiaries are deemed to be partners and the trustee is deemed to be their agent. The control issue is an inherent and irreconcilable tension with beneficiaries, especially if there are not many of them in a trust. When a small number of individuals pool their capital together for investment, it is more likely than not that they would want a degree of activc influence and control. Conversely, with a group consisting of thousands of disparate investors, their desire for and entitlement to influence and control reduces proportionately with the relative sizes of their investment. In the end, only statutory intervention can wipe away centuries-old trust rules and give rise to entity-trusts. With watertight asset-partitioning and legal personality, entity-trusts these days are much closer to corporations than they are to common law trusts. The need to legislate for entity-trusts demonstrates that the common law trust is not as entity-like as the corporation when it comes to asset-partitioning. Trusts do partition assets to a large extent, but not enough to cross the threshold of becoming an entity.

Historical Asset-Partitioning and Legal Entities

Asset-partitioning is said to be the essential role of organizational law and there appears to be a widespread belief that only legal entities can provide it.[27]

[25] The law on piercing the corporate veil is complex. Situations where the court has pierced the veil include fraud, tax, employment law, tort, and where one company is the agent of another. See A. Dignam and J. Lowry, *Company Law* (5th edn. Oxford University Press, Oxford 2009), Chapter 3.

[26] See generally R. S. Stevens, *supra* note 22.

[27] See J. Getzler and M. Macnair, 'The Firm as an Entity Before the Companies Act', 2006, <http://papers.ssrn.com/sol3/papers.cfm?abstract_id=941231>, last accessed 7 January 2010, 1–2.

Because they are creatures of the legislature, they are not bound by any existing limitations of property or contract law and can have whatever asset-partitioning attributes legislators deem suitable. HKM, for example, treat organizational law almost exclusively as the domain of legal entities.[28] In the case of trusts, they equate asset-partitioning and separate patrimonies with legal entities. But, historically, asset-partitioning existed in primitive forms well before corporations emerged and became available for general use. Joshua Getzler and Mike Macnair argue that before the emergence of general incorporation, courts were able to adapt 'basic concepts of contract, property and debt priorities... [which could] result in a workable organizational law... '.[29]

Getzler and Macnair show that with some help from statutes, the courts constructed a doctrinal machinery based on a theory of interpersonal transacting. This machinery relies on doctrines such as presumptive fraud, *bona fide* purchase, reputed ownership, estoppel, and the treatment of trusts as rights sounding through *in personam* claims. The end result is 'a pre-incorporation system that offered many of the effects of separate personality, asset partitioning and limited liability'.[30] Of particular interest here—and as proof that asset-partitioning is possible without entities—is the jingle rule found in the laws of partnership insolvency. According to Getzler and Macnair, 'the jingle rule states that the joint creditors of a partnership cannot access individual assets of the partners until the partnership funds are exhausted; and the individual creditors of individual partners cannot access other partners' assets until the personal assets of the partner (including his share of the partnership capital) is exhausted.'[31]

The rule, which pre-dates the first modern Companies Act by almost 100 years, shields the partnership (as a going concern) and the partners (as individuals) up to the value of each individual partner's asset and the partnership capital respectively. This rule alone shows that asset-partitioning can exist without the use of legal entities. Clearly, a legal entity is not a conceptual prerequisite to asset-partitioning. The essential role of organizational law is indeed its ability to partition assets, but organizational law is not the exclusive domain of legal entities. Of course, the imposition of legal personality significantly accelerated the development of organizational law.

[28] Apart from briefly mentioning state marital laws and their asset-partitioning effects, Hansmann and Kraakman's influential article discusses organizational law in the exclusive context of legal entities. See *Essential Role*, *supra* note 1, 390.

[29] J. Getzler and M. Macnair, *supra* note 27, 3.

[30] Ibid. 5.

[31] Ibid. 10. Obviously, other partners' personal assets outside the partnership cannot be used to satisfy the personal debts of an insolvent partner.

Judges can only develop creditor priority rules slowly whilst respecting judicial precedents and the socio-economic environment of the times; whereas legislative imposition of legal personality can legitimately sweep away precedents and established understandings of creditor priorities. What is important to draw from history is that asset-partitioning can exist without the use of legal entities.

The Differences Between Trust Law and Organizational Law

The essential feature of all legal entities, which is more important than any asset-partitioning attributes, is that they are separate from the individuals that participate in them.[32] In the case of a corporation, it has its own legal personality with it own rights and duties that are separate from those of its management and shareholders. What the corporation owns does not belong to the shareholders; at best, shareholders own the corporation, which in turn owns the assets.

The same cannot be said for the trust. The beneficiary's relationship with the trust asset is a lot more direct than that between a corporate shareholder and corporate assets. Under both English and United States trust laws, the beneficiary by default has a right to call for the delivery of the trust asset because he has a proprietary right in it; whereas the corporate shareholder does not have an equivalent right to call for corporate assets. It is true that the beneficiary's relationship with the trust asset is intermediated by rules such as the *bona fide* purchaser exception and the doctrine of overreaching,[33] but they simply exist to facilitate the trust as a fluctuating fund concept.[34]

In the case of a corporation selling assets, a buyer only needs to be concerned with actual knowledge of an *ultra vires* transaction (which in any case has nothing to do with shareholders' property rights in the underlying

[32] *Black's Law Dictionary* defines an entity as 'an organization that has a legal identity apart from its members or owners'. 'Entity' in *Black's Law Dictionary* (9th edn. 2009).

[33] Overreaching is the English term for the doctrine where a purchaser of a trust asset takes it free of any beneficial interest. The beneficiary's interest in the trust asset attaches instead to the sales proceeds. In English law, this is embodied in s 2 of the Law of Property Act 1925. In the United States, this doctrine is reflected in §283 and 284 of the Restatement (Second) of Trusts. See generally D. J. Hayton, P. Matthews, and C. Mitchell. (eds.) *Underhill and Hayton The Law Relating to Trusts and Trustees* (17th edn. LexisNexis Butterworths, London 2006), art 45.1 (16). See also C. Harpum, 'Overreaching, Trustee's Powers and the Reform of the 1925 Legislation' 49 *CLJ* 277 (1990) and D. Fox. 'Overreaching' in P. Birks and A. Pretto (eds.) *Breach of Trust* (Hart, Oxford 2002).

[34] See Part III.

asset).[35] The doctrine of overreaching also has no corporate counterpart. It exists in trust law as part of the mechanism that enables the beneficiary's proprietary interest to shift from one asset into another as the trustee transacts; there is no need for a corporate equivalent because it is the corporation as a separate legal person that is changing the composition of its assets, not its shareholders.

As long as the beneficiary's proprietary position is governed by these rules, it is difficult to assert that the trust is a legal entity that is separate from its members or managers. This also raises a salient point about the usefulness of the term 'entity'. To be considered as a legal entity for general purposes, an organization or vehicle must meet many conceptual requirements. But to be deemed as an entity, or juridical unit,[36] for tax or special legal reasons, all that is required is legislative or judicial will. Trusts are treated as juridical units most frequently for tax purposes; marriages or households are treated as accounting units for tax benefits; even investment accounts are deemed to be legal persons for regulatory purposes.[37] With the widespread use of the trust as an estate planning and tax avoidance device, it should come as no surprise that governments often classify and tax trusts as entities so to better capture them within the revenue net. Interestingly, the United States is almost alone in the common law world to push for the entity-trust idea. In England the idea is almost unheard of and in the offshore jurisdictions, it would be counterproductive to use entity-trusts as confidentiality and avoiding entity-level taxation are leading motivations for end-users.

That the United States has entity-trusts may be comprehensible from a tax perspective. In any developed country, the structure of its tax and organizational laws means that the choice of entity for a particular transaction will have some tax consequences; that is why the tax planning industry exists. In some jurisdictions, the planned and diligent use of trusts may result in very significant tax savings for individuals and businesses; in other jurisdictions, because of their catch-all tax codes and long-arm jurisdictions, the tax savings may be significantly reduced, if not minimal. Compared to other industrialized countries, the United States may belong to the latter group and the

[35] The importance of the *ultra vires* doctrine has been significantly reduced in modern corporate law. Sections 31 and 39 of the UK Companies Act 2006 provide companies with an unrestricted corporate objective by default and provides that the validity of an act done by a company shall not be called into question on the ground of lack of capacity by reason of anything in the company's constitution.

[36] For a useful discussion on legal entities, see P. I. Blumberg, *The Multinational Challenge to Corporation Law* (Oxford University Press, Oxford 1993), Chapters 9 and 10.

[37] Ibid. 225; see also T. J. Finnegan and J. P. Garner, 'The Separate Account as an Investment Company: Structural Problems of the "Ectoplasmic Theory"' 3 *Conn. L. Rev.* 106 (1970).

choice between trusts and other vehicles for certain transactions may only have minor effects. Ironically, this environment that lacks tax advantages is conducive to developing novel trust concepts like the revocable trust. Since the revocable trust is taxed just like a decedent's estate, the revocable trust is allowed to appear and behave as though the settlor has never parted with his assets.[38] This is both interesting and ironic because both ends of the tax jurisdiction spectrum—the United States and the Caribbean islands—foster novel trust concepts for basically opposite reasons.

The Supportive Role of Trusts in Commerce

HKM point out the trust's role in commerce to demonstrate its corporation-like importance. Business trusts, especially those with legal personalities, are often cited as evidence of the trust's commercial success. Statistical figures are used to support their importance, for example by stating the value of assets they hold for the mutual fund industry.[39] However, their dollar values and contributions to the economy are not as significant as they purport to be. Asset securitization is an important activity in financial markets, but the purported market size of $4 trillion is dwarfed, for example, by the notional value of credit default swaps (which are contracts) at the end of 2008: $38.6 trillion.[40] This is further outnumbered by the notional value of interest rate derivatives at the end of 2008: $403.1 trillion.[41] It is true that these enormous figures are only the notional values and the actual amounts that change hands may only be a tiny fraction of the notional values. But such is the problem of using such statistics to assess a legal vehicle's contribution to commerce. Whether one uses a trust, a corporation, or a contract, if it is the right legal form, it is scalable at almost zero cost. A $10 million asset securitization deal involves just as much legal and administrative work as a $100 million one; the same can be said about mutual funds of differing sizes.

[38] Settlors and beneficiaries of revocable trusts are treated in like manner as testators and will beneficiaries respectively under the federal income and transfer tax systems. See Restatement (Third) of Trusts, §25 General Comment.

[39] For example, Hansmann and Mattei note that asset securitization trusts hold $2 trillion worth of assets. John Langbein states that the trust form holds half of the $4 trillion worth of mutual fund assets. See *Trust Law in the United States*, *supra* note 1, 133; and J. H. Langbein, 'The Secret Life of the Trust: The Trust as an Instrument of Commerce' 107 *Yale L. J.* 165 (1997), 170.

[40] International Swaps and Derivatives Association, 'News Release, ISDA Publishes Year-End 2008 Market Survey Results', 22 April 2009, <http://www.isda.org/press/press042209market.html>, last accessed 7 January 2010.

[41] International Swaps and Derivatives Association, *supra* note 40.

What is important to note, however, is where the money goes. In the case of an asset securitization, investors ultimately lend money to issuers who securitize assets to provide as collateral. Unless it is a refinancing exercise, issuers usually reinvest the money into their business operations. In the case of mutual funds, investors entrust funds to fund managers who invest in equities (and other financial instruments). Whether their equity investments take the form of an initial public offering or a purchase in the secondary market, mutual funds assume the role of shareholders and owners of real businesses; and corporations are still the dominant vehicle for businesses that produce goods and services. There have been various discussions as to why trusts are ill-suited for this role.[42] But what is important to note here is that the role trusts perform in financial markets is merely a supportive one, namely, to hold assets. In dollar terms, trusts may hold more financial assets than the market capitalization of the entire US equities market, but it is business corporations that create jobs and innovate. If one insists on celebrating the commercial success of trusts, one should also do the same for contracts or property, which are even greater commercial successes.

Civilian Conceptions of Trusts and the Entity Model

HKM are not alone in arguing that the trust is a legal entity. The civil law world has struggled to conceive of the trust in common law terms. The most significant conceptual challenge to introducing English trusts to civil law systems is often said to be the duality of titles in English trusts.[43] The contemporaneous existence of legal and beneficial titles appears to be in clear violation of the civilian notion of absolute dominium, which only allows the totality of ownership to reside with one owner at any one time.

Because of this irreconcilable difference in conceiving property, there is not a civilian proprietary conception of trust, at least in modern times.[44] Roman law recognized the *fideicommissum*, where a testator can leave property to one

[42] See Chapters 4 and 5 and also T. Frankel, 'The Delaware Business Trust Act Failure as the New Corporate Law' 23 *Cardozo L. Rev.* 325 (2002).

[43] G. L. Gretton, 'Trusts Without Equity' 49 *ICLQ* 599 (2000), hereafter *Trusts Without Equity*, 600.

[44] The closest 'proprietary' conception civilians have is an encumbrance on an asset legally owned by the 'trustee'. In the Netherlands, this is known as a *goederenrechtelijk verband*. But this is materially different from the proprietary approach that is familiar to English scholars where the trustee is holding the trust asset for the benefit of the beneficiary; the Dutch approach is proprietary in the sense that there is an all-encompassing lien attached to the asset. See D. J. Hayton, S. C. J. J. Kortmann, and H. L. E. Verhagen. (eds.) *Principles of European Trust Law* (Kluwer Law International, The Hague 1999), hereafter *Principles of European Trust Law*, 207.

for life and upon one's death pass it on to another.[45] This is like a modern life tenant and remainderman arrangement only the 'life tenant' here is meant to be the trustee holding for the 'remainderman'; the trustee's life tenancy is seen as his trustee remuneration. Although it can only be used as a post mortem device, the *fideicommissum* stands out because the remainderman's interest cannot be defeated by the *bona fide* purchaser.

In modern times, there are two civilian models to deal with the trust. The first is the obligational model which posits that the trust 'is an obligation between the creator of the trust and the trustee. The remedies for interference with that obligation, or for its non-performance, are therefore in principle personal. The beneficiary being not a party to the obligation may or may not have remedy, though the usual statute or code provision is to confer rights of some kind upon the beneficiary'.[46] Such devices are usually deemed to be contracts or agencies and strictly speaking fall under the law of obligations.[47] For example, the Luxembourg *fiducie* is a fiduciary contract between the settlor and the *fiduciaire* and it resonates with the trust because *fiducie* assets are held according to the terms of the contract and *fiducie* assets do not form part of the *fiduciaire's* property in case of his insolvency. In this way, the *fiducie* is like an asset-partitioned contract. The Swiss-German *treuhand* involves the *treuhander* managing assets from the *treugeber*. To outsiders, the *treuhander* appears to be the owner of the asset but in actual fact it belongs to the *treugeber*. Under Swiss law, the *treuhand* is considered to be part of the law of agency and it resembles an English nomineeship, or perhaps an asset-partitioned agency. While the civilian obligational model is closest to the English trust, it is interesting to note that devices like the *fiducie* or the *treuhand* are largely bilateral relationships between the settlor and the trustee and trustees here typically do not have as much discretion as their English counterparts.

The second model is the patrimony model. As George Gretton explains, the patrimony is the 'totality of a person's assets, and, in its broader sense, his liabilities also'.[48] In principle, each individual only has one patrimony, but there are exceptions to this rule, such as a special patrimony for matrimonial property. Assets and, to a certain extent, liabilities are segregated from an individual's general patrimony. Gretton posits that the trust is a trustee's special patrimony and also notes that this is recognized by The Hague Convention and the *Principles of European Trust Law*.[49]

[45] See generally P. Matthews. 'Some Alternatives to Trusts' 5 *OTPR* 31 (1995).
[46] D. Waters. 'The Future of the Trust Part I' 13 *JITCP* 179 (2006), 187.
[47] See generally P. Matthews, *supra* note 45.
[48] *Trusts Without Equity, supra* note 43, 608.
[49] The Hague Convention on the Law Applicable to Trusts and on their Recognition 1984.

There are two offshoots of the patrimony model: the pure patrimony by appropriation and the patrimony with legal personality. The French jurist Pierre Lepaulle conceives of the trust as a patrimony by appropriation.[50] Here, the trust assets belong to a special patrimony and have the asset-partitioning effects of a trust. Crucially, however, the special patrimony is not held by the trustee; in fact, the trust special patrimony belongs to nobody. According to Lepaulle, the settlor, the trustee, and the beneficiary are all inessential to the trust; what is required is that a trust asset is appropriated to further a certain object, be it a person or a purpose.[51] This 'patrimony by appropriation' view of the trust is reflected in Article 1261 of the Quebec Civil Code, which states that 'the trust patrimony, consisting of the property transferred in trust, constitutes a patrimony by appropriation, autonomous and distinct from that of the settlor, trustee or beneficiary and in which none of them has any real right.' From an English lawyer's point of view, the trust assets are 'owned' by nobody, not even the trustee.[52]

As the 'patrimony by appropriation' concept clearly segregates the trust assets from all human parties, it can be argued that it is an entity in all but name. Therefore, granting the trust legal personality is just a token step towards recognizing the reality of trusts. Lepaulle later also proposed granting legal personality to the trust. In discussing the problems common law scholars themselves face when trying to classify rights and duties according to the *in personam* and *in rem* categories, he suggested that the most effective solution to these problems is to grant the trust legal personality.[53] Lepaulle is by no means alone in this endeavour. In modern times, Gretton argues for granting the trust legal personality, but not because it solves certain conceptual problems. Rather, because special patrimonies 'tend to function as persons, and historically they have shown a tendency to become persons.'[54]

Of the two models, the legal entity one is more attractive because civilian lawyers can relate an entity-trust a lot more easily with existing civilian foundations (the French *fondation* or the Germanic *Stiftung*). In fact, there are very few special patrimonies that do not have legal personalities. For

[50] See generally P. Lepaulle, *Traité Théorique et Pratique des Trusts en Droit Interne, en Droit Fiscal et en Droit International* (Rousseau & Cie, Paris 1932); see also P. Lepaulle, 'An Outsider's View Point of the Nature of Trusts' 14 *C.L.Q.* 52 (1929), 55.

[51] Ibid. 55.

[52] Even Louisiana, the only other civilian jurisdiction in North America, adopted the common law conception of trusts when it defines it as a 'relationship resulting from the transfer of title to property to a person to be administered by him as a fiduciary for the benefit of another.' See La. R.S. 9:1731.

[53] P. Lepaulle, 'Book Review' 4 *Revue Internationale de Droit Comparé* 377 (1952).

[54] *Trusts Without Equity, supra* note 43, 617.

export purposes, the entity-trust should gain more acceptance than the patrimony by appropriation as the former is better known. Another advantage of the entity-trust is that it is easier to administer and regulate than the patrimony by appropriation. The beneficiary and the trustee's creditors ought to have lower monitoring costs because assets are held by and transactions are made with the entity-trust, not the trustee personally. There is a much lower risk of the trustee co-mingling assets from other separate patrimonies.[55]

But perhaps the biggest reason of all for granting legal personality is administrative workability. As Waters observes, Lepaulle's concept of patrimony by appropriation is a legal entity without the actual persona and jurisdictions who adopt it must resolve how the patrimony will transact with others and defend its own interests.[56] It is simply difficult to sue or be sued in court by a non-person. Perhaps Lepaulle's proposal to grant legal personality is a concession to his critics on administrative workability.

There may be practical reasons for grating legal personality to trusts, but conceptually it is not necessary. Special patrimonies held by another legal person have long existed in the civil law world and the closest civilian cousins to trusts are obligational *fiducie* that do not have legal personalities. The civil law trust could arguably be developed by improving the special patrimony held by another legal person or by reifying concepts like the *fiducie*. In any case, it is clear that trusts need not be legal entities in order to be accepted in civilian jurisdictions.[57] Conceiving patrimonies by appropriation as legal entities is just a fix for a badly transplanted legal concept.

But these days it is not civil lawyers who argue for trust entities, but—of all people—common law scholars like HKM and Gretton.[58] The reason is that the patrimony model of trusts exhibits much stronger asset-partitioning features. In theory, because everything happens in a special patrimony, the trustee and beneficiary will not be personally responsible for, say, tort liabilities or *Hardoon v Belilios* obligations arising from ownership of the trust assets. As a result, asset-partitioning scholars and supporters of entity-trusts will tend to argue that the trust ought to be a special patrimony, a legal entity, or ideally both. The cruel irony here is that the separate patrimony and legal entity ideas started off as an approximate explanation of the trust's

[55] But then again, English trusts—where the trustee can potentially co-mingle assets—have functioned for centuries without posing any systemic administrative problem.

[56] D. Waters, *supra* note 46, 193.

[57] In fact, the *Principles of European Trust Law* specifically excludes patrimonies by appropriation and, more importantly, trust-like devices that have legal personalities. *Principles of European Trust Law*, *supra* note 44, 30.

[58] George Gretton is a professor of Scottish Law, which, of course, involves elements of civil law.

asset-partitioning features for civilian lawyers, but they have now become the aspiration of many common law scholars.

Conclusion

Like characterizing trusts as contracts, labelling trusts as entities has a lot of aesthetic and pragmatic appeal. The trust provides a reasonable degree of asset-partitioning and when the legal niceties are overlooked, it does appear and behave like a legal entity. Also, by reforming trust law along the lines of entities, trusts will gain stronger-than-ever asset-partitioning attributes, putting them truly on par with corporations. Furthermore, the best way to export trusts to civilian jurisdictions is to treat them as legal entities, which are recognized in virtually all legal systems and avoids the English duality-of-title problem.

But the 'trust' that entity advocates are describing is not the trust that the common law knows. The 'trust' that HKM and others are describing is the one that they wish to see, the one that fits into their overall organizational law taxonomy project. Trusts do exhibit a degree of asset-partitioning features but they are porous when compared to the corporation. History also tells us that asset-partitioning does not require legal personality, a point seemingly overlooked by organizational law scholars. But most importantly, the relationship that beneficiaries have with trust assets is not intermediated by a fictitious legal person; the relationship is a lot more direct and strong but the same cannot be said for members of legal entities and their assets.

As for civilian conceptions of trusts, it is clear that trusts can be conceived using patrimonies alone and without legal personalities. True, it is much easier for civilian trust-like devices to be conceived as entities so that when they are used abroad there are no recognition problems. Therefore, out of pragmatism, civilian trusts ought to be conceived of as legal entities. But this does not mean common law trusts are or should be legal entities.

4

Trusts as Economic Firms

Introduction

That trusts are not legal entities and that they are not as popular as corporations for organizing businesses that produce goods and services is clear. Yet they are commonly associated with business and commerce. Not only is there a very business feel to trusts, Langbein's and Sitkoff's accounts of trusts borrow ideas from the branch of economics that seeks to explain why firms exist and how they are organized. As a result, for reasons yet to be understood, trusts are intricately linked with firms and businesses. This chapter examines this relationship by applying economic theories of the firm to the trust. If these theories of the firm can explain why trusts exist, then there is a genuine link. If not, then either the trust's relationship with firms and businesses is completely illusory or something else is fostering this relationship.

Economic theories of the firm explain why individuals band together as an organization to conduct economic activities. In this respect, they transcend legal forms and can be related to any economic organization, be it a corporation, partnership, sole proprietorship, or perhaps even a trust. It is not what we call it that counts, but what happens inside it. Trusts and their uses, on the other hand, defy stereotyping. If terminology is any guide, *Black's Law Dictionary* lists out over 160 different types of trusts; so it is difficult to claim any specific uses as prototypical.[1]

This chapter will focus on donative managerial and business trusts. Donative managerial trusts usually involve a settlor entrusting assets to the trustee who will manage investments and distribution for beneficiaries. Business trusts involve a trustee who manages a business for non-donative beneficiaries, who are investors of capital. Defining 'business' will simply lead us into a morass, as any form of activity for economic gain appears to meet the definition. It is better to consider the classic business trust activities of managing equities or real estate mutual funds. The donative trust and the

[1] 'Trusts' in *Black's Law Dictionary* (9th edn. 2009)

business trust are good examples for several reasons. First, scholars who apply theories of the firm to trusts generally focus on the donative trust so it is only appropriate to see whether the donative trust can be explained by these theories. Second, the business trust epitomizes the use of trusts in commerce and resembles an economic organization more than any other types of trusts. Therefore, if theories of the firm possess any explanatory power, they should be able to relate to the activities and relationships that exist inside donative and business trusts.

Three leading theories of the firm will be applied to the trust. They offer different explanations as to why individuals form economic firms to conduct their activities. However, none of these theories could adequately explain why trusts exist, even if one stretches these theories and the trust concept to their limits. Each of these theories focuses on specific features at prototypical firms, such as the use of administrative fiats, the monitoring of multiple workers, and the need to invest in assets specific to a particular contract or relationship. But none of these features can be found in trusts. Even the straightforward idea of residual control over a firm cannot be consistently applied to trusts. There is a reason why these theories cannot explain the existence of trusts. The activities conducted in donative and business trusts lack the two crucial features that can be found in any economic firm. Firms have what is known as intra-firm transfers, which refers to firm participants passing on a partly finished product or service to others. For example, in a car factory one worker may pass the chassis on to another to install the engine, who in turn passes it on to another to paint the body. These are examples of intra-firm transfers and if a car firm was not established, it is possible that each worker is a separate business specializing in one part of car manufacturing. Each business would sell on a partly finished product to the next one in the value chain until the completed car reaches the business that markets it to the public. This seemingly mundane idea is a key assumption in all theories of the firm but it does not exist in trusts. The other crucial feature that trusts lack is market transactions. All the intra-firm transfers notwithstanding, a car factory or a law firm ultimately transacts with the market by selling their goods or services. The end of the 'production cycle' in a trust is not characterized by market transactions, but by distribution of trust assets to beneficiaries. These two differences may appear to be subtle and innocuous, but they make all the difference in distinguishing trusts from firms.

This chapter is organized as follows. First, it introduces the ideas of institutions, organizations, and transaction costs, which are the conceptual prerequisites to understanding firms. Second, it examines three leading theories of the firm and applies them to the functions and activities of trusts to see if they can explain why trusts exist. Third, it explains the differences between trusts and firms and why these theories cannot account for trusts.

Institutions, Organizations, and Transaction Costs

Theories of the firm came to prominence as part of a broader movement known as institutional economics, which developed as a response to the perceived inadequacies of neoclassical economics. Broadly speaking, neoclassical economics ignore the role that man-made institutions play in economic behaviour and is over-simplistic. Institutional economics seek to better understand economic behaviour by taking into account institutions and organizations and in doing so, better capture reality. For example, in neoclassical economics, a factory may be assumed to be able to emit pollution at its discretion; all that matters was input of supplies and output of goods. Institutional economics, however, will recognize that there may be regulatory limitations to a factory's emissions and pollutions and will factor in such constraints.

An economic institution is any form of constraint that human beings devise to shape their interactions;[2] and those such as democratic government and the rule of law are deemed to be necessary for and beneficial to market economies. An organization, on the other hand, is a group of individuals bound by some common purpose to achieve objectives.[3] Trade unions, political parties, universities, marriages, and firms are all considered to be organizations. A trust may be considered an organization under this definition as it has three principal parties, who may be bound by some common purpose.[4]

How and why organizations form have been the subject of many studies but theories of the firm focus on why economic ones exist. All these theories recognize an important constraint within the economic framework: transaction costs. There is no precise definition of transaction costs but it is an all-encompassing idea that can explain most inefficiencies in economic life. Ronald Coase describes it as the cost of using the price mechanism and gives examples: price discovery, negotiating and concluding a contract, and

[2] D. C. North, *Institutions, Institutional Change and Economic Performance* (Political Economy of Institutions and Decisions, Cambridge University Press, Cambridge 1990), 4–5.

[3] Ibid. 5.

[4] This does not negate the fact that the three trust parties have conflicts of interests. On the other hand, the internal conflicts of interest among participants of trade unions and political parties are equally significant.

possibly enforcing a contract.[5] Organizational economists describe transaction costs as the imperfections and inefficiencies arising out of the structure of a transaction.

It has been said that if transaction costs were zero, every possible contingency would be negotiated and agreed upon *ex ante*, and, by definition, all contracts would be complete. If transaction costs were zero, there would be no need for firms as contract and property laws would suffice. In other words, in the case of a trust, if transaction costs were zero, the settlor and trustee can agree to a trust instrument that will specify in detail what the trustee will do in every conceivable scenario. In fact, if transaction costs were really zero, there would be no need for trusts at all as the trust parties can simply contract with the whole world complete contracts to achieve the trust terms and asset-partitioning effects.

But humans suffer from bounded rationality, which is the phenomenon where individuals intend to be rational, but because of their limited cognitive ability to be rational, they are only rational to a limited extent.[6] Because of bounded rationality, transaction costs will always be positive, even in trusts. It is precisely because of positive transaction costs that Easterbrook and Fischel interpreted the duty of good faith as a hypothetical bargaining mechanism that resolves our inability to agree *ex ante* to all possible contingencies.[7]

Among transaction costs, organizational economists distinguish between coordination costs and motivation costs.[8] Coordination costs are costs incurred when determining prices, supply and demand quantities, and when bringing together buyers and sellers. A stock exchange reduces coordination costs in the trading of stocks as it houses all these activities under one roof. Motivation costs can be further subdivided into information incompleteness and asymmetries and imperfect commitments. Information incompleteness occurs when one party has private information about the transaction and he may use that information to his advantage. The disadvantaged party either walks away from the transaction or imposes significantly costlier arrangements to ensure proper performance. Imperfect commitment occurs when one party has to make a large financial investment as part of a

[5] R. H. Coase, 'The Problem of Social Cost' 3 *J. L. & Econ.* 1 (1960), 15.

[6] This limit consists of neuro-physiological limits of processing and storing information and linguistic limits of expressing knowledge or ideas with absolute precision. In other words, humans are not perfect. The term was first coined by Herbert Simon, but was later popularized by Williamson. See O. E. Williamson, *Markets and Hierarchies: Analysis and Antitrust Implications* (Free Press, New York 1975), 11.

[7] See Chapter 1.

[8] P. Milgrom and J. Roberts, *Economics, Organization, and Management* (Prentice Hall, Englewood Cliffs 1992), 29.

transaction, but fearing that the other party may renege on his promise, the former is deterred from transacting in the first place. Trusts do not suffer from much coordination costs but there are plenty of motivation costs. Sitkoff's agency costs theory of trust law is an offshoot of the motivation cost idea as there is significant information asymmetry between the parties.

Most theories seek to explain the rise of the firm as solutions to motivation costs. More importantly, these theories stem from Coase's original theory of the firm. It states that individuals will structure their activities within a firm—instead of in the open market—if there are transaction cost savings to be made.[9] Although too generalized for detailed application, Coase's idea forms the basis for the theories of Williamson, Alchian and Demsetz, and Grossman, Hart, and Moore. As a refinement to Coase's generalized idea, they all rely on the idea that transaction costs inevitably result in incomplete contracts. Incomplete contracts create *ex post* contractual 'gaps' that need to be resolved by the parties, often expensively. Firms are understood as being cheaper than post-contractual bargaining.

In the case of donative and business trusts, the parties involved also suffer from bounded rationality and whatever terms they agree upon, they are inevitably incomplete. Just as disparate individuals can move away from open market transactions and conduct their activities within a firm, perhaps trust parties can move their activities away from a simple contract and into a trust in order to reduce transaction costs. If trusts resemble firms, the transaction cost savings found in firms should also be readily identifiable in trusts. In Langbein's account, trust law provides the default rules that help lower transaction costs but this alone does not support the idea of the trust as a firm. In Sitkoff's account, the trust is a firm by way of a nexus of contracts but he does not explain what transaction cost savings there are by banding these contractual parties inside such a firm.

Williamson: Fiats and Firms

Oliver Williamson argues that individuals will exploit any unspecified contractual terms to their advantage, and that there are two ways to deal with this opportunistic behaviour. The first is to negotiate and set out contractual terms in as much detail as possible, which is not only costly but also never perfect. The second is to integrate activities into a firm. A unified governance structure within a firm is likely to have an economizing effect on transaction

[9] R. H. Coase, 'The Nature of the Firm' 4 *Economica* 386 (1937).

costs.[10] The economizing effect comes in several forms, and relies on the concept of 'fiats'. Williamson does not provide a definition of 'fiat', but from his usage in the context of a hierarchical firm structure (manager versus worker), it can be said to mean an administrative directive issued by a superior to a subordinate to do something. With production integrated into a firm, the number of intra-firm transactions decreases as hierarchical fiat replaces the market pricing system and negotiations. The same is true with adapting to unforeseen circumstances, as hierarchical fiat takes the place of costly renegotiations. As Williamson says, 'fiat is frequently a more efficient way to settle minor conflicts . . . than is haggling or litigation'.[11] For example, within a car manufacturer, instead of the various departments (for example, design, assembly, marketing) haggling with each other over transfer pricing and other issues, they would all follow the orders of a manager. Nowadays, it is almost unimaginable for a car to be manufactured in a way other than by an integrated firm.[12]

Williamson argues that there are three distinctive advantages that firms possess when compared to market transactions.[13] First, common ownership reduces the incentives of trading units to pursue local goals. Second, the ability to issue internal fiats to resolve differences is often cheaper than adjudication between traders. Third, the internal nature of a firm means that there is better access to information that can be used when resolving disputes. It is the second point, as far as transaction costs and incomplete contracts are concerned, that best represents his theory of the firm.

At the heart of Williamson's idea is the issuance of fiats to deal with new and unforeseen circumstances. In theory, trusts with incomplete agreements can benefit from either the settlor or beneficiary issuing fiats to the trustee as new circumstances emerge. This idea can be applied to investments or distributions of trust assets. The workings of bare trusts and revocable trusts come closest to Williamson's idea of the firm. In these trusts, the settlor can be considered as the owner of the firm and the trustee the worker. If the relationship was governed by a simple contract, any post-contractual dispute would be subject to contentious bargaining; whereas with a revocable trust,

[10] O. E. Williamson, *The Economic Institutions of Capitalism: Firms, Markets, Relational Contracting* (Free Press, New York 1985), 85–6.

[11] O. E. Williamson, 'The Vertical Integration of Production: Market Failure Considerations' 61 *Am. Econ. Rev.* 112 (1971), 114.

[12] Clearly other factors such as economies of scale influence the decision to integrate economic activities into a firm.

[13] O. E. Williamson, 'The Modern Corporation: Origin, Evolution, Attributes' 19 *J. Econ. Lit.* 1537 (1981), 1549.

the settlor's instructions are akin to fiats and the trustee is under an employee-like obligation to follow the settlor's instructions.

But apart from these two types of trusts, it is difficult to relate Williamson's idea to trusts at large. In the case of non-revocable donative trusts, neither the settlor nor the beneficiary is in a clear position to issue fiats to the trustee. When either sees the trustee doing something they do not like, there is generally no feedback mechanism and if the trustee duly exercises his discretionary powers, he is unimpeachable. Of course the settlor or a third party (as protector) can retain various powers, as offshore legislations nowadays provide; but such arrangements bring it closer to revocable trusts than prototypical donative ones. In the case of business trusts, it is even clearer that settlors and beneficiaries do not want to issue fiats, as they risk being deemed a partnership with the trustee as agent. In donative and business trusts, it is precisely the settlor's intention to confer discretion and powers to the trustee to manage the trust assets and to generally remove himself from management and control. So, if Williamson's idea is applicable at all, it is the trustee who is making decisions on unforeseen circumstances. This, of course, turns the theory on its head with the 'worker' being left to his own device.

Alchian and Demsetz: Metering

Alchian and Demsetz disagree with Williamson over his fiat theory of the firm. They argue that the fiat relationship in Williamson's firm is no different from a relationship between two parties in the open market.[14] They point to the fact that the remedy for worker insubordination in a Williamsonian firm is termination, but this is no different from a customer terminating his custom with a grocer that he no longer favours. In other words, the boundary between the firm and the market is ill-defined in Williamson's idea. Alchian and Demsetz argue that the difference between the firm and the market is that in the firm there is team use of inputs, and a centralized position of one party in the contractual arrangements for all other inputs.[15]

They presume that there are economic benefits to be gained from individuals teaming up to produce together and for them the problem begins once the firm is formed. Once individuals produce as a team, its output cannot easily be attributed to individual members for the purpose of allocating rewards and punishments. For example, in a choir with dozens of singers, it

[14] A. A. Alchian and H. Demsetz, 'Production, Information Costs, and Economic Organization' 62 *Am. Econ. Rev.* 777 (1972), 777–8.

[15] Ibid. 778.

is difficult to ascertain the exact contribution of each individual singer. Because of this problem, each member may have an incentive to shirk and expend less effort in the process, thereby saving his own costs. As a solution to what they call the metering problem, Alchian and Demsetz propose appointing a monitor who can manage or examine each member's input and adjust rewards accordingly.[16] To maximize his incentives to monitor, they propose that the individual monitoring should receive the residual claim. In other words, he should be the owner of the firm.[17] Furthermore, the owner-monitor must also have the right to alter or terminate team members (without terminating the team as a whole) and he must be able to sell his residual claim and monitor rights to others.[18] These features make up their idea of the firm.

Superficially, the trust fits into Alchian and Demsetz's team production model as the beneficiary holds the residual claim and may monitor the trustee's work. But on closer inspection, their model does not fit well with donative or business trusts. For instance, the only output that these trusts have is investment returns and they are all attributable to the trustee or his delegates, for whom he is responsible. When investment returns are subpar, there is no one else to blame other than the trustee. As a result, trusts do not suffer from the sort of team-based measurement problem that exists in Alchian and Demsetz's firm. In the case of donative trusts, although the beneficiary is the residual claimant, he is not often considered to be a good monitor. As Daniel Fischel and John Langbein say, fiduciary duties replace beneficiary monitoring.[19] More importantly, the beneficiary is not often in the position to alter or terminate the trustee, as Alchian and Demsetz envisioned. The rule in *Saunders v Vautier* is difficult to apply in trusts with disparate beneficiaries and in the United States, there may be a material purpose preventing beneficiaries from jointly terminating the trust prematurely.

In the case of business trusts, beneficiaries come very close to realizing Alchian and Demsetz's idea of an owner of the firm. Beneficiaries, as residual claimants, perform a monitoring role and have voting rights that empower them to remove the trustee so they can alter the membership of the team. However, the beneficiaries are not monitoring the performance of a team with numerous members, just that of the trustee—for the trustee is

[16] Ibid. 781–2.

[17] Residual claim is the income and cash flow from the asset or business that remains after all fixed obligations are met.

[18] A. A. Alchian and H. Demsetz, *supra* note 14, 782–3.

[19] D. Fischel and J. H. Langbein, 'ERISA's Fundamental Contradiction: The Exclusive Benefit Rule ' 55 *U. Chi. L. Rev.* 1105 (1988), 1114.

responsible for his delegates' actions. Because there is only one 'owner' monitoring one 'worker', there is not much team performance to speak of in the Alchian and Demsetz sense; there is also no reason to form a firm. A simple contract can also accommodate such a bilateral relationship.

Grossman, Hart, and Moore: Holdups

Grossman, Hart, and Moore (GHM)'s property rights theory of the firm specifically ties firms to the ownership of non-human assets.[20] A party is the owner of a non-human asset if he possesses residual control, which is the ability to restrict or grant access to the asset, subject to existing contractual obligations. Whereas assets are not integral to other theories, they are crucial to GHM's explanation of the rise of the firm. To them, ownership of an asset is authority over people. This is because the owner's control over access to the asset means that workers are more likely to act in the owner's interests as this will strengthen the workers' bargaining position when their access to the asset (that is, employment) comes under review. This is better known as Hart's 'power' theory, where 'ownership is a source of power when contracts are incomplete'.[21]

Ownership of assets is also seen as a solution to the holdup problem. A holdup occurs when one party threatens to terminate the relationship with a view to extracting better terms. For example, a key joint venture partner may threaten to walk away if he does not gain better terms or a bigger share of the profits. Holdups not only increase bargaining costs, they deter vulnerable parties from making the initial investment. The GHM model predicts that the vulnerable party who values the investment and transaction the most will end up owning the asset in question and retaining power, so as to avoid being held up.[22] Firms reduce or prevent holdups between parties that seek to cooperate.

GHM's theory appears to be applicable to the trust because it requires a non-human asset, just as the trust requires an asset to be valid. On the other

[20] This particular property rights approach is closely identified with Grossman, Hart, and Moore, though they did not work together throughout their project. Rather, Grossman and Hart delivered the seminal article on defining property rights and Hart and Moore developed the property rights theory of the firm. See S. J. Grossman and O. D. Hart. 'The Costs and Benefits of Ownership: A Theory of Vertical and Lateral Integration' 94 *J. Polit. Economy* 691 (1986) and O. Hart and J. Moore, 'Property Rights and the Nature of the Firm' 98 *J. Polit. Economy* 1119 (1990).

[21] O. Hart, *Firms, Contracts, and Financial Structure* (Oxford University Press, Oxford 1995), 29.

[22] The classic example economists use to illustrate this idea—the case of General Motors and Fischer Body—has been discredited as being factually incorrect. See R. H. Coase, 'The Conduct of Economics: The Example of Fisher Body and General Motors' 15 *J. Econ. Manage. Strategy* 255 (2006). Despite this, the holdup problem and its contribution to theories of the firm remain a staple of organizational economics.

hand, the issue of who possesses residual control in a trust relationship is open to debate. The trustee retains legal title and, subject to contractual obligations, he can restrict or grant others access to the asset. But he must exercise his residual control rights in a manner that is for the benefit of the beneficiary. Even then, the beneficiary who possesses the residual claim does not possess any meaningful form of residual control. Therefore, the idea of residual control is difficult to apply consistently in trusts.

More importantly, however, the holdup situation is rare in donative, business, or any kind of trusts. Consider the case of the trustee holding up the beneficiary, who possesses residual control. What are the costs to the beneficiary if the trustee threatens to leave unless he is paid a higher trustee fee? What if the trustee resigns? In both donative and business trusts, the trustee's investment skills are replaceable. The only additional consideration for donative trusts is the trustee's personal knowledge of and experience with specific beneficiaries, which will enable him to make better distribution decisions. Even then, this knowledge and experience can be regained by a new trustee. In any case, the beneficiary has not made a significant financial commitment that could be jeopardized by the trustee's termination of services.

Where the trustee is deemed to have residual control of the asset, one may consider the bizarre case where the beneficiary holds up the trustee, for example, by demanding lower fees. To begin with, beneficiaries often cannot fire the trustee. Even if the trustee could be fired, the consequences for him are minimal. In the case of professional trustees, their investment (office space, computers, etc.) is not specific to one particular trust relationship; they can be redeployed to another relationship with minimal costs. For lay trustees, there is hardly any relationship-specific investments apart from the time and effort spent. Given the lack of a holdup problem to solve in trusts, GHM's theory cannot be used to explain why trusts exist.

Intra-Firm Transfers and Market Transactions

It is clear that the various theories of the firm cannot explain the existence of trusts. Trusts do not have fiats, team productions, or holdup problems. This leads to a more interesting question: why do trusts not have these features? It is because they lack intra-firm transfers and market transactions.[23] These

[23] Even Robert Sitkoff readily admits that the trust lacks intra-firm transfers, but the significance of this fact does not appear to be appreciated. R. H. Sitkoff, 'An Agency Costs Theory of Trust Law' 89 *Cornell L. Rev.* 621 (2004), 635.

fundamental attributes of firms ultimately give rise to theories of the firm and the trust's lack of them means that the theories are not applicable.

Intra-firm transfer is the idea that one unit within a firm passes on a product or service that is still work-in-progress to another unit within the firm for further processing. To use the car manufacturer example again, the design department would pass the design on to the assembly department to build the car; it would then pass it on to the marketing department to sell the car. Virtually all car manufacturers today integrate all the above activities into a single firm. But it is entirely possible to have a car design company sell the design to a car building company, who then builds a car and sells it to a car marketing company, who finally sells it to the general public. This modular method would have involved each company selling to others at market prices. In Coase's firm, these activities would have been integrated and there would be intra-firm transfers. Intra-firm transfers are not limited to manufacturing activities. A trainee lawyer who drafts a contract and passes it on to his supervising partner for review is also considered a form of intra-firm transfer. Again, what is being conducted within a (law) firm could have been conducted as independent market transactions.

The various problems that the theories claim firms help solve—such as litigation, holdups, or team production monitoring—exist only when there are intra-firm transfers. There would be no need for fiats to override haggling or pricing if multiple parties transferring goods and services within an organization did not exist. There would also be no need to have a residual claimant monitor if a metering problem—which requires multiple team members working together—did not exist. There would be no holdups (or less of it anyway) if the activity in question does not involve multiple parties using one asset to produce another. Without intra-firm transfers, firms will not be firms, and these theories would be meaningless.

In the trust, the three principal parties are not replacing a series of market transactions with transfers within a firm. The only transfer that takes place is the transfer of the trust asset from the settlor to the trustee and, eventually, from the trustee to the beneficiary. It is true that the trustee would add value to the asset through investments. But, crucially, the trustee neither buys the asset from the settlor nor sells it to the beneficiary; no haggling or transfer pricing is involved. It is also true that the trustee can delegate his duties to other parties and each delegate may be responsible for tasks akin to the car design, building, and marketing activities. But given the trustee's legal responsibility for his delegates' action, the trustee and his delegates ought to be considered as one integrated party.[24]

[24] In such a case, the trustee and his delegates would be considered as an integrated firm in itself interacting with another firm comprising the settlor and the beneficiary. This, of course, spoils the

In addition to lacking intra-firm transfers, the trust also lacks market transactions, which helps explain the poor fit between theories of the firm and trusts. Firms interact with the market during the production stage by buying materials and other inputs. Crucially, they interact with the market at the end stage when they sell goods or services. In a trust, the trustee may conduct market transactions such as buying and selling financial securities or real estate, but this only occurs during the asset management stage. The trust's end stage is characterized by distributions to beneficiaries, not commercial exchanges with the market.

The trust's lack of intra-firm transfers and market transactions explains why it does not fit within the traditional description of a firm. However, it is important to remember that form and function must be distinguished. What has been established is the simple idea that prototypical trust activities conducted by trust parties are very different from the activities of other economic organizations.

Conclusion

Donative trusts and business trusts may band several parties together with a common purpose but the economic activities conducted within them are very different from those typically conducted by economic firms. Whereas the theories of the firm studied can explain the existence of, say, car manufacturers and law firms, they are not at all applicable to trusts. This conundrum can be explained by the lack of intra-firm transfers and market transactions in trusts. Without them, the problems that firms are meant to resolve simply do not exist. Trusts are not firms.

These findings do not render all applications of theories of the firm irrelevant. For example, Sitkoff's agency costs analysis of the tensions among the three principal parties is somewhat insightful.[25] Yet many questions remain: despite the rather tenuous conceptual link, why is the trust so intricately associated with firms and businesses? What is the contribution of trusts to commerce? What truly differentiates them from corporations? The next chapter offers an explanation.

whole idea that the three principal parties' activities are conducted within one firm and brings us back to open market transactions.

[25] But then again Jensen and Meckling's theory is not *a* theory of the firm. Also, agency costs can be insightfully applied to most socio-economic activities involving more than one party. As Eric Posner says, once the agency model is mastered, 'it is a fine game, especially on long car trips, to apply it to everything in the universe'. E. A. Posner, 'Agency Models in Law and Economics' in E. A. Posner (ed.) *Chicago Lectures in Law and Economics* (Foundation Press, New York 2000), 240.

5

The Function of Trusts in Business and Commerce

Introduction

Trusts are neither legal entities nor economic firms, yet they are popular and successful commercial vehicles. Legal entities have strong asset-partitioning features that protect the parties from unintended creditor claims and economic firms have intra-firm transfers that are an essential feature of goods and services production. Why then do trusts make good commercial vehicles when they lack both essential attributes? This chapter reviews the legal and economic attributes that the trust either possesses or lacks, and explains why the trust is useful for certain commercial activities.

It is often said that the trustee's stricter duties of care and impartiality make the trust useful for certain kinds of commercial activities. There are two insights to this widely held belief. The first is that these duties are part of the trust's governance structure and, like that of the corporation, this structure is dictated by the type of asset held and the investment activities conducted. But equally important in the trust is the quality and strength of the beneficial interest. The weaker the beneficial interest (as in discretionary trusts), the stronger these duties become; and vice versa. This is because there ought to be a correlation between the beneficiary's rights and the trustee's duties, for the stronger the beneficiary becomes, the more he is able to monitor and judge the trustee's actions himself. The second insight is that these duties are easily replicable by corporations. With some customization, corporate directors can also have stricter duties of care and impartiality. Therefore, these duties alone do not give the trust a competitive edge over the corporation.

Rather, these and other legal features of the trust shape its economic attributes that make it uniquely suitable for certain commercial activities. Without legal personality and, consequently, without intra-firm transfers, trustees come to rely on market transactions and prices. As a result, their workload and information burden significantly decreases along with the risk of liability. These legal and economic attributes mean that trusts are geared towards doing one thing really well: holding assets and, to some extent, managing them.

This chapter is organized as follows. First, it argues that although the nature of trust asset and the type of investment activities have a bearing on how a trust is governed, it is the strength of the beneficial interest that should be key determinant on the level of trustee duties. Second, it reviews why the duty of impartiality is a commercially attractive trust feature, but argues that both the duties of care and impartiality can be replicated by corporations. Third, it demonstrates how the trust's unique legal and economic attributes make it particularly useful for holding and managing assets.

Duty of Care and Risk-Taking

In contrast to corporations, trusts are not conducive to high-risk activities because, among other reasons, trustees are held to a stricter duty of care and they cannot hide behind a legal entity. To understand the difference between corporations and trusts, one can borrow more ideas from organizational economics. Organizational economists associate a firm's capital structure with its governance mechanisms, type of assets held, and type of activities conducted. The optimal capital structure for any firm—typically in terms of the composition of debt and equity—is a function of its assets and the nature of its operations.[1] In turn, the type of capital largely dictates the governance structure and relationship between the key parties to the firm.

A firm's manager will behave according to the firm's capital composition. Equity holders possess the residual claim to the firm's assets. This, by definition, means they are also last in priority during insolvency. These characteristics of equity mean that equity holders will want the firm to engage in comparatively risky activities to generate a higher return to compensate them for the risk they are taking. Holders of debt capital are only entitled to a fixed claim, namely, principal and interest. Therefore, they ideally want the firm to engage only in activities that are risky enough to generate cash flow to satisfy their claims, and no more.

A firm engaging in high-risk activities or holding risky and uncertain assets will find it more difficult to raise debt and is likely to have a higher equity component in its capital structure. Conversely, a firm with stable operations

[1] See E. M. Iacobucci and G. G. Triantis, 'Economic and Legal Boundaries of Firms' 93 *Va. L. Rev.* 515 (2007) and G. S. Geis, 'The Space Between Markets and Hierarchies' 95 *Va. L. Rev.* 99 (2009).

and a predictable cash flow may find a balanced capital structure of both equity and debt more attractive. Assuming such a firm's debt payments are manageable, the debt component serves to lever up the equity holders' return. And debt holders are willing to serve this role because there is a significant likelihood of repayment. Debt capital here also serves as a disciplinary device for equity holders: the burden of periodic debt payments will focus managers' minds to manage the firm prudently and productively.[2]

Obviously, there are tensions among and between the two classes of capital providers. Equity and debt holders have different return objectives: debt holders only want the firm to generate returns and risks sufficient to satisfy their claims. Equity holders, on the other hand, will want higher returns and risks, since they only start making a return on their investments after all claimants have been satisfied. Within equity and debt holders, there will also be tensions between senior and junior creditors and between majority and minority shareholders. To address these tensions, governance mechanisms are devised to strike a balance between the interests of the various class members. For example, board seats may be allocated to certain equity and debt holders with significant stakes in the firm. Debt covenants may dictate to some extent what the firm can and cannot do with its assets, operations, or finances. Also, certain corporate actions (such as issuing new equity) may require equity and debt holder approval.

Much of capital structure theories' findings can be applied to trusts. Just like firms, there is a complex relationship between the trust's governance mechanisms, its assets and investment activities, and beneficiaries' rights. In trusts, there are also two possible types of capital, or claims: debt and equity (that is, beneficial interest, as the beneficiaries hold the residual claim to trust assets). Debts in trusts are neither common nor encouraged. In England, trustees can purchase real estate with the assistance of a mortgage.[3] However, this is only because the purchasing and mortgaging of the property are deemed to be one indivisible transaction. Unless expressly authorized to do so, trustees cannot borrow money from, say, real estate and use the proceeds to invest in financial securities; in other words, trusts by default cannot 'gear up'. In the United States, the English position was followed in the Restatement (Second) of Trusts. Trustees could not mortgage or pledge trust assets or borrow money on the credit of the trust estate unless authorized by the court or the trust instrument.[4] In the Restatement (Third) of Trusts, however, the position has been reversed and trustees now have a general power to

[2] See G. Geis, *supra* note 1, 117.

[3] D. J. Hayton, P. Matthews, and C. Mitchell (eds.), *Underhill and Hayton The Law Relating to Trusts and Trustees* (17th edn. LexisNexis Butterworths, London 2006), art 52.31.

[4] Restatement (Second) of Trusts, §191.

borrow money on the credit of the trust estate and pledge trust assets.[5] Where debt exists, its governance effect is the same as that found in any economic organization or individual. Because he must repay interest and principal, debt focuses the trustee's mind in generating investment returns or, even better, not getting into debt in the first place. Debt in trusts coupled with the trustee's personal liability makes it a much more potent governance mechanism than debt found in corporations with legal personalities.[6] In any case, debt is not often a key feature of trusts.

If debt was out of the question and the beneficial interest (equity) is considered as the only source of capital, the main determinants of the trust's governance mechanism may be the type of assets held and the type of investment activities conducted. A trustee who only holds cash for a beneficiary obviously has lesser duties than a trustee who manages a portfolio of complex financial investments. This can be easily understood from trustee risk-taking and beneficiary monitoring perspectives. But the nature of the trust's assets is only a minor factor in a trust's governance mechanisms.

A more important determinant is arguably the strength of the beneficiary's rights. In the same way that a corporation with a majority, controlling shareholder (for example, a family business) may have a comparatively weaker corporate governance structure, trusts with strong beneficiaries may have correspondingly weaker trustee governance structures. In this way, the stronger the beneficiary's rights under the trust are, the more likely that the trust's assets could be put to riskier investments. Trusts where beneficiaries have strong rights to, say, trust information and trustee removal are more conducive to riskier investments. Such trusts include bare trusts (which give almost total control to the beneficiary) and business trusts of mutual funds (which give strong rights to information and voting to remove trustees and managers). Trusts where beneficiaries have weaker rights are less likely to be involved in risky assets and investments. These include discretionary trusts (with very little beneficiary control) and trusts used in asset securitization (with very limited affirmative beneficiary rights until a bankruptcy event occurs).

This pattern arguably exists because of the trustee's liability to beneficiaries; the more rights and powers beneficiaries assume, the less duties and liabilities the trustee owes to them. With less duties and liabilities, the trustee can undertake riskier investments not because he can now be negligent or reckless, but because the lesser trustee duties and liabilities imply a higher risk tolerance on the beneficiary's part. As a result, where the beneficiary can

[5] Restatement (Third) of Trusts, §86 comment d; see also Uniform Trust Code §816(5).

[6] In the United States, the trustee's limited liability only applies if he is not at fault; if he recklessly incurs debt on the trust estate's credit, he remains liable as he owes a duty of care.

actually take charge or be fully informed of the riskiness of trust investments, all else being equal, risky investments are more likely to be undertaken. Conversely, it is difficult for a trustee to justify pursuing risky investments if he has to answer to ignorant widows and orphans.

Duty of Care and Risk-Taking: Trusts and Corporations

Within trusts, there are different types of beneficial interests and corresponding governance mechanisms. Trusts with stronger forms of beneficial interests and control are more capable of undertaking risky investments and vice versa. Can this theory be empirically proven? It is difficult to undertake studies of trusts, especially private donative ones. But trusts and corporations sometimes appear to be the same thing and the difference is just a matter of degree. Trustees by default are held to the higher standard of the prudent man, whereas corporate directors are held to the less onerous business judgement rule.[7] The lower corporate standard can be understood from the fact that shareholders have various recourses, including the right to vote at meetings and to remove directors. Therefore, they collectively have greater control over the director and, to some extent, can control the risks he takes. On the other hand, not all trust beneficiaries are of the same stature as corporate shareholders. Because some may have very weak rights against the trustee, a higher default standard is appropriate. So as far as governance and risk-taking are concerned, the average corporation can be understood as a riskier version of the average trust.

In this respect, Joseph Warburton compares the performance of trusts and corporations in the context of the British mutual fund industry.[8] He finds that mutual funds set up as trusts tend to choose portfolios with lower risks than those set up as corporations. However, the risk-adjusted performance of both trust- and corporate- mutual funds are largely the same. This means that

[7] The business judgement rule has been described by Henry Manne as 'one of the least understood concepts in the entire corporate field' and continues to stir contentious debates. Put simply, the rule makes a 'presumption that in making a business decision the directors of a corporation acted on an informed basis, in good faith and in the honest belief that the action taken was in the best interest of the company'. As Lyman Johnson observes, 'unless the plaintiff succeeds in rebutting the rule, the court will not substitute its views for those of the board's if the latter's decision can be "attributed to any rational business purposes"'. See H. G. Manne, 'Our Two Corporation Systems: Law and Economics' 53 *Va. L. Rev.* 259 (1967), *Aronson v Lewis* 473 A.2d 805 (Del. 1984), and L. P. Q. Johnson, 'Corporate Officers and the Business Judgment Rule' 60 *Bus. Law* 439 (2005).

[8] A. J. Warburton, 'Commercial Trusts Versus Corporations: Evidence from the British Mutual Fund Industry', 2009, <http://papers.ssrn.com/sol3/papers.cfm?abstract_id=1290722>, last accessed 7 January 2010.

when trustees and directors choose the same level of risk, their investment performances are comparable; it is just that trustees generally choose lower levels of risk. Warburton attributes these differences to the inherent governance measures found in trusts and corporations and concludes that trusts are better at curtailing opportunistic behaviour whilst corporations' flexibility encourages greater risk-taking behaviour. Although the study does not characterize the strength of beneficiaries' or shareholders' interests,[9] it is telling that risk preferences are dictated largely by trustee and director duties.

Duty of Impartiality and Risk-Taking

In addition to the trustee's duty of care, an important duty regulates the type of asset and investments trustees undertake. Steven Schwarcz argues that the trustee's duty of impartiality significantly differentiates trusts from corporations.[10] In the commercial context, it is important because there are often beneficiaries with different classes of claims. Schwarcz observes that where there are different classes of claims, it is difficult to strike a balance between them when determining how much risk to take with the assets.[11] Investors of senior, lower risk tranches (for example, debt) have a lower risk/reward appetite and will want the manager to prioritize asset safety over returns. Conversely, investors of deeply subordinated, higher risk tranches (for example, equity) will want the manager to take risks in order to generate profits commensurate with the risks they are taking.

According to Schwarcz, corporations are not suitable for catering to the needs of multiple classes of claimants because there is no duty of impartiality that can protect all classes of claimants; managers of corporations serve the interests of its shareholders.[12] Trusts, on the other hand, are suitable for balancing the interests of different classes of claimants. Just as the trustee of a donative trust must be impartial when dealing with life tenants and remaindermen, the trustee of a commercial trust must be fair to beneficiaries with different classes of entitlement. Because it must be impartial and because

[9] In the context of mutual funds, they ought to be very similar.

[10] S. L. Schwarcz, 'Commercial Trusts as Business Organizations: Unraveling the Mystery' 58 *Bus. Law* 559 (2003).

[11] Ibid. 578–9.

[12] Ibid. 575–6. However, this traditional view of shareholder supremacy is changing. Increasingly, directors have a duty to take into account the interests of other stakeholders when discharging their corporate duties. For example, s 172(1) of the UK Companies Act 2006 requires directors, when discharging their duties, to have due regard to the interests of the company's employees, suppliers, customers, community, and environment. It also requires directors to have regard to the need to act fairly as between members of the company. Crucially, this provision does not mention creditors so, in the normal course of things, the directors still primarily answer to the equity holders.

different classes may have very divergent risk/return expectations, the trustee's set of possible actions is quite limited.

As a result, it is not unusual to see trusts that benefit multiple classes of beneficiaries doing nothing besides safekeeping the trust asset and distributing according to predetermined terms.[13] These mundane activities serve a valuable role in financial transactions such as asset securitizations. The trustee's mere holding of assets and distribution according to the trust deed meet the expectations of different beneficiaries; they may have different claim seniorities but their interests are collectively served by the simple preservation of trust assets in accordance with the trust terms.

The Imitable Nature of the Duties of Care and Impartiality

The duties of care and impartiality steer the trustee towards prudent investments and ensure that different classes of interests are treated equally and fairly. This may be why trusts make good commercial vehicles for mutual funds or asset securitization. But by and large these legal attributes are not unique to trusts; most of them can be cheaply emulated by corporations. The director's duty of care can be easily strengthened to the prudent man trustee level. Different classes of interests can be catered for by creating different securities classes and further modifying directors' duties and the corporate constitution. For example, holders of preferred shares may have a risk profile that is different from holders of common equity. Directors' duties and the articles of association can be modified to ensure that directors must treat holders of preferred shares and common equity equally and assets are to be held and distributed on predetermined terms. The end result is the same: corporate directors are so constrained that they are nothing more than conduits of fund and asset flows, just like commercial trustees. It is true that a corporation cannot be 'de-personified', but directors can equally undertake to indemnify the corporation for all losses and liabilities unless they are not at fault. By having such a provision, corporations can largely replicate the trust's governance effect of not having legal personality.[14] So it is clear that the legal attributes of trusts are not unique and, with a bit of customization, corporations can emulate them. The reverse can also be said about trusts as trustee duties can be watered down and exemption from liability

[13] Ibid. 578–9.

[14] Another possibility is to use a corporation with unlimited liability, but this imposes liability not only on directors, but also shareholders; this would make corporate shareholders worse off than trust beneficiaries.

can also be granted. The only advantage trusts have over corporations when it comes to the stricter duties of care and impartiality is that trusts have them built in by default whereas deliberate customization is required if corporations are to have them. In this respect, Langbein is correct in that trusts provide transaction costs savings when parties want to adopt trust-like terms. In any case, as Henry Hansmann and Ugo Mattei observe, the line between trusts and corporations is blurring as statutory enactments interweave the two ever closer together. The distinction between trusts and corporations lies elsewhere.

The Economic Attributes of Trusts as Commercial Vehicles

Instead, it is the trust's economic attributes that make it useful for commercial activities such as mutual funds or asset securitization. The trust lacks both intra-firm transfers and legal personality and these two features complement each other. Without legal personality, it is difficult for the various parties to contract with each other in the same way that a corporation acts as a central counterparty in the nexus of contracts. As a result, the number of people participating in intra-firm transfers and the complexity of their activities is also diminished by the lack of a fictitious central counterparty. It is this corporate legal fiction that serves as a nexus of contractual relationships, which enables the multiple inputs from various parties that characterize modern productive businesses. Legal personality also enables the corporate owner to sell the entire bundle of contracts as an integrated whole, rather than having to go through the cumbersome process of contractual assignments.[15] Clearly, legal personality has become an important feature of business organizations.

It is entirely possible for the trust to behave like a corporation, even without legal personality. The trustee could be the central counterparty to the various inputs but doing so is very disadvantageous. The burden of managing multiple inputs (for example, suppliers, creditors, employees, customers, etc.) is roughly the same for trusts and corporations; in both cases, there are plenty of transaction and monitoring costs. But if things go wrong and liabilities arise, the trust's porous asset-partitioning attributes place its human participants at a legal disadvantage to their corporate counterparts: trustees and even beneficiaries may be sued whilst directors and shareholders are shielded comfortably behind

[15] K. Ayotte and H. Hansmann, 'Legal Entities as Transferable Bundles of Contracts', 2009, <http://www.kernbureau.uva.nl/template/downloadAsset.cfm?objectid=7BA63183-AE57-4DE0-A8EEA2AB9673374E>, last accessed 16 September 2010

the corporation. This lack of legal personality (and the limited liability it entails) explains why trusts are not conducive to accommodating intra-firm transfers. As for selling away the business as a bundle of contracts, the trustee could indeed be the central counterparty to the contracts and the beneficiary can sell or assign his beneficial interest to third parties.[16] By doing this, the cumbersome process of contractual reassignment can also be avoided. But the costs of the trustee becoming the central counterparty clearly outweigh the benefits. This is why trusts are not in the business of operating real businesses.

The lack of intra-firm transfers also means that the only kind of transfers that take place with the trust are market transfers (that is, investing in the stock market or hiring an external contractor for certain services). The corporate director may assume that he has superior economies and knowledge and opts for intra-firm transfers. A car manufacturer may choose to design and build its own engines rather than use those produced by others because it feels that producing them in-house may give it an edge over just buying them from the market. On the other hand, the trustee acts alone and relies on the market for contracts and assets. Rather than assuming that he has superior skills and knowledge, the trustee relies on the superiority of the market's competition and pricing mechanisms. This certainly presents a much lighter workload and lower information intensity for the trustee and the beneficiary and explains why financial assets are often found in trusts. Financial assets usually have reliable market prices and are easier to manage than, say, a complex manufacturing business. The nature of assets also reinforces the idea why trusts do not need strong asset-partitioning that legal personality entails: the risks of legal liabilities arising from managing assets with market prices are much lower than complex businesses. In the normal course of things, trust risks can be reduced to a manageable level and strong asset-partitioning is not essential.[17]

Conclusion

The trust's legal attributes may be unique at the default level but they can be easily and cost-effectively replicated by corporations. As a result, the popularity of trusts in commerce cannot be explained by the trustee's duties alone.

[16] A complete sale and exit from the enterprise only works if there is a sole beneficiary or if multiple beneficiaries act unanimously.

[17] Ironically, most professional trustees take the form of corporations. This does not negate the low workload and informational intensity argument posited; professional trustees who manage hundreds, if not thousands, of trusts are effectively placed in the situation of managing a complex business and the risks are high, thereby justifying the protection of strong asset-partitioning that a corporation provides.

Rather, the legal limitations of trusts shape their economic features. The fact that trusts are popular for mutual funds and asset securitization is telling because it shows that they are particularly good for one thing: holding assets.

Trustees of asset securitization trusts do nothing more than hold and distribute assets on predetermined terms. Trustees of mutual funds do more than just hold property; they have to put the funds to work and generate investment returns. But this investment function is usually outsourced to a portfolio manager whose relationship with the trustee is governed by contract. By virtue of his duties of care and loyalty, the trustee is still responsible for monitoring the performance of the portfolio manger and safeguarding the interests of mutual fund beneficiaries. The workload of monitoring is manageable as portfolio manager performance can easily be ascertained by financial benchmarks and market information. This means the trustee's position is still similar to that of the asset securitization trustee—passively holding and administering assets. In the commercial context, trusts are most useful for passive activities that are performed according to terms to which beneficiaries have agreed. Seldom can one find commercial trusts where trustees exercise genuine discretion over investment or distribution, which would expose beneficiaries to the judgement and will of trustees. In this respect, trusts are successful in commerce, again, because of their role as passive conduits.

Therefore, the trust owes its immense popularity in business and commerce to its ability to act as a sophisticated property-holding vehicle. This is the reason why trusts are so commonly associated with commercial deals. Where transactions do not involve actual production of goods and services but demand complex structuring of rights and duties over a period of time, property alone is inadequate and is replaced by the trust. Bernard Rudden's remark about the donative trust, that it is 'a gift projected on the plane of time and, meanwhile, in need of management'[18] can be reinterpreted in the commercial context where the gift simply becomes a commercial asset transfer.

[18] B. Rudden, 'Book Review' 44 *MLR* 610 (1981), 610.

PART III
TRUSTS AS PROPERTY
Property Makes an Unlikely Comeback

Neither contracts nor entities provide a good theoretical basis for understanding trusts, which realistically leaves only property. But is property up to this daunting task? As the first chapter of this part will explain, property as a coherent concept has been in decline for many years. But this is primarily because it has not changed in the last few centuries, even as society and the economy have fundamentally been transformed. As a functioning institution today, English property law retains a distinctly feudal feel. Property has been losing out to other ideas in the competition to explain trusts not only because contract and entity accounts are superficially appealing, but, more importantly, because property is losing its explanatory power.

For the property idea to recapture trusts, what is needed—and indeed what has happened—is for this concept to be reformed. The key stumbling block has been the persistent idea of exclusion, which very few property theorists have been willing to abandon. Because the right to exclude is so central to our understanding of property, only by discarding or perhaps reforming it can property carry on as a useful idea. And, coincidentally, lawyers and economists renewed their understanding of property at almost the same time a decade ago. Lawyers have de-emphasized the right to exclude or interpreted it in a new light while economists gave it an important economic justification by associating it with information-processing costs.

Not only is property understood under a new light, but another widespread form of ownership—the fund—is rationalized in legal property terms. This bodes well for the trust because it is a fund and the beneficial interest is an interest in a fund. With legal understandings of trusts as property and economic understandings of property on solid footing, an economic account of trusts as property is appropriate and timely. It is appropriate because other economic accounts of trusts completely overlook the proprietary aspects of trusts and it is timely because modern trust developments tend to de-emphasize the proprietary nature of the beneficial interest. Trusts are funds and their functions can be traced back to property. Once these concepts are properly grasped, many trust rules and doctrines become clear. Only by understanding that the trust institution is rooted in property can one appreciate why novel trust developments are not good.

6

The Decline of Property and Trust

Introduction

Donovan Waters divides the current developments of trusts into three categories: the obligational, the entity, and the proprietary approaches.[1] Whereas the entity approach—epitomized by the works of Hansmann, Kraakman, and Mattei and embodied in the draft Uniform Statutory Trust Entity Act—is predominantly a niche American phenomenon, the obligational approach has achieved global recognition. The proprietary approach, however, is nowhere to be found. Why are the contract and entity approaches so successful? It is because contracts and entities are unambiguously defined concepts, lawyers and lay people alike can describe them without much disagreement arising. It is easy to describe trusts as contracts or entities because people can visualize the two and draw similarities or differences.

The same cannot be said for property. From ancient philosophers to law and economics scholars, everyone seems to hold a different view of property. In legal and philosophical thinking, property can be justified on various grounds such as labour, value, identity, and liberty. There is no consensus on what property is and, to some extent, what it encompasses. This is so despite property being one of the most widely used socio-economic institutions in the world. The difficulty of understanding trusts as property is clear: to assert that the trust is based on something that is vague and undefined simply does not work.

Since the obligational and entity approaches are largely based on the works of law and economics, perhaps the discipline's work on property would help. But here the literature simply does a great disservice to property and trust. From the start, economists and law and economic scholars have never conceived of property properly. Instead, they conceive of it exclusively as fragmented rights and duties. Apart from atomizing the property concept, they have only studied property in a piecemeal manner. The most important contributions to the

[1] D. Waters, 'The Future of the Trust Part I' 13 *JITCP* 179 (2006).

literature claim to be generally applicable to the field of 'property', but have actually been developed with specific topics in mind, such as nuisance and rights to natural resources. As a result, there is a diverse and rich set of ideas on animal grazing rights, radio wave spectra, and common fishery grounds, but not so much in mundane areas like land registration and covenants.[2] With the law and economics of property in disarray, it is almost impossible to construct a property-based understanding of trusts.

On the legal front, property as traditionally understood has become anachronistic. In light of intangible wealth such as bank accounts and shares, any concept of property that relies on the physical right to exclude trespassers will not be able to keep up with modern property practices. By extension, attempts to explain the nature of the beneficial interest with the physical right to exclude are riddled with inconsistencies and qualifications: there simply is not a right-duty relationship between the beneficiary and the rest of the world over specific trust assets.

To quote Thomas Merrill and Henry Smith, 'property has fallen out of fashion'[3] and this can be said about both legal and economic property. This chapter traces the decline of property and, consequently, the disintegration of the property-based concept of trusts. The ascent of the obligational and entity approaches has simply rendered the law of trusts internally inconsistent. This chapter is organized as follows. First, it reviews and criticizes the predominant economic approach to property, which is characterized by bilateral use rights over resources. Second, it charts the decline of legal property from the days of Blackstone's characterization of property as the sole despotic dominion to Hohfeld's atomization of *in rem* rights. Third, it explains the inherent weaknesses of traditional, exclusion-based concepts of property, which contributed to its own demise. Fourth, it shows how trusts cannot comfortably exist within this traditional, exclusion-based framework of property. Fifth, it observes how the obligational and entity approaches ascended to fill the vacuum left by the disappearing proprietary approach.

The Fragmented Approach to Property in Economics

Economic conceptions of property did not get off to a good start. Unlike contracts and firms, property has never been studied in economics as an independent concept. The economics of property has always revolved around

[2] A key exception to this is intellectual property, which perhaps has been less dragged down by historical and conceptual baggage.

[3] T. W. Merrill and H. E. Smith, 'What Happened to Property in Law and Economics?' 111 *Yale L. J.* 357 (2001), hereafter *What Happened?*, 357.

other topics such as nuisance and resource management. Clearly, property rights are an important factor in these areas of law, but they are just that: a means with which resource use conflicts can be resolved. Economists never held a conceptualist view of property or recognized it as a standalone legal institution.[4] This is most evident in Ronald Coase's works, which remains the cornerstone of the economic analysis of property rights.

In an article that lays out the idea of transaction costs and what will become his eponymous theorem, Coase briefly discussed property rights. He says: 'we may speak of a person owning land and using it as a factor of production but what the land-owner in fact possesses is the right to carry out a circumscribed list of actions.'[5] These actions include, for example, the right to quarry, the right of others to cross one's land, and the right to erect certain buildings. Later, Coase likens use rights such as those regarding land as being bought and sold in bundles, or bundles of rights.[6]

The individualized nature of use rights is not meant only for the nuisance context, which is Coase's focus in his seminal article. In other articles, Coase continues his bilateral and fragmented idea of property rights. In dealing with government auction and regulation of radio broadcast frequencies in the 1950s, there was opposition to creating private property rights in the radio spectrum as they were too difficult to define and enforce. Coase overcame this problem by rationalizing the auction as creating rights to operate radio broadcast equipment in certain ways, rather than creating traditional property rights in invisible radio waves.[7] Putting it succinctly, he said 'whether we have the right to shoot over another man's land has been thought of as depending on who owns the airspace over the land. It would be simpler to discuss what we should be allowed to do with the gun'.[8] From this, it is clear that Coase's conception of property rights is very different from that of lawyers and lay people.

Coase fragments the property concept into 'property rights'. Whereas traditional property philosophy conceives of property as a relationship between a person and a thing, the 'property rights' approach conceives of property as bilateral relationships between persons over use rights. However, even for Coase, this novel conception of property is not without flaws, especially when it comes to exchanging property rights. As property rights create a baseline for future bilateral exchanges, their appeal diminishes when

[4] For a useful overview, see T. W. Merrill and H. E. Smith, *supra* note 3.

[5] R. H. Coase, 'The Problem of Social Cost' 3 *J. L. & Econ.* 1 (1960), 44.

[6] R. H. Coase, *The Firm, the Market, and the Law* (University of Chicago Press, Chicago 1988), 11.

[7] R. H. Coase, 'The Federal Communications Commission' 2 *J. L. & Econ.* 1 (1959).

[8] Ibid. 34.

the number of parties involved increases. He says 'when large numbers of people are involved, the argument for the institution of property is weakened and that for general regulation becomes stronger'.[9] Merrill and Smith observe that the list-of-use conception 'can explain how conflicts can be resolved by contract when small numbers of claimants are involved. But when the number gets too large, this conception has no solution to the coordination problem other than to call upon public regulation'.[10] Despite these inherent flaws, the Coasean bilateral approach to property has captured the minds of economists and lawyers and continues to exert significant influence on the property discourse.

Yoram Barzel takes the bilateral approach to property much further than Coase and integrates the understanding of property with that of contracts.[11] In fact, Barzel considers property to be contract and says 'at the heart of the study of property rights lies the study of contracts'.[12] Barzel turns the common understanding of property on its head. Whereas Coase considers that property sets the baseline for contractual exchange, Barzel considers property to be the leftovers of contractual exchange. According to Barzel, an asset has many attributes that can be exchanged or assigned. To an owner, property in an asset is the bundle of attributes which has not been contracted or assigned away. Barzel also distinguishes between economic property rights and legal property rights. An economic property right is 'the individual's ability, in expected terms, to consume the good (or services of the asset) directly or indirectly through exchange'.[13] If a thief could steal an asset, he also has economic property rights in it. Legal property rights are a subset of economic property rights recognized and protected by the state and they play a prominent but merely supportive role to economic property rights.

Although Barzel's conception of economic property rights can sometimes find application in real life legal examples,[14] it can hardly be related to legal property as a normative system regulating society's use of resources. Not only are all rights to resources economic property rights, but legitimacy is not meaningfully distinguished from ability. Given its bilateral nature, Barzel's conception of property rights can hardly tell us the owner's relationship with non-contractual third parties.

[9] Ibid. 29.

[10] *What Happened?*, *supra* note 3, 374.

[11] Y. Barzel, *Economic Analysis of Property Rights* (2nd edn. Cambridge University Press, Cambridge 1997).

[12] Ibid. 33.

[13] Ibid. 3.

[14] For example, the holder of a reversionary interest in land indeed owns all the attributes that have not been contracted out to the tenant.

In their celebrated article, Guido Calabresi and Douglas Melamed also propel the bilateral view of property through the lens of legal remedies.[15] Calabresi and Melamed are less concerned with contracts and transaction costs than the legal system's protection of legal entitlements. They argue that legal entitlements can be protected through three rules. Legal entitlements that fall under the inalienability rule cannot be traded or infringed upon; those that fall under the liability rule can simply be infringed upon, but the offender must make market value compensation for the infringement; and finally, and more importantly, those that fall under the property rule cannot be infringed or be taken away unless the holder of the entitlement agrees.

Calabresi and Melamed's 'property rule' is just another name for injunctive relief and 'liability rule' is merely a short hand for relief by way of compensation, or damages. What is proprietary about the property rule is that many (but not all) recognized property rights have available injunctive relief as a remedy. The proprietary nature of the property rule is epitomized by property in land. However, injunctive relief is available in many non-property situations, such as injunctions granted to prevent certain information disclosures or to prevent businesses from operating. At the same time, damage or trespass to one's property often occurs too late for injunctive relief, and the victim would only be 'protected' by the liability rule and the monetary compensation that it provides; this is evident in the tort of conversion in chattels. Calabresi and Melamed's property rule does not advance our economic understanding of property in law but instead further develops its bilateral nature. Such was the state of the property economics literature throughout most of the twentieth century. Only at the turn of this century did neo-conceptualists rightfully relate economic conceptions of property to the legal system.[16]

The Historical Decline of Legal Property

Economic ideas of property got off to such a wrong start for two reasons. First, by the time economists started to study it, the legal conceptions of property had already disintegrated.[17] This meant that even if economists chose to analyse property along traditionally understood lines, there was no legal account upon which they could rely. Second, the classical idea of property only works for tangible things and it struggled to account for modern social and economic

[15] G. Calabresi and A. D. Melamed, 'Property Rules, Liability Rules, and Inalienability: One View of the Cathedral' 85 *Harv. L. Rev.* 1089 (1972).

[16] See Chapter 7.

[17] See generally *What Happened?*, *supra* note 3.

practices where assets of value are often intangible. In the case of invisible radio waves, Blackstone's conception of property has nothing meaningful to say. Therefore it should not come as a surprise that economists took the realist route and constructed 'property rights' out of bilateral relationships.

The philosophy of property is at least as old as Plato and Aristotle and although it is impossible to survey, even briefly, all the literature here, a good starting point is the golden age of property in law during the times of William Blackstone and Jeremy Bentham. Blackstone defines property as 'that sole despotic dominion which one man claims and exercises over the external things of the world, in total exclusion of the right of any other individual in the universe'.[18] This rhetorically powerful slogan is perhaps the most widely quoted description of property in the common law world.

Yet, as Merrill and Smith observe, much of this is just hyperbole.[19] Behind the slogan's chest-thumping appearance lies a legal reality that is eclipsed by qualifications and exceptions. The state has an important role to play in Blackstone's conception of property. Blackstone accepts that, to a large extent, the state and society generally have the right to craft and mould property owners' rights.[20] Much of Blackstone's analyses of property rights contradict the absolutist view his statement suggests. To reconcile this, state- or society- imposed limitations on property rights are rationalized as limitations inherent in the nature of the thing or the owner.[21]

Even if flaws can be pointed at Blackstone's famous slogan, it still represents the peak of property in law for two reasons. First, Blackstone's conception of property is that between a person and an external thing.[22] Second, as a result of protecting the person-thing relationship, Blackstone's property is primarily concerned with the right to exclude others—even if there are state-imposed limitations on exercising this right. These features, especially the right to exclude, make Blackstone's idea of property a quintessentially conceptualist one. Merrill and Smith observe another important factor contributing to the exclusive nature of property.[23] Blackstone functionally justifies property on grounds of labour and security of expectations, in that a farmer would not be

[18] W. Blackstone, *Commentaries on the Laws of England* (Clarendon Press, Oxford 1765), hereafter *Commentaries*, 3.

[19] *What Happened?*, *supra* note 3, 361; see also R. P. Burns, 'Blackstone's Theory of the "Absolute" Rights of Property' 54 *U. Cin. L. Rev.* 67 (1985).

[20] *Commentaries*, *supra* note 18, 125; others go as far as to say that Blackstone's property rhetoric betrays owners' anxieties over the bases of their property rights. See C. M. Rose, 'Canons of Property Talk, or, Blackstone's Anxiety' 108 *Yale L. J.* 601 (1998).

[21] *Commentaries*, *supra* note 18, 389.

[22] Blackstone recognizes intangible property and to reconcile them with the person-thing framework, he calls them things 'in contemplation'. Ibid. 20.

[23] *What Happened?*, *supra* note 3, 361.

incentivized to farm if his crops are liable to be taken and he is left with no recourse. To this end, property's underlying rationale can only be served by way of excluding others with an *in rem* right. Other philosophers during Blackstone's times echo the same ideas of property. Adam Smith and Jeremy Bentham, although at times critical of Blackstone, also support the exclusive nature of property and its labour and industry justifications.[24]

For more than two centuries, Blackstonian property was the staple of lawyers and political philosophers in both England and the United States. This changed in the early twentieth century when Wesley Hohfeld the legal taxonomist wrote about *in rem* and *in personam* rights.[25] According to Hohfeld, an *in rem* right is merely an aggregate of *in personam* rights and the nature and quality of the two types of rights are indistinguishable. Although Hohfeld did not label his idea as a 'bundle of rights', his conception of *in rem* rights is indeed a bundle of *in personam* rights. According to his critics, what Hohfeld fails to appreciate is that the two types of rights are very different. James Penner argues that with an *in personam* right, the content of that right is known to the right-holder and duty-holder and they are aware of each other's identity.[26] An example of this would be a simple contract where the contracting parties know each other and are fully aware of the terms of their contract. With an *in rem* right, however, the duty-holders are generally not aware of the identity of the right-holder. For example, a rambler may not know who the owner of a house is, but he does know that he is under a duty not to trespass. James Harris also criticizes Hohfeld's treatment of *in rem* and *in personam* rights.[27] Not only does Hohfeld's analysis overlook the person-thing nature of property, but it is devoid of an underlying, open-ended ownership idea; it de-conceptualizes the property idea. Harris argues that Hohfeld's analysis becomes unhelpful when the content of the present law is subject to controversy and ownership principles need to be drawn in to resolve disputes.[28]

Although Hohfeld is not mentioned by name in any of Coase's work, one can almost credit Coase for the 'economification' of Hohfeld's property

[24] See A. Smith, *Lectures on Jurisprudence* (Clarendon Press, Oxford 1978); J. Bentham, *The Limits of Jurisprudence Defined* (Columbia University Press, New York 1945); and *What Happened?*, *supra* note 3, 362–3.

[25] W. N. Hohfeld, 'Fundamental Legal Conceptions as Applied in Judicial Reasoning' 26 *Yale L. J.* 710 (1917).

[26] See generally J. E. Penner, *The Idea of Property in Law* (Oxford University Press, Oxford 1997), hereafter *Idea of Property in Law*.

[27] J. W. Harris, *Property and Justice* (Oxford University Press, Oxford 1996), 120–5.

[28] This viewed is also echoed by Hanoch Dagan, who says that while the bundle of rights metaphor can 'liberate us from the imaginary methodology of deduction from frozen forms... it cannot substitute for normative analysis'. See H. Dagan, 'The Craft of Property' 91 *Cal. L. R.* 1517 (2003), 1533–4.

rights ideas. Both believe in the bilateral nature of property rights and both are primarily concerned with specific use rights. This historical coincidence also sets the scene for the development of the economic literature on property rights. Yet it still beggars belief that the works of two scholars can change centuries-old understandings of property. Merrill and Smith note that Blackstone and his contemporaries may be more concerned with securing ownership and property rights and upholding the *in rem* right to exclude was paramount to their efforts.[29] In modern times when property rights are relatively secure, scholars are more concerned with the fine details of property, which may be better analysed with *in personam* rights. But this explanation cannot be the only reason for Hohfeld and Coase's success.

The Inherent Weaknesses of Blackstonian Property

A more plausible cause of *in rem* property's demise is its inability to keep up with property practices. Blackstonian property works best when applied to land or tangible chattels. But when one moves away from tangible assets and into intangible ones, the idea of exclusion-based property starts to falter. Blackstone included as property intangible things such as easements and rationalized their thing-ness as one being in contemplation, but he does not explain how intangible properties come under the protection of an owner's right to exclude.[30] In his times, reconciling intangible properties with the right to exclude was not very important because most intangible properties were not of significant economic nature. Blackstone listed eleven types of intangible things capable of being property and all but two (commons and ways) are unrelated to land; the others include rights to offices, dignities, and advowsons.[31] These rights may have economic value, but they are not as easy to trespass on and interfere with, and are not as commercially important as intangible property such as bank accounts and shares.

And in modern times it is bank accounts and shares that expose Blackstonian property's weakness. James Penner's book *The Idea of Property in Law* is one of the more prominent resurrections of Blackstonian property in recent years. Scrutinizing his account of property serves to illustrate the inherent

[29] *What Happened?*, *supra* note 3, 398.

[30] According to Blackstone, intangible property may be protected through various legal means, such as the laws of nuisance or trespass. But such protections lack the *in rem*, exclusionary nature that is found in the right to tangible property and are dangerously similar to Hohfeld and Coase's notions of protecting property rights.

[31] This is the right to nominate a person to hold a church office.

weaknesses of any exclusion-based property idea. He defined property as 'the right to determine the use or disposition of a separable thing (that is, a thing whose contingent association with any particular person is essentially impersonal and so imports nothing of normative consequence), in so far as that can be achieved or aided by others excluding themselves from it, and includes the rights to abandon it, to share it, to license it to others (either exclusively or not), and to give it to others in its entirety'.[32]

Penner's idea of property consisted of the exclusion thesis and the separability thesis. The exclusion thesis states 'the right to property is a right to exclude others from things which is grounded by the interest we have in the use of things'.[33] The separability thesis is highlighted by the thing-ness and personality-poor nature of property. He says 'only those "things" in the world which are contingently associated with any particular owner may be objects of property'.[34] What may be one's property must be capable of being someone else's. As he said, our talents, personalities, and eyesight are not capable of being property as they are not contingently associated with us and it is not capable of being owned by someone else. In these respects, Penner's definition of property resonates with Blackstone and others to the extent that it focuses on the person-thing relationship and relies on the right to exclude others.

The challenge to any Blackstonian conception of property is to reconcile intangible properties with the exclusion idea, and Penner recognizes this when he says choses in action and in equity are the most difficult kinds of property to explain.[35] Bank accounts and shares are choses in action, which in turn are '. . . all personal rights of property which can only be claimed or enforced by action, and not by taking physical possession'.[36] Although lay people consider money in their bank accounts to be 'theirs', Penner acknowledges that 'a creditor has no right in the property of his debtor'.[37] What a

[32] *Idea of Property in Law, supra* note 26, 152.
[33] Ibid. 71.
[34] Ibid. 111.
[35] Ibid. 138.
[36] In Halsbury's Laws of England, the editors further elaborate: 'the expression . . . in the literal sense means a thing recoverable by action . . . ', and they also qualified the issue of definition by saying 'the expression is found in the history of English law with so many meanings attached to it, and has been and still is employed to denote so many and such various classes of things, that it is impossible to give an accurate and complete definition of what it means and may include at the present day'. By extension, a chose in equity is any personal right to property which can only be claimed or enforced through the Chancery court. 'Choses in Action' in *Halsbury's Laws of England* (4th edn. Butterworths, London 2003), para 1–6.
[37] *Idea of Property in Law, supra* note 26, 129.

creditor has instead is a right to demand and recover a sum of money from his debtor.

The right to exclude and the duty of non-interference are difficult to apply to choses in action because of their intangibility and the legal reality that chose-holders do not 'own' specific properties of their debtors. Instead, Penner argued that 'the general duty of non-interference with property does not directly shape the nature of the chose-holder's right... The protection is indirect, as it protects... the wherewithal[38] of the entity or person against which the chose is held... that wherewithal is what is protected from depredation by the general duty of non-interference'.[39] He continued, 'choses in action, therefore, are rights in respect of the property of other legal owners which the law is happy to allow their holders to treat as "things" in their own right'.[40] With choses in action, Penner upholds the exclusion criterion by arguing that the chose-holder is indirectly protected by the chose-issuer's right to exclude others from his wherewithal. In other words, a creditor is indirectly protected by his debtor's right to property insofar as the rest of the world must not interfere with the debtor's property. To the extent that the debtor will have funds to pay the creditor, the creditor is protected.

This application of the exclusion idea, however, is difficult to accept, because the rest of the world does not owe the creditor any duty not to interfere with his debtor's property. In fact, one does not have a property owner's creditors in mind when one respects an owner's right to property. From a right-duty perspective, if a third party destroys or misappropriates a debtor's entire wherewithal, the creditor's access to the debtor's wherewithal may have been interfered with, but the creditor's rights have not been violated. At best, the creditor is merely a causal beneficiary of the debtor's right to exclude.

Another key criterion to Penner's idea of property is personality-poverty,[41] which the personal nature of rights requiring personal performances seems to contradict. Choses in action, Penner argues, inevitably involve the transfer of a sum of money so whatever personal relationship exists (say, between creditor and debtor), it is reduced to an impersonal one because of the

[38] Being 'all the property held by those entities or persons which provide the assets from which the chose may be satisfied...' Penner also invoked the civilian concept of the patrimony as a comparison.

[39] *Idea of Property in Law*, *supra* note 26, 129.

[40] Ibid. 129–30.

[41] This is the idea that property is about the human practice of dealing with things, rather than dealing with people or relationships with other people that involve their personal qualities. See generally *Idea of Property in Law*, *supra* note 26, Chapter 5.

creditor's wherewithal providing the sum in question. This, he argues, renders choses in action different from other *in personam* rights and fit to be classified as property.

The weakness of this argument, which Penner himself acknowledged, is that when things are fine, legal choses in action behave like property, but when things go wrong, the relationship and the character of the property revert back to being strictly *in personam* in nature. Despite this, he argued that such property rights retain their proprietary character. In the case of a bad debt, the debt holder retains a form of proprietary protection as the law of bankruptcy is triggered and he obtains an actual share of the debtor's wherewithal, along with all the protection the trustee in bankruptcy is meant to provide.[42]

Despite Penner's best efforts, it is clear that intangible assets such as choses in action are very difficult to reconcile with the exclusion criterion as it is known. Holders of such rights are not directly owed a duty of non-interference by the rest of the world. As Roscoe Pound says, '. . . in a commercial age . . . wealth is largely made up of promises.'[43] And most promises come in the form of choses in action or choses in equity. As land is no longer the predominant form of wealth or factor of economic production, the Blackstonian idea of exclusion-based property struggles to find relevance in a world of bank accounts, shares, and collateralized debt obligations.

Trusts under the Existing Legal Proprietary Framework

Given the regrettable state of property in law and in economics, it should come as no surprise that the proprietary conception of trusts is, at best, weak with a negative outlook on the horizon. Indeed, trusts and beneficial interests fare badly under conceptions of property. To continue with Penner's idea of property, his analysis of the beneficial interest (being a chose in equity) is an extension of his ideas on choses in action. Beneficial interests are generally assignable and can even be the subject-matter of trusts, so they appear to meet his separability criterion. However they do not always meet the personality-poverty criterion. The primary duty of trustees of bare trusts is to deliver the trust property when called on to do so. In this respect, the relationship between the trustee and the beneficiary is as personality-poor as that between a bank and its customer. But in other trusts where trustees are under a duty to

[42] Ibid. 131–2.
[43] R. Pound, *Jurisprudence* (West Publishing, St Paul 1959), 163–4.

consider the interests and unique personal needs of, say, life tenants or discretionary objects, the relationship is anything but personality-poor.

More importantly, on the exclusion criterion, Penner argued that beneficial interests are even more proprietary than choses in action. This is because the trust property is kept separate from the trustee's other property. And because the trustee is not able to use it for his own purposes, the beneficiary benefits much more directly from the general duties *in rem* not to interfere with the property of others. That beneficial interests are more 'proprietary' than run of the mill choses in action is not doubted, but once again the notion heavily relies on the indirect relationship, if it exists at all, between the beneficiary and the rest of the world.

This is precisely the point of contention between Frederic Maitland and Austin Scott in the early twentieth century. Regarding *in rem* and *in personam* rights, Maitland and Scott argue over who owes the beneficiary a duty to respect his rights in the trust property. According to Maitland, the beneficiary's interest is a right *in personam* against the trustee, and only misleadingly appears to be a right *in rem.*[44] To support this, he invokes two valid statements in his analysis of beneficial interests.[45] The first is that 'the *cestui que trust* has rights enforceable against any person who has undertaken the trust, against all who claim through or under as volunteers, against his creditors, and against those who acquire the thing with notice actual or constructive of the trust'. The second is that 'the *cestui que trust* has rights enforceable against all save a *bona fide* purchaser...who for value has obtained a legal right in the thing without notice of the trust express or constructive'.

In actual fact, both statements contain the same set of people, but Maitland prefers the former and argues that the latter gives the misleading impression that the beneficial interest is a right *in rem.* Maitland traces the judicial development of the beneficiary's enforcement rights. Naturally, it began with the trustee, but gradually expanded to cover volunteers and purchasers with notice. Eventually, the second statement took hold, and today we define the beneficiary's interest as one that is enforceable against an indefinite class of persons except the excluded class, rather than the other way round, as Maitland prefers. For him, the problem with the modern formulation is that it misleads people into believing that the beneficiary's right is proprietary, when, clearly, the beneficiary's right is composed of a series of *in personam* rights against a multitude of (but not all) people. The

[44] F. W. Maitland, *Equity: a course of lectures* (2nd edn. Cambridge University Press, London 1936), 117.

[45] Ibid. 115.

heart of Maitland's argument is that because it is not enforceable against literally everyone, it cannot possibly be a right *in rem*.

Scott takes the opposite view, namely, that the *cestui que trust's* interest is one that is good against the world at large.[46] He states that the *cestui que trust* has two classes of rights: 'he has a number of rights, positive and negative, available against the trustee alone; he has in addition, as equitable owner of the trust *res*, and a right against the world at large to insist that it respect his ownership, to insist that it refrain from using the trust property for any purpose which is inconsistent with the trust; that right is not available against a purchaser for value and without notice; and if, unlike some equitable interests, it is not available against one who acts adversely to the trustee, as disseisor or converter, it is not because equity does not regard the *cestui que trust* as beneficial owner of the trust *res*, but because it considers that the trustee adequately represents him.'[47]

Scott's description of the beneficiary's right against the rest of the world is one step stronger than Penner's as Scott maintains that the rest of the world owes the beneficiary a duty not to interfere. However, Harlan Stone finds Scott's conception of rights *in rem* difficult to accept and points out the dangers of abusing Latin notions.[48] Although the beneficiary indeed has a right against the world at large not to improperly 'interfere' with the trust, it is difficult to characterize this right as property. He said that to call such a right a right *in rem* without establishing 'any substantial identity in character of the rights of the *cestui* with the rights of property hitherto commonly spoken of as rights *in rem* [may] destroy a useful although not altogether scientific generalization expressed by the phrase "rights *in rem*"'.[49]

It may be apparent by now that Maitland and Scott's debate is bogged down by what Donovan Waters calls the 'deceiving dichotomy'.[50] Their positions are qualitatively similar but for the Latinisms and semantics. They agree that the content of the beneficiary's interest is less than that of a legal owner, but disagree about how this interest is expressed. Also, framing the debate within the narrow confines of Roman *in rem* and *in personam* rights severely limits the scope of discussion. Needless to say, the controversy over the nature of an *in rem* right remains; so to assert that the beneficial

[46] A. W. Scott, 'The Nature of the Rights of the Cestui Que Trust' 17 *Colum. L. Rev.* 269 (1917).
[47] Ibid. 290.
[48] H. F. Stone, 'The Nature of the Rights of the Cestui Que Trust' 17 *Colum. L. Rev.* 467 (1917).
[49] Ibid. 470.
[50] D. Waters, 'The Nature of the Trust Beneficiary's Interest' 45 *Can B.R.* 219 (1967).

interest must be either an *in rem* or an *in personam* right does not further anyone's cause.

Apart from the right to exclude and the duty of non-interference, another oft-cited proprietary quality of the beneficial interest is questionable. In his account of property, Harris considers trusts to be one of many cashable rights. Civil trespassory rules protect the trustee's domain and it is the trustee who *prima facie* possesses ownership privileges and powers to the trust property. But, crucially, trust rules are designed so that the trustee exercises these powers and privileges for the benefit of the beneficiaries. Furthermore, beneficiaries have certain rights against third party meddlers. The net effect, Harris says, is that 'beneficiaries enjoy, as part of their private wealth, the totality of ownership privileges and powers vested in the trustee'.[51]

The problem with Harris's conclusion is that it is more often than not an exaggeration. In the case of a bare trust, the beneficiary may be exercising all his full-blooded ownership rights through the trustee. In this way, the trustee of a bare trust is just a conduit or an agent for the beneficiary. But in virtually any other kind of trusts, beneficiaries cannot simply enjoy the totality of ownership privileges and powers vested in the trustee at their whim. The trustee may be exercising these privileges and powers in the best interest of the beneficiaries, but this is very different from having all of these privileges and powers at their own disposal.

From these various debates and accounts, it is clear that neither the exclusionary feature nor the positive entitlement aspect of beneficial interests is properly defined, let alone understood. When the trust's most fundamental concept is not even properly understood, it should surprise nobody that trust law is internally inconsistent. By internal inconsistency, whatever a trust rule is supposed to mean or to protect, there will always be exceptions or even contradicting rules. A case in point is beneficiaries' right to trust information. We have always been taught that beneficiaries with fixed interests have equitable title or ownership of the trust assets and it would seem logical that, because of their vested interests, they are always entitled to trust information. But, as the current law (*Schmidt v Rosewood Trust*) stands, even they are not automatically entitled to trust information. The Privy Council in this case held that any beneficiary or object's right to seek disclosure of trust documents was an aspect of the court's inherent jurisdiction to supervise and, if necessary, to intervene in the administration of trusts.[52] In other words, it is up to the court to decide who has the right to trust information.

[51] Ibid. 53.
[52] [2003] 2 WLR 1520.

The bogeyman behind this deeply unsatisfactory case is the nature of a discretionary object's interest. Whereas the previous rule tied a beneficiary's proprietary interest to his right to trust information,[53] it could not be applied to a trust where all the 'intended beneficiaries' were merely discretionary objects. Because the nature of a discretionary object's interest is not well defined, it is difficult to continue applying a rule based on beneficial interests, vested or otherwise. As an equitable fudge, the court decided that the right to trust information is based on accountability and it can decide who is entitled to the information. Therefore, what we end up having are two generally valid statements: beneficiaries with vested interests are so powerful that they can even terminate the trust; yet it is up to the court to decide whether they are entitled to trust information. In this respect, trust law is internally inconsistent. As Penner observes in a different context, our understanding of trust law is 'unstable, oscillating between an obligational and proprietary perspective'.[54]

The Ascent of the Obligational and Entity Approaches

Much that trust law and beneficial interests lack coherence and consistency, they are also being influenced by the obligational and entity approaches. Through academic discussions and legislative and judicial developments, these approaches have been making inroads into trust law for some years. The modern academic literature, especially in the field of law and economics, is monopolized by the two approaches. More importantly, in the United States these ideas have found their way into the Restatement and also in the Uniform Trust Code.

Globally, trust law is developing along the lines mapped out by both approaches. The clearest example of this is the development of non-charitable purpose (NCP) trusts. NCP trusts are trusts that do not have beneficiaries; instead, trustees administer them for the benefit of purposes. These 'purposes' can be as mundane as tending to a testator's grave or to provide financial support to unincorporated associations such as political parties. Purposes can also be deliberately logically circular ('the purpose of this

[53] 'The beneficiary is entitled to see all trust documents because they are trust documents and because he is a beneficiary. They are in a sense his own.' Wrenbury L.J. in *O'Rourke v Darbishire* [1920] AC 581. See generally D. J. Hayton, P. Matthews, and C. Mitchell, (eds.) *Underhill and Hayton The Law Relating to Trusts and Trustees* (17th edn. LexisNexis Butterworths, London 2006), para 60.23.

[54] J. E. Penner, 'Exemptions' in P. Birks and A. Pretto (eds.) *Breach of Trust* (Hart, Oxford 2002), 267.

trust is to hold trust assets'). In any case, NCP trusts violate the fundamental tenet of trust law that a trust must have a beneficiary.

That NCP trusts can hide the true identity of human beneficiaries and aid tax and creditor evasion is beside the point.[55] What matters is that they have analytical supporters. David Hayton argues that a beneficiary is necessary only to enforce the trust and that the settlor can appoint an enforcer to perform the same function.[56] He observes that a lot of the beneficiary's rights to trace and claim misappropriated trust assets exist just as well in charitable purpose trusts, which have no beneficiaries. Furthermore, Hayton points out that objects of discretionary trusts have 'proprietary' rights that hardly resemble ownership interests and that the right to trust information no longer has a proprietary basis.[57] These justifications lead Hayton to argue that NCP trusts can be recognized as long as they are administratively workable and are restricted to a valid perpetuity period.

On the other hand, Paul Matthews states the case against NCP trusts.[58] For him, to separate enforcement from enjoyment is to change radically the nature of the legal institution involved. He does not reject outright vehicles that separate enforcement from enjoyment, but he says '[the legal institution] might have to be a contract, a foundation, a company, or something else. But not a trust'.[59] Legal taxonomy aside, Matthews points out that duties can be considered as 'annexed to the [trust] property' and owed to the beneficiaries.[60] In this way, an action for a breach of contract is very different from that for a breach of trust because in the latter, one is not seeking to enforce a bargain but rather to recover for damage done to a vested interest. Furthermore, Matthews finds it difficult to explain how an enforcer can have claims against third parties; the trustee may have undertaken a duty to him at the outset, but surely not the rest of the world. Only holders of beneficial interests

[55] See generally P. Matthews, 'Shooting STAR: the new special trusts regime from the Cayman Islands' 11 *TLI* 67 (1997); A. G. D. Duckworth, 'STAR WARS: The colony strikes back' 12 *TLI* 16 (1998); P. Matthews, 'STAR WARS: Big Bang or Red Dwarf?' 12 *TLI* 98 (1998); A. G. D. Duckworth, 'STAR WARS: Smiting the bull' 13 *TLI* 158 (1999); Financial Services and the Treasury Bureau (Hong Kong), 'Review of the Trustee Ordinance and Related Matters—Consultation Paper', 2009, <http://www.fstb.gov.hk/fsb/ppr/consult/doc/to_review_consultation_e.pdfM>, last accessed 15 June 2010, para 6.28.

[56] D. J. Hayton, 'Developing the Obligation Characteristic of the Trust' 117 *LQR* 96 (2001).

[57] *Schmidt v Rosewood Trust* [2003] 2 WLR 1520.

[58] P. Matthews, 'From Obligations to Property, and Back Again? The Future of the Non-Charitable Purpose Trust' in D. J. Hayton (ed.) *Extending the Boundaries of Trusts and Similar Ring-Fenced Funds* (Kluwer Law International, London 2002), hereafter *From Obligations to Property, and Back Again?*

[59] Ibid. 218.

[60] Ibid. 216.

can enforce their right against the rest of the world and an enforcer does not have a beneficial interest in the trust asset.

Consistent with Blackstone who asserts the unity of ownership rights ('that sole despotic dominion'), Matthews argues that the rights to enforcement and enjoyment must always exist together. In this respect, those who argue for NCP trusts based on an 'enforcer principle' are playing the role of Hohfeld and Coase. By splitting up enforcement and enjoyment rights, scholars turn the beneficial interest into a bundle of use rights. Recall that Coase says 'whether we have the right to shoot over another man's land has been thought of as depending on who owns the airspace over the land. It would be simpler to discuss what we should be allowed to do with the gun'.[61] In the same spirit, apologists of NCP trusts can say 'whether someone has the right to enforce a trust has been thought of as depending on who holds the beneficial interest. It would be simpler to discuss what rights he has been allocated against the trustee'.

This unbundling of the beneficial interest need not stop, and has not stopped, with the enforcement/enjoyment dichotomy. The offshore trend of recognizing the validity of settlor retention of powers is also another example of integral sets of rights being broken up. This phenomenon, however, is quite different from splitting enforcement rights from enjoyment rights in NCP trusts. The powers that settlors typically retain belong to not only the beneficiary, but also the trustee and even an absolute owner.

A settlor may retain a beneficial interest and may appoint himself as a protector (whose rights and powers may overlap with those of an enforcer). However, he could also retain investment and dispositive powers, which traditionally belong to the trustee. In extreme cases, he can even retain the power to give any directions to the trustee or even to terminate the trust. Such powers cannot properly be attributed to either the trustee or the beneficiary and—if there is meant to be a logical basis for such powers—can only belong to the settlor *cum* absolute owner. Just as an absolute owner can choose to never settle a trust, only the settlor can 'undo' the settlement of the trust.

Legal scholars typically frown on settlors retaining such powers because settlors risk being deemed not to have beneficially parted with the trust asset. In turn, this thinking seems to depend on there being an irreducible core content of trusteeship (and for that matter beneficiary-ship). By usurping a certain amount of rights and powers from trustees and beneficiaries, the argument goes, trustees stop being trustees and beneficiaries stop being beneficiaries. To put it in Blackstonian terms, such an arrangement would

[61] R. Coase, *supra* note 7, 34.

be frowned upon because the trustee and the beneficiary no longer have sole despotic dominion of legal ownership and equitable ownership respectively.

However, if Hohfeld and Coase were trust lawyers, there would be no problem because all rights and duties would be considered bilateral and could be disaggregated and distributed to any parties. For them, it is entirely conceivable for the rights to an asset to be divided among not just the three principal trust parties, but among any number of people. The powers and rights of the settlor, the trustee, and the beneficiary broadly correspond with the functions of origination, management, and enjoyment. If all rights and powers can be disaggregated and distributed, then one can truly mix and match them among three, or even hundreds of, individuals.

This *in personam* approach is a trust lawyer's dream as it can conceptually justify any kind of trust customization. Witness its appearance in the issue of the beneficiary's right to trust information. Turning to *Schmidt v Rosewood Trust* again, no doubt the nature of the beneficial interest is key to understanding any beneficiary-related rights. But insofar as it is up to the court to discover whether an applicant has a right to trust documents, this approach strongly resonates with Coase's preference to rely on asking what onc can do with one's gun rather than what one can do to another's field. Essentially, the court will be asking whether an applicant specifically has (or ought to have) the right to trust information rather than examining the totality of his rights. Rightly or wrongly, this is precisely the kind of legal reasoning that the bundle of rights idea encourages.

Conclusion

Our idea of property has been in decline. We have moved from the Blackstonian idea of exclusive property in things to a very loose concept where any valuable rights that are given state protection are deemed to be property. That our legal systems and capitalist economies have not come crashing down because of the disintegration of the property concept demonstrates the trivial and academic nature of this decline. But the same cannot be said about trusts. Like ill-thought out company or insolvency laws, shoddily conceived trust laws have a direct and real impact on society. All of this is happening because the trust concept has lost its property-based foundation and in its place are the obligational and entity approaches.

To paraphrase Merrill and Smith, one must ask 'what happened to the proprietary conception of trusts in law and economics?' Much of the 'how' has been answered in this chapter. We now know that legal ideas of property have been in a downward spiral and its economic conception never got off to a proper start. This does not leave much to be desired for the idea of trusts as property. But the question of 'why' remains. Why has no one sought the revival of the proprietary basis of trusts in law and in economics? One possible reason is that trusts—just like property—suffer from post-establishment neglect.

Recall that Merrill and Smith argue that the study of property has moved from emphasizing its exclusive and absolute qualities to analysing day-to-day problems. This is explained by the fact that in Blackstone's times, security of property was not yet fully guaranteed by the state and much of his rhetoric is geared towards reifying the concept. Once security of property is guaranteed, we take it for granted and have embarked on the study of other property problems. The same may be said about trusts in that its proprietary qualities are emphasized during its infancy to secure its place as a standalone institution. But once this is accomplished, we also take its proprietary qualities for granted and analyse other trust problems, and the obligational and entity approaches may appear to be better suited for the task. As the remainder of this book will show, this need not be the case.

7

Reconceptualizing Property and Funds in Law and Economics

Introduction

Despite the conclusions of the previous chapter, property is not in a hopeless state. In fact, where it concerns trusts and beneficial interests, the future looks bright. After decades, if not centuries, of denial, property theorists have in recent years finally let go of the exclusion requirement of property. With hindsight, dispensing with the exclusion requirement makes property a much more flexible and coherent concept. What is more, this modern idea of property accommodates an advanced and sophisticated form of property ownership—the fund, which traditional property could never have. This chapter introduces the new idea of property, which does not solely rely on exclusion and, from this, the fund concept.

Why did it take so long for us to let go of the exclusion requirement? Perhaps in part because of dogma and inertia, property theorists have been slow to react to changing socio-economic circumstances. More importantly, however, is the traditional uni-dimensional treatment of the right to exclude. For most, it meant a right physically to exclude trespassers off one's land and this did not fare well with the introduction of new forms of intangible economic wealth. The physical right to exclude others is of limited economic value in the age of intellectual property and financial wealth.

To deal with this, the exclusion requirement has not been completely abandoned. Rather, it has been reinterpreted. Through a more flexible right to exclude—one that only binds successors to title—the trust and the beneficial interest can be sustained and developed as property concepts. But rationalizing the right to exclude is only the beginning. What is more important is to recognize the fund concept as a distinct property interest. This concept, as epitomized by trusts and beneficial interests, goes a long way towards understanding the fungibility and ever-changing nature of assets in funds and other types of pooled resources.

Just as legal ideas of property are given a breath of fresh air, the economic literature has also revived the idea of property. The works of Thomas Merrill and Henry Smith argue for a neo-conceptualist view of property and justifies the *in rem* right to exclude largely on economic grounds. To a large extent, Blackstone has made a comeback. The contemporaneous revival of property, in law and in economics, as one coherent concept lays the groundwork for the reformation of the property-based understanding of trusts.

This chapter is organized as follows. First, it shows why the exclusion requirement is no longer necessary in the modern conception of property. Second, it looks at how James Penner's successor version of the right to exclude operates in the beneficial interest. Third, it introduces the fund concept and compares Penner's and Nolan's accounts. Fourth, it presents Merrill and Smith's revival of the *in rem* right to exclude as key to understanding the economics of property. The next chapter offers an economic account of the trust as a fund.

De-emphasizing the Exclusion Requirement

The right to exclude is Blackstonian property's greatest strength as well as its Achilles' heel. The physical nature of the right to exclude means that an intangible thing is afforded no protection. There are two ways to overcome this. The first is simply to divorce excludability from separability; that is, excludability should no longer be seen as a prerequisite to the property concept. The second is to reconceptualize the right to exclude to catch up with modern times. Scholars have done both, and in doing so, they have further extended the idea of property in law.

Giving up the right to exclude may appear at first defeatist, but it is not so upon closer examination. Bank accounts, shares, and beneficial interests are treated as property because owners and non-owners alike interact with these assets with almost the same degree of security and confidence as owners who enjoy physical exclusion rights. A better question to ask, therefore, is whether the absence of the right to exclude is detrimental to owners' use and enjoyment of their property in bank accounts and shares. To have the right to exclude others from bank accounts or shares would be to have a security interest over a bank or company's wherewithal; this would be a lot more than what bank customers and shareholders have bargained for. To be sure, having a security interest over a bank or company's wherewithal significantly increases the probability of payment, but this is not the 'property' being discussed here—this would just be a matter of creditor priorities.

In most cases, having the right to exclude others from intangible assets is simply security overkill, and the absence of such a right is not detrimental to enjoying such properties.[1] Penner now considers the idea of property to be better understood with the separability thesis alone; the right physically to exclude and the correlative duty of non-interference are not necessary in finding property in assets generally.[2] Robert Chambers divides property into two categories: a smaller, traditional category of rights *in rem*, which are rights to things enforceable generally against other members of society; and a larger category of assignable rights, which include rights *in rem* and *in personam*.[3] James Harris also describes property as '. . . comprising items which are either the subject of direct trespassory protection or separately assignable as part of private wealth'.[4] Most scholars have simply detached excludability from separability in order to accommodate intangible assets.

The Exclusive Nature of the Beneficial Interest

Penner, however, takes the exclusion thesis one step further. Although he now argues that the exclusion thesis is inessential to the idea of property, he further develops it where it is still relevant. Penner divides the right to exclude into trespassory and successor versions.[5] The trespassory version is the well-known *in rem* right to exclude others from tangible things, whereas the successor version primarily caters to explaining the beneficial interest. Since the beneficial interest binds the whole world except the *bona fide* purchaser for value without notice, there is something *in rem* about it. Penner calls the *in rem* right observed in the beneficial interest the 'successor' version because 'such a right *in rem* is one which in [principle], may bind all others, not because of the fact that each of us all presently owe a duty to the [beneficiary], but because of the fact that in principle all persons may become successor in

[1] Herein lies the difference between property in tangible things and property in intangible things. With tangible things like land, the protection afforded to the owner is absolute in the sense that if someone commits trespass, he can be assured that the trespasser will be evicted. With intangible things like bank accounts, there is no absolute protection and there is always a risk that the owner will not be able to secure repayment. Short of using security interests, this appears to be the trade off between tangible and intangible properties.

[2] Statement by J. E. Penner. (Personal Email Correspondence. 17 September 2009).

[3] R. Chambers, 'Two Kinds of Enrichment' in R. Chambers, C. Mitchell and J. Penner (eds.) *Philosophical Foundations of the Law of Unjust Enrichment* (Oxford University Press, Oxford 2009), 254–5.

[4] J. W. Harris, *Property and Justice* (Oxford University Press, Oxford 1996), 13.

[5] J. E. Penner, 'Duty and Liability in Respect of Funds' in J. Lowry and L. Mistelis (eds.) *Commercial Law: Perspectives and Practice* (Lexis Nexis Butterworths, London, 2006).

title or possession to property which is bound by the [beneficiary's] right'.[6] This successor *in rem* right can be found in all beneficial interests, and is much more suitable than the trespassory version because the beneficial interest is intangible, and is always derivative of an underlying asset.

The Nature of the Trust Fund

The question facing the successor version is: just how big a hole does the *bona fide* purchaser exception blow to the net catching subsequent takers of the property?[7] Ironically, this hole is meant to be there and only with it can the successor version *in rem* right work. To appreciate this point, one must understand the nature of a fund. A fund is a pool of assets, the composition of which changes from time to time. For lawyers and philosophers, the challenge is to characterize the nature of beneficiaries' interests in the fund or its underlying assets.

In the case of a trust, the trustee usually has the power to sell trust assets; it is this crucial power that gives the trust assets the dynamic and fluctuating characteristics of a fund. That the trustee has the power to change the composition of the trust fund and the beneficiary has some kind of an interest are clear; what is debated is the nature and extent of that interest. What, if anything, does the beneficiary own and what does ownership mean in the context of trust funds?

The beneficiary has neither 'full ownership' of nor legal title to the trust assets; to do so would contradict the trustee's position and potentially create an anticommon.[8] The beneficiary's interest is clearly not ownership as we know it, but this less-than-full-ownership arrangement is not a weakness of the fund concept. Crucially, it makes the fund concept possible and the *bona fide* purchaser exception is part and parcel of the fund concept. The fund concept requires *bona fide* purchasers to take free of the beneficial interest.

[6] Ibid. Para 12.23. The successor version is very similar to Merrill and Smith's 'quasi-multital' relationship, where one has a right against singular, unidentified persons. See T. W. Merrill and H. E. Smith, 'The Property/Contract Interface' 101 *Colum. L. Rev.* 773 (2001), 845–7. See also Chapter 8.

[7] J. E. Penner, *The Idea of Property in Law* (Oxford University Press, Oxford 1997), 136–8.

[8] This refers to the situation where property rights are too fragmented and too many people have the right to exclude; the end result is that an asset is underutilized, if utilized at all. If both the trustee and the beneficiary have legal titles, they become joint owners rather than trustee and beneficiary. If too many beneficiaries have veto power over asset sales, the trustee may never be able to obtain unanimous consent and the asset may never be sold or properly utilized. See M. A. Heller, 'The Tragedy of the Anticommons: Property in the Transition From Marx to Markets' 111 *Harv. L. Rev.* 622 (1998).

Failure to have this not only leads to the non-marketability of trust assets, the fund also loses is fluctuating nature—it ceases to be a fund. The *bona fide* purchaser taking title free of the beneficial interest is merely one-half of the equation. The other half is that the beneficiary's interest in the sold asset is extinguished and instead attaches to the newly exchanged asset. This, of course, is the doctrine of overreaching.[9] As David Fox says, 'overreaching is an incident of the powers of disposition conferred on [the trustee]'.[10]

Interestingly, where an unauthorized transaction takes place between the trustee and a *bona fide* purchaser without notice, the same result occurs: the *bona fide* purchaser takes title to the asset free of the beneficial interest and, through the evidentiary tracing process, the beneficiary's interest in the original asset is extinguished and attaches to the sales proceeds or exchanged asset. Therefore, whenever a trustee transacts with a *bona fide* purchaser, the beneficiary's interest in the original asset is replaced by an interest in another asset—regardless of whether one calls it overreaching or tracing. Needless to say, in the normal course of things, cases of overreaching far outnumber cases of tracing.

The doctrine of overreaching is so prevalent and so important to the fund concept that Richard Nolan says 'the "trust fund" is defined as a set of assets; the beneficiary has rights in the "trust fund", and so the beneficiary has rights in those assets, subject to the possibility that those rights might be overreached'.[11] In other words, a trust fund is merely a shorthand for a set of assets that are liable to substitution through overreaching. Penner calls this the 'minimalist' approach and criticizes it on several grounds.[12] He argues that the minimalist view suggests that beneficiaries have full proprietary rights in individual trust assets but this is inconsistent with the practice of disposing of beneficial interests.[13]

[9] See generally C. Harpum, 'Overreaching, Trustee's Powers and the Reform of the 1925 Legislation' 49 *CLJ* 277 (1990) and D. Fox. 'Overreaching' in P. Birks and A. Pretto (eds.) *Breach of Trust* (Hart, Oxford 2002). Curiously, the term 'overreaching' is never used in the United States. In the Restatement (Second) of Trusts, this simple yet essential idea is reflected in § 283 under the heading 'Where Transfer is Not in Breach of Trust'.

[10] D. Fox, *supra* note 9, 97.

[11] R. Nolan, 'Property in a Fund' 120 *LQR* 108 (2004), 116. See also R. Nolan, 'Equitable Property' 122 *LQR* 232 (2006) and R. Nolan, 'Understanding the Limits of Equitable Property' 1 *J. Eq.* 18 (2006).

[12] J. E. Penner, *supra* note 5, para 12.15–12.21.

[13] If the minimalist approach is correct, then a beneficiary who disposes of his interest in the trust assets would be required under s 53(1)(c) of the Law of Property Act 1925 to record each disposition of each individual asset in writing. This is neither the practice nor the understanding of the operation of s 53(1)(c). See J. E. Penner, *The Law of Trusts* (6th edn. Oxford University Press, Oxford 2008), para 6.13–6.14. On the other hand, there is no similar controversy in the United States as there is no general requirement to record such dispositions in writing. See Restatement (Third) of Trusts, §53.

In addition, Nolan's minimalist idea fails to explain why beneficiaries are entitled to 'future assets', such as gratuitous asset additions to the trust by the settlor. Nolan does note that in addition to rights to substitutes, beneficiaries also have rights to 'future assets', including any further assets settled on the same terms. However, the minimalist idea—proprietary rights in assets coupled with the doctrine of overreaching—cannot provide a basis for beneficiaries' entitlement to such future assets. Neither their present interest in current assets nor the right to substitute assets justify why they are automatically entitled to future assets. There is simply no conceptual basis for beneficiaries being entitled to future assets under the minimalist approach.

Another issue that the minimalist approach cannot resolve is the relationships between beneficiaries *inter se.* The minimalist approach focuses on the relationships between the beneficiary and the outside world and between the beneficiary and the trustee. Crucially, the minimalist approach does not account for the relationships between multiple beneficiaries or objects. In particular, if discretionary objects have a proprietary interest in the trust assets subject to overreaching, who owns what and how? The minimalist approach caters solely for the case of a single beneficiary or, at best, the beneficiary class as a whole. Nolan states that beneficiaries are entitled to whatever interest the trust instrument so provides, but this leaves something to be desired.[14]

Not only are the property relationships between beneficiaries unclear, conceiving of equitable property as outright ownership of assets (subject to overreaching) neglects the fact that the modern trustee does not normally administer the trust fund as a collection of individual assets. Whether it is providing trust accounts or making trust investments, trustees consider the collection of assets as a composite fund. The summing up of asset values is not just to inform beneficiaries of the total value of their assets, but to inform them of the total value of their fund. For trust investments to work, both modern portfolio theory and total return investing require the set of trust assets to be treated as a composite fund for investment purposes. Although the minimalist approach is not concerned with how trustees prepare their accounts or invest, it is very telling that, from the trustee's perspective, trust assets are best understood as a composite fund.

In contrast, Penner conceives of the beneficiary's interest as a distinct interest in a fund. He says, 'it is not merely an interest in multiple items of property, which items may fluctuate because of the exercise of the powers of the fund manager. The interest the fund beneficiary has is one in which [the

[14] R. Nolan (2004), *supra* note 11, 116–17; and R. Nolan (2006), *supra* note 11, 237.

beneficiary] has no present interest in any of the properties comprising the fund; his interest is only in whatever rights are given under the terms of his interest in the fund. However it is one of the incidents of title in the fund that when certain events occur—the most obvious example being a breach of trust—the beneficiary may elect to enforce a direct proprietary interest in individual items of the fund'.[15]

Understanding the beneficiary's interest as a distinct interest in a fund resolves many conceptual difficulties posed by the minimalist approach. The fund concept can explain why beneficiaries are entitled to future assets added into the trust fund on the same terms. Beneficiaries own an interest in the fund, which is comprised of a collection of assets that may fluctuate—either intangibly through changes in value or tangibly through dispositions, distributions, or additions. As far as trust accounting and investments are concerned, the fund concept is fully consistent with the presentation of trust accounts and modern investment theories.

The fund concept also provides a better foundation for both Nolan's and Penner's description of the beneficiary's positive entitlement and explains the relationship between beneficiaries *inter se.* Nolan states that the positive aspect of the beneficial interest is whatever the trust instrument provides and that it is highly variable and enforceable only against a very limited number of people.[16] Similarly, Penner states that the beneficiary's interest is only in whatever rights are given under the terms of his interest in the fund. While both Nolan and Penner understand that the content of the beneficiary's positive rights are highly variable and ultimately rest on the terms of the trust instrument, only Penner's fund concept is compatible with this variable-entitlement idea. The idea that beneficiaries have ownership interests in individual assets under the minimalist approach is simply incompatible with the variability of positive entitlements as provided by the trust instrument. Beneficiaries under the minimalist approach would *prima facie* have equal rights and standings, presumably as tenants in common. However, with the fund concept, the burden of explaining asset-specific entitlement is removed and the primacy of the trust instrument in dictating entitlements can be justified at the fund level.

In addition to better explaining the trust and its beneficiaries in the normal course of things, Penner's fund concept is also able to explain the consequences of breaches of trust, in particular the beneficiary's rights against trustees and third parties.[17] When a trustee makes an unauthorized

[15] J. E. Penner, *supra* note 5, para 12.16.
[16] R. Nolan (2006), *supra* note 11, 237–8.
[17] J. E. Penner, *supra* note 5, para 12.20.

disposition of trust asset, the beneficiary can choose between falsifying the accounts (as though the transaction never took place) or taking the new asset that the trustee may have wrongfully acquired (retrospectively authorizing the disposition); both choices are compatible with the idea that a fund's assets will fluctuate. When a trustee misappropriates trust assets outright, the beneficiary can elect to take the new asset or to treat the misappropriation as a loan to the trustee. Again, in both cases, the beneficiary's interest in the original asset is replaced with an interest in the asset he elects to adopt.

Finally, with transfers to third parties in breach of trust, it is known that those who are liable do not owe the beneficiary the full plethora of trustee duties.[18] Rather, such transfers are better conceived as the original express trustee transferring the trust asset to the third party as a custodian trustee, who holds it to the order of the express trustee. As custodian trustee, he is not under active trustee duties such as that to invest. Yet the fluctuating nature of funds continues to subsist with the custodian trustee. If the custodian trustee disposes of the trust asset, the beneficiary can trace and claim the substituted asset. To the extent that the custodian trustee is merely following the express trustee's directions (and is not aware of the actual trust terms and breaches thereof), he cannot be liable to the beneficiary for wrongful misapplication of trust assets.

Whichever account of the fund one adopts, it is useful to acknowledge and appreciate its practice as it plays an important role in modern business and finance. To be clear, one can have a fund without involving any third party fund manager; but a fund managed by oneself for oneself is more of a mental accounting phenomenon than the property practice that we are considering. It is the tripartite, or sometimes bipartite, fund like the modern donative trust that poses the most analytical challenge. Rationalizing the fund in legal terms provides a foundation for an economic account of trust funds.

The Economic Rationale of the Right to Exclude

Just as new ideas about property and funds have recently emerged, Merrill and Smith offer an economic account of property that resonates with the Blackstonian tradition.[19] Their account departs from other ones in several

[18] Ibid. Para 12.38.

[19] See T. W. Merrill, 'Property and the Right to Exclude' 77 *Neb. L. Rev.* 730 (1998); T. W. Merrill and H. E. Smith, 'What Happened to Property in Law and Economics?' 111 *Yale L. J.* 357 (2001), hereafter *What Happened?*; T. W. Merrill and H. E. Smith, 'Optimal Standardization in the Law of Property: The Numerus Clausus Principle' 110 *Yale L. J.* 1 (2000); T. W. Merrill and H. E. Smith, 'The Property/Contract Interface' 101 *Colum. L. Rev.* 773 (2001); H. E. Smith, 'Exclusion Versus Governance: Two Strategies for Delineating Property Rights' 31 *J. Leg. Stud.* 453 (2002); H. E. Smith, 'The

meaningful ways. First, they recognize the indefinite nature of *in rem* rights and do not subscribe to the view that property rights are generally bilateral in nature. Second, their account relies significantly, though not exclusively, on the right to exclude. In these ways, at least, Merrill and Smith's account is consistent with those of Blackstone and Penner. Third, and most importantly, their account rationalizes property as a coherent concept and locates it among other legal relations such as contracts. This neo-conceptualist account is made possible by one of its key ideas: the costs of discovering and processing information for right- and duty-holders.

Merrill and Smith advocate the *in rem* nature of property rights because only it can explain many property phenomena. As they say, although the *in personam* account of property rights is useful in analysing transaction costs and incentives, it has nothing to offer in explaining other important aspects of property.[20] For example, virtually all property systems limit the number of forms of ownership and permissible forms are largely standardized.[21] In England, the Law of Property Act 1925 limits legal estates to two forms: the fee simple absolute and the term of years absolute; all other estates must take effect as equitable interests.[22] For Hohfeld and Coase, their flexible *in personam* conception of property rights has no explanation for this restrictive phenomenon.

According to Merrill and Smith, the *numerus clausus* principle is 'a device to standardize property rights, and thereby reduce the widespread information-gathering and processing costs imposed on third parties by any system of *in rem* rights'. Since property rights are *in rem* rights and the world at large as duty-holders must respect them, it is incumbent upon the duty-holders to study the form and content of such rights so that they can be respected. If the property system permits the creation of all kinds of unusual and novel property rights, then duty-holders face the prospect of having to study property rights in order to find out their unique content so that they can be respected. Merrill and Smith assert that this imposes high information-gathering and processing costs for duty-holders. By mandating that property rights conform to standardized forms, the *numerus clausus* principle allows duty-holders to know the content of property rights without going into

Language of Property: Form, Context and Audience' 55 *Stan. L. Rev.* 1105 (2003); H. E. Smith, 'Property and Property Rules' 79 *N. Y. U. L. Rev.* 1719 (2004); H. E. Smith, 'Exclusion and Property Rules in the Law of Nuisance' 90 *Va. L. Rev.* 965 (2004); and H. E. Smith, 'Intellectual Property as Property: Delineating Entitlements in Information' 116 *Yale L. J.* 1742 (2007).

[20] *What Happened?*, *supra* note 19, 385.

[21] This is known as the *numerus clausus* principle in civil law but it is not accorded official recognition in the common law world. See T. W. Merrill and H. E. Smith (2000), *supra* note 19.

[22] Law of Property Act 1925, s 1.

detailed discovery, which reduces information-gathering and processing costs. Conversely, the *numerus clausus* principle cannot be explained when property rights take on a bilateral, *in personam* nature because under the *in personam* framework, the idea that the world at large must respect property rights—and therefore suffer from significant information costs—does not exist.

Another important analytical contribution of *in rem* property rights is that they anchor the idea of causation.[23] We normally regard trespassers as causing harm to landowners. But for Coase and his followers, the issue of causation hinges on who values the right the most or is the cheapest cost avoider. If the cattle-owner values the land for grazing more than the landowner values it for farming, then the farmer is the 'cause' of this conflict of land use. This causal agnosticism, Merrill and Smith argue, does not stand if property rights are conceived of as being *in rem.* This is because it is costlier to communicate the cattle-owners' 'rights to grazing' than it is to communicate the landowner's rights to be free from trespass. For the landowner, simple fencing provides effective communication to the rest of the world that his land shall not be trespassed upon. For the cattle-owner and those who would owe him a 'duty', there is no cost-effective way to communicate his particular cattle's right to graze to the rest of the world. As Merrill and Smith observe, this is why the commonsensical default rule is that landowners have the right not to be trespassed by strangers.

What is important about Merrill and Smith's account of property is that it actually corresponds with legal and lay understandings of property. One of the enduring criticisms of the law and economics movement is that many of the theories and accounts produced bear no relation to how lawyers or lay people understand the law.[24] Economic theories of the law may make sense from the economist's perspective, but often judges do not make decision on grounds of, say, economic efficiency. The same decision may be reached by judges, but on grounds of corrective justice or other non-economic reasons. For a long time, Coase's and Barzel's economic accounts of property have become completely detached from legal and practical reality. Merrill and Smith's account brings property back to its roots.

[23] *What Happened?, supra* note 19, 391–4.

[24] See S. A. Smith, *Contract Theory* (Oxford University Press, Oxford 2004), J. L. Coleman, *The Practice of Principle: In Defence of a Pragmatist Approach to Legal Theory* (Oxford University Press, Oxford 2001); and for a spirited response: J. S. Kraus, 'Transparency and Determinancy in Common Law Adjudication: A Philosophical Defense of Explanatory Economic Analysis' 93 *Va. L. Rev.* 287 (2007).

Conclusion

For most of the twentieth century, the idea of property in law and in economics was on a downward path. This is because our understanding of it could not adapt to modern times and in its place came a fragmented, obligation-like reinterpretation of property. For a long time, commentators have fretted about the pending demise of property, but have done little about it. This only changed about a decade ago when neo-conceptualist legal and economic accounts of property were offered. But by no means has the fragmented, obligation-like approach been discredited or put aside. No matter how convincing neo-conceptualist accounts are, there is no absolute, universal truth when it comes to ideas like property. In fact, property is at best a fluid concept that evolves with time and socio-economic practices.

At the very least, scholars such as Penner, Nolan, Merrill, and Smith have contributed to a better understanding of property, especially on aspects that the previous approach failed to explain. More importantly, however, is the rationalization of the fund concept. Funds touch on our everyday lives to almost the same extent that property does, but for too long there has been too little enquiry into the nature of funds. Regardless of whether one subscribes to Nolan's minimalist approach or Penner's fund-as-an-interest approach, there is now active discussion on the funds idea. With a legal understanding of funds and an economic conceptualist account of property in place, it is now possible to analyse and justify trusts in economic terms of property.

8

The Economic Structure of Trusts

Introduction

The previous chapter showed that the beneficial interest can be understood as an interest in a fund, and that its ability to bind most third parties can be explained by the successor version of the right to exclude. At the same time, the *in rem*, exclusion-based conception of property rights is justified by, among other things, its information-processing cost-saving attributes. By integrating these important ideas, an economic account of trusts based on property can be constructed. But before such an account can be offered, one must understand something even more crucial than how beneficial interests are conceived or how property rights operate. To appreciate the trust, one must appreciate why we have property at all. Anthropologists, philosophers, and political scientists will offer different justifications for property but it is the economist's explanation that matters here.

The institution of property incentivizes economic activities and coordinates exchange, but there are limits to these incentivizing and coordinating effects. Individuals are mortal and cannot be incentivized forever. Equally, the basic mechanism of property—the right to exclude—is a low cost but very blunt tool to coordinate exchanges and sharing of resources. The trust extends both functions of property in two ways: it serves as a sophisticated intergenerational wealth transmission device and it enables a form of ownership that cannot easily be replicated by property and contracts alone. In essence, the trust fund concept requires allocating total control over a pool of fluctuating assets to the trustee while excluding the trustee from it. This paradox is compounded by the need of the trust to perform all the above at minimal information-processing costs. As will be seen, much of the wonders performed by the trust are reflected in the well-known but misunderstood legal and beneficial title split. Ultimately, the trust fund is a derivative form of property ownership.

Trust law rarely affords beneficiaries rights at the asset level, for doing so defeats the objectives of a fund. Instead, trust law is primarily concerned with protecting assets and wealth and accordingly is structured along these two levels. At the asset level, trust law protects assets. For example, the trustee is required to segregate trust assets so to allow the trust fund to subsist unambiguously. More importantly, the various trustee duties of care and investments ensure that assets are put to productive and efficient use. On this, Lepaulle is to some extent correct in noting that trusts are not primarily about the individual parties. At the wealth level, the beneficiary's wealth in the trust fund is protected. This is primarily achieved by the *bona fide* purchaser exception, the rules on damages for breach of trust, and the rules on tracing. Equally important, the rule against perpetuities and the rule in *Saunders v Vautier* should be understood as exit strategies that allow the beneficiary to transition from having wealth to possessing things.

This chapter is organized as follows. First, it reviews the incentivizing and coordination functions of property. Second, it argues that there are limitations to the incentivizing function and that trusts temporarily augment it. Third, it describes the well-known information cost reduction role that trusts play in creating unconventional property interests. Fourth, it highlights the limits of property as a coordinating mechanism in that property must often work in conjunction with contract and other rules to regulate resource uses. Fifth, it sets out what the trust is actually trying to do with the asset and the principal parties. Sixth, it demonstrates why the basic tools of property and contracts are inadequate for achieving the goals of the trust arrangement. Seventh, it shows how the trust employs governance-based exclusion as a strategy and how this is reflected in the legal and beneficial title split. Eighth, it argues that trust law is doctrinally asset- and wealth-centric in that it first and foremost protects assets and wealth. Finally, it briefly explains why trusts must terminate and why the beneficiary must be provided with a strategy to exit wealth and gain access to assets.

The Functions of Property

Much has already been said about how we conceive of property rights and funds. But beyond the *in rem* and *in personam* debate or the rights and wrongs of the minimalist approach to funds, a more fundamental question remains. Why do we have property? If trusts are indeed based on property, then the rationale for the latter must also be applicable to the former. The previous chapters alluded to one of the strongest justifications of property: to incentivize labour and industry. As will be seen, this is certainly applicable to trusts. But there is much more to property and trusts than just encouraging people to work. Both Richard Posner and Harold Demsetz explain why property rights exist and, although their accounts differ, they agree that property is designed to promote the efficient use of resources.

Posner argues that property rights confer two kinds of benefits: dynamic and static.[1] Roughly speaking, the dynamic aspect of property is Blackstone and Bentham's labour justification of property. Because most economic activities—including farming—do not produce instantaneous results, individuals face a dynamic, or temporal problem. Without property rights in land or its output, a farmer who farms a plot of land throughout the year risks wasting his efforts if at harvest time someone seizes the harvest. With property rights, a farmer can be assured that his efforts will not be wasted as he will have recourse against trespassers and thieves. Property rights secure expectations and incentivize time-consuming economic activities.

Posner's static aspect of property is less understood and consequently less discussed outside the academic literature. Property serves to coordinate the efficient use of resources. If a pasture for grazing is not owned by anyone, it is a commons and anyone can access and use it. When anyone can let their cows graze in the pasture, the pasture would inevitably be overgrazed because no one bears the costs of overgrazing and no one has the incentive to manage the pasture.[2] To avoid overgrazing and to promote the efficient use of the pasture, someone must be assigned the role of gatekeeper to control the grazing or other uses of the field. To ensure that the gatekeeper is incentivized, he should be given ownership rights to the pasture. By being the owner, he will suffer from the consequences of poor management and coordination. Conversely, he will also enjoy the benefits of good management and proper utilization of the pasture.

Another crucial coordinating function that property serves is setting the baseline for exchanges. If a farmer is physically no longer able to farm and leaves idle a plot of land, then resources are not being put to good use. If the farmer can exchange the plot of land for something that he values more highly, he will be better off. The farmer's counterpart will also be better off because he is exchanging something in return for the plot of land, which he presumably values more highly. Property sets the baseline for such exchanges because without it, parties cannot be certain what is being exchanged and thereafter be protected by the state. By having a basic framework for exchange, individuals can own assets and pursue economic activities that they value most. This is good because by giving people a free hand over what they own and what they do, society's scarce resources will be optimally utilized.

[1] R. A. Posner, *Economic Analysis of Law* (6th edn. Aspen Publishers, New York 2003), 32–4.

[2] This phenomenon is also known as the tragedy of the commons. See G. Hardin, 'The Tragedy of the Commons' 162 *Science* 1243 (1968).

In contrast, Demsetz's account focuses exclusively on the coordination function of property rights. For him, when cows graze in a common pasture, the cow's owners are creating negative externalities. Externality is an ambiguous concept that includes 'external costs, external benefits, and pecuniary and non-pecuniary externalities'. Demsetz states 'no harmful or beneficial effect is external to the world. Some person or persons suffer or enjoy these effects. What converts a harmful or beneficial effect into an externality is that the cost of bringing the effect to bear on the decisions of one or more of the interacting persons is too high to make it worthwhile . . . '.[3]

In the common pasture example, overgrazing produces a harmful effect on all pasture users but no individual cow owner needs to bear the full cost or responsibility. Another example is a factory that emits pollution. If left unregulated, the factory will produce a harmful external effect on its neighbours without suffering from the consequences. Conversely, an owner who manicures his garden in plain view is producing a beneficial external effect: the public gets to admire his garden for free.

Demsetz theorizes that property rights are developed 'to internalize externalities when the gains of internalization become larger than the cost of internalization'.[4] He says, internalizing such effects is 'the process that enables these effects to bear (in greater degree) on all interacting persons . . . a primary function of property rights is that of guiding incentives to achieve a greater internalization of externalities'.[5] To the extent that property allows the owner to internalize the positive effects, Demsetz also agrees with the incentivizing effects of property. Demsetz further theorizes the emergence of property rights. He argues that new property rights emerge as new harmful and beneficial effects emerge (when new knowledge or technologies are developed).

The Temporal Limits of Property and the Rise of the Trust

Much that property incentivizes and coordinates economic activities and conserves information costs along the way, there are limits to these functions. With the incentivizing effect of property, it is limited by human mortality. Property incentivizes labour and other economic activities because individuals reap benefits and also burdens. An owner of a farm is incentivized to use and

[3] H. Demsetz, 'Towards a Theory of Property Rights' 57 *Am. Econ. Rev.* 347 (1967), 348.
[4] Ibid. 350.
[5] Note that property only internalizes externalities to a greater degree, but never completely.

maintain it to the fullest extent because, whilst he is still owner, he is exposed to all the losses and gains. However, he cannot be the owner forever because he will die eventually. Just as a tenant does not own the house he lives in and does not have an incentive to maintain the property to the best of his ability, especially towards the end of his lease, the mortal farm owner suffers from the same problem. In a system where there is only 'ownership for life'—in other words a 100 per cent inheritance tax regime—one can expect a gradual decrease in the incentivizing effects of property. If the owner cannot reap the benefits of his farmland because he thinks he will die soon, he has no reason to farm it, let alone maintain it.

But because no one knows exactly when one will die, the incentivizing effect does not only fade out when an owner grows old. Rather, the uncertainty of the timing of death generally overshadows and disincentivizes economic activities because there is always the possibility that one will unexpectedly meet a premature demise. To mitigate these effects, we have a private inheritance system whereby the testator can name others to succeed him in owning his properties. As Richard Epstein sums up: 'allowing the present owner to choose the persons who enjoy the property after death reduces the likelihood of wasteful subterfuges designed to minimize the impact of the tax, or for a pattern of immediate consumption, which may be easily approximated by the sale of fixed assets and the purchase of a lifetime annuity. It also cuts down on the premature or hidden transfer of assets to children or other family members. With a strong bequest motive, the benefits to the next generation will be treated largely as though they were benefits to present owners, thereby reducing the dislocations that time may impose upon consumption and investment preferences.'[6]

Private inheritance, however, is not enough. At its core, private inheritance is just a future property transfer system whereby ownership of assets is transferred to others according to a testamentary instrument. An alternative to this is simply to transfer assets during one's lifetime; the same results are achieved, just earlier. While private inheritance is a giant leap from no inheritance, it is quite blunt and inflexible. It only works if everyone—the testator and his heirs—find simple, outright transfers suitable. In the case of young children or other vulnerable individuals, it is impossible to quantify how much money is needed to take care of them and, even if it is quantifiable, an outright transfer may not be prudent because they may commit waste or be defrauded. What is needed is a smarter, more sophisticated transfer system.

[6] R. A. Epstein, 'Past and Future: The Temporal Dimension in the Law of Property' 64 *Wash. U. L. Q.* 667 (1986), 697.

But this in itself did not give rise to the trust—the trust is the descendant of the use, which in turn arose as a result of several converging practices in medieval times.[7] One of these practices was the use of testaments and executors, which dates back to as early as the thirteenth century.[8] Executors back then were capable of possessing land and when they did so, they looked very much like feoffees (the predecessors of trustees), and vice versa. The historical dividing line between executors and feoffees is at best blurred. What is clear, however, is that other historical factors lifted the use and the trust from mere post mortem administration to a standalone property institution.

Whether the trust owes its origin to the mythical crusader or the thirteenth century executor *cum* feoffee, it is clear that the trust began life as an intergenerational property transmission device. And for this reason, the trust is historically about extending the incentivizing effects of property. With the trust, the crusader could go into battle with peace of mind, knowing that his land would be properly transferred to his heirs, thereby incentivizing him to focus on what was then a productive economic activity: reclaiming the Holy Land. This function of trusts continues to this very day and although trusts are multi-faceted, they are fundamentally a property transmission device.

Information Costs and Trusts

But trusts have other historically important functions, one of which was to circumvent medieval land-owning restrictions.[9] A basic principle of land law is that one cannot grant land to oneself. In order to change the terms on how land was held, one must grant it to a third party before having the third party re-grant the land on new terms.[10] Such grant-and-re-grant transactions enabled fee simple estates to be turned into, say, life and fee tail estates. Joseph Biancalana argues that these transactions slowly disappeared in the fourteenth-century because they transformed into intergenerational uses.[11] Apart from explaining the rise of the trust, these grant-and-re-grant transactions also demonstrate that there is a historically consistent demand to avoid ownership restrictions. What individuals wanted in medieval times—customization or restructuring of ownership rights—still holds true. The

[7] See the Introduction.

[8] J. Biancalana, 'Medieval Uses' in R. Helmholz and R. Zimmermann (eds.) *Itinera Fiduciae: Trust and Treuhand in Historical Perspective* (Duncker & Humblot, Berlin 1998), 117.

[9] See the Introduction.

[10] J. Biancalana, *supra* note 8, 119.

[11] Ibid. 121.

difference is back then it was a dubious practice of regulatory arbitrage. Today, the use of trusts to create highly-customized ownership arrangements is not only sanctioned, but also mandated by law.

This need for customization highlights the information-processing limit of property. Merrill and Smith argue that property rights are *in rem* because they are respected by the world at large. And in order for the world at large to cost-effectively respect the content of property rights, they must be in simple and standardized forms. The trade off of restricting property rights to simple and standardized forms, of course, is that they are not easily customizable. The use and later the trust fill this functional gap. By having the trustee as legal owner of the property, the rest of the world only need to deal with one person with one standardized title. Behind the façade of the trustee's legal ownership of property may lie numerous beneficiaries with complex and unusual beneficial interests. But persons dealing with the trustee need not be concerned with the content of those beneficial interests; they only need to be sure that the trustee has good legal title. Bernard Rudden calls this simple yet effective arrangement of dealing with the outside world the 'trust-screen'.[12]

As Merrill and Smith explain, 'the trust as an institution dramatically reduces the information costs of having a system of property rights that includes exotic interests such as life estates, remainders, possibilities of reverter, and executory interests. If life estates and remainders were commonly held as legal interests, then third parties dealing with property owners would face substantial risks that any particular parcel would be subject to an undisclosed future interest.'[13] They continue: 'in effect, the trust is a brilliant device that allows for considerable customization of beneficial interests using the building blocks of the old common law—thereby reducing the frustration costs associated with strict regimentation of property forms—while at the same time consolidating the assets used to fund these beneficial interests in a form that minimizes third-party information costs.'[14]

That trusts allow people to better manage property distributions during and after their lives and that they enable the creation of unconventional property interests is nothing new. These functions of trusts are practised by lawyers and estate planners every day and have been praised by countless commentators. What is rarely mentioned, however, is that these functions—the greater incentivizing effect and the creation of complex property rights

12 B. Rudden, 'Things as Thing and Things as Wealth' 14 *OJLS* 81 (1994), 90.

13 T. W. Merrill and H. E. Smith, 'The Property/Contract Interface' 101 *Colum. L. Rev.* 773 (2001), 848.

14 Ibid. 849.

behind a simple one—are better viewed as extending the limits of the property institution.

The trust is a functional extension of property—not contracts or entities. As we have seen, many arguments have been made as to why trusts are contracts or entities. In the case of contracts, trusts are neither contracts nor functional extensions of them. John Langbein and others' observation that there is nothing special about trusts and that they are easily replaceable by highly specialized contracts misses the point. There really is nothing special about trusts as contracts precisely because trusts do not exist primarily to enforce economic exchanges; this is why the 'contractual elements' of trusts appear so ordinary. As to trusts as entities and trust law as a branch of organizational law, this view is also mistaken. Given the weak and porous asset-partitioning that trusts provide, they are not a functional equivalent—let alone extension—of entities; if anything, they are a functional regression of them.

Exclusion and Governance

Providing greater incentives to engage in economic activities and enabling the creation of complex property rights at a low information cost may be important justifications for the trust, but its unique contribution to property lies in its coordination function. The fund concept, the *bona fide* purchaser exception, and the nature of the beneficial interest can all be accounted for by the coordination function of trusts. Recall that property provides a coordination function by assigning ownership of an asset to one individual who will optimize its utilization because he bears all the benefits and burdens stemming from the asset. The asset owner can utilize the asset optimally because he can use it by himself, share it with others, rent it out, or even sell it. He can do these things because he has the right to exclude others from the asset and to dictate its use.

In modern times, however, it is rare that assets are exclusively used by an owner alone. In one way or another, the benefits and burdens of assets are often shared. We may share our house with friends and relatives (whether or not for rent) and we may share the burden of maintaining it with a building repairman (most certainly for a fee). Ownership of an asset enables us to do these things because we have the right to exclude others and, in the case of sharing, we abstain from exercising that right. Clearly, ownership and the right to exclude are insufficient in most cases; they only work in law and economics textbook examples involving ranchers and pastures. In the case of the building repairman, it would be impractical if we could only choose to deny him access or to grant him access to the asset, and nothing more. This is essentially the choice presented by the right to exclude—it is binary and very blunt.

Instead ownership of an asset merely sets the baseline for more sophisticated dealings. What normally happens is that one abstains from exercising the right to exclude for the repairman and regulate his activities inside the house. Regulating the repairman's activities may take the form of contracts, tort law, government health and safety regulations, and so on. In Smith's account of how resource uses can be regulated, these are all examples of the governance strategy.[15] The governance strategy employs detailed rules to regulate how a resource is used and this stands in contrast to the exclusion strategy, which also regulates resource uses by relying on low-cost proxies such as boundaries and fencings. With finer regulations, the governance strategy enables specialization of economic activities. The trustee's management activities count as a form of specialization.

The pros and cons of the two strategies should be obvious. The exclusion strategy imposes very little information measurement or processing costs precisely because it conveys so little information. A lot of the times, the exclusion strategy is adequate. If an owner simply wants to keep unwanted strangers away from his land, then erecting fences along the boundaries provides sufficient information for him and the strangers. If a stranger is within the fenced area, he is trespassing; if he is outside of it, he is not trespassing. For both the owner and the stranger, the fence-based exclusion strategy here provides enough information for enforcement and compliance, respectively. At the same time, as Smith says, 'if enough uses are bunched together [under an exclusion strategy], we can speak approximately of regulating 'access' to the thing or even of having a right to the thing itself.'[16] On the other hand, governance is much more precise because one can specify to a high degree how a resource is used but this specification is also expensive as it involves negotiation, implementation, and monitoring. For activities demanding high precision, governance is a lot better than exclusion, but it

[15] In this respect, Merrill and Smith diverge on the exclusion concept. Merrill holds a solidly trespass-based conception of the right to exclude (like Blackstone and Penner previously) whereas Smith views it as a strategy to govern resource uses. The right to exclude can also be analysed along a spectrum of firmness, ranging from the right against physical trespass to, say, binding successor third parties. See T. W. Merrill, 'Property and the Right to Exclude' 77 *Neb. L. Rev.* 730 (1998) and H. E. Smith, 'Exclusion Versus Governance: Two Strategies for Delineating Property Rights' 31 *J. Leg. Stud.* 453 (2002).

[16] H. E. Smith, *supra* note 15, 469. What he means is that if enough uses come under the protection of the exclusion strategy, we can reify these uses and call it a thing. As will be discussed shortly, the 'ownership feel' that we derive from beneficial interests can be attributed to this exclusion-based reification of uses.

is by no means perfect. Because of its high costs, no governance arrangement can be complete.

In the case of trusts, the contractarian and agency costs accounts are solely based on the governance strategy. In Langbein's account, default trust rules save costs by minimizing the negotiation of common trust terms, and the duty of good faith acts as a catch all default term in any *ex post* dispute. For Sitkoff, trustee duties replace beneficiary monitoring, and agency costs only exist because trust terms can never be complete. Notice that Langbein and Sitkoff rely on the governance strategy while acknowledging its shortcomings, namely, transaction costs and incomplete contracts. As will be seen, trusts are a lot more than just cheap, imitable governance rules.

Why We Have Trusts and Why Assets Fluctuate

It must be obvious that most owners' dealings of assets with strangers involve a combination of the exclusion and governance strategies. What is not obvious is how the trust does not conform to conventional understandings of exclusion and governance. To appreciate this, one must understand why we have trusts and what we are trying to do with them. In the case of an express trust, practitioners and lawyers may say that trusts are settled for tax, probate, asset-management, insolvency, or structuring reasons. These can be distilled into a simple, if not glaringly obvious, reason: settlors settle trust because they derive benefits from doing so. These benefits can stem from having the trustee hold and manage the asset or specific trust terms, or, often, a combination of both.

One must ask why would the owner of an asset transfer it to a stranger without intending him to benefit from it? It must be because the settlor finds it useful for the trustee to hold the trustee property in lieu of himself. There are many reasons for this: for example, the trustee may be expected to outlive the settlor; the trustee may have special skills that the settlor does not have; or the trustee may be in a comparatively superior tax position. With specific trust terms, the settlor may derive a benefit when he settles the property on trust for others on particular terms. The benefit may be tangible if the trust is in pursuance of a commercial exchange or it may be intangible if he simply feels good about bestowing assets to friends and family. Either way, having the ability to structure rights and interests is a benefit of settling trusts.

More often than not, the case of settling a trust is strongest if there are both trustee-related and trust terms-related benefits. For example, an aged settlor who wants to benefit his children but is afraid that they become spendthrifts will find the use of a trust compelling. This is because he can find a trustee—who is expected to outlive him and who possesses superior investment skills—to manage the asset on specified trust terms, which could be refined to take into account the children's unique circumstances. In the case of a commercial trust, a settlor may find the trustee to be in a fiscally superior position and that the trust terms can be specified in such a way that the beneficiaries—the settlor's commercial counterparties—deem to be beneficial; an example would be an asset securitization trust.[17]

For these reasons, the settlor embarks on the unnatural act of transferring control of an asset to a stranger without intending him to ever benefit from it.[18] But often compounding the unconventional nature of this act is the fact that trust assets may fluctuate. To be sure, there are express trusts that purely hold assets *in specie* and nothing more. But that may not be the norm for trusts, and definitely not so for non-trust assets. The vast majority of non-trust assets are not static, at least not forever. In the private and personal context, almost everything that we own as individuals is liable to be consumed, wasted, disposed of, or sold. Think of the clothes we wear, the computers we use, the cars we drive, and the houses we live in. All of these objects will eventually be consumed, sold, or simply dissipated. The main exceptions to this are land and the buildings built on them, though in modern urban societies, it is becoming increasingly difficult to find individuals who actually live in the same house throughout their entire lives. Family heirlooms and objects of great sentimental value are also exceptions, but they are liable to be lost or disposed of by future generations.

In the commercial context, assets such as furniture, computers, equipment, vehicles, and buildings are also eventually consumed or sold. Even intangible assets are dissipated or sold: intellectual properties expire; bonds and debt are repaid and become cash or other choses in action; and shares, while theoretically retainable forever, are often sold or involuntarily bought out in takeovers. What this demonstrates is that assets are rarely held forever, and economic advancement and efficiency dictates that they be disposed of or exchanged for something else.

That assets are rarely static must not be confused with the idea that every asset in the world is part of someone's fund.[19] In an abstract, philosophical

[17] See S. L. Schwarcz, 'Commercial Trusts as Business Organizations: Unraveling the Mystery' 58 *Bus. Law* 559 (2003).

[18] What follows is an account for the tripartite modern donative trust. But it is equally applicable to the case where a settlor declares himself as trustee for a beneficiary. The rules applicable to the trustee and the beneficiary's rights against him can equally be found in cases where the settlor doubles up as the trustee.

[19] James Penner sought to defuse this over-expansive idea of the fund concept by drawing on Lionel Smith's arguments that '(1) equity will regard [the obligation with respect to property] as wider than the original obligor, and will extend it to others; (2) equity will regard that obligation as fixing not only to

sense this may be true; but in practice the fund concept is only invoked intentionally or by operation of law (for example, bankruptcy or probate). When one sells one's house, one does not treat it as a transaction for one's fund, unless of course the house is held on trust or being sold by a trustee in bankruptcy or an executor. The fund concept only exists because the law affords it a degree of regulation and asset protection; it only exists in the contemplation of the law. One may create a bank account and deposit money in it specifically to support a child's university education and call it a child education fund. But unless certain steps are taken to formalize this arrangement, such a 'fund' carries no legal validity and at death or bankruptcy, it would simply fall under one's general estate. The point being made here is that, for various reasons, assets are rarely held *in specie* for perpetuity, whether they are part of a specific fund or not.

With these observations in mind, one can now understand what the trust is trying to achieve. In a modern donative trust, the settlor transfers legal title to an asset to the trustee. The legal title, in theory, gives the trustee complete control and dominion over the trust asset. Yet the trustee must not benefit from the trust asset in any way unless authorized (that is, approved trustee remuneration). Instead, all the benefits must flow to the beneficiaries, who are not in control of the trust asset. Often (but not always) complicating this arrangement is the fact that trust assets may fluctuate, usually by virtue of a power of investment. It is incredibly difficult to achieve these conditions using the conventional exclusion and governance strategies.

The Difficulties of the Trust Structure

It is difficult to achieve the objectives of the trust using conventional exclusion and governance strategies because their aims are inherently contradictory. Not only is the exclusion strategy low cost, it is also all-encompassing. If a stranger is excluded, he simply must not trespass or interfere with the asset—no ifs or buts. The contradiction lies in the fact that the settlor gives total control over the asset to the trustee but at the same time wants the trustee to be excluded from its benefits. In everyday life, we grant to strangers

the property which was the original subject matter of the obligation, but to property which "represents it", that is, to property which is the proceeds of an exchange of the original property; in short, equity will treat interests in trust property as fund interests'. See J. E. Penner, 'Value, Property, and Unjust Enrichment: Trusts of Traceable Proceeds' in R. Chambers, C. Mitchell, and J. Penner (eds.) *Philosophical Foundations of the Law of Unjust Enrichment* (Oxford University Press, Oxford 2009), 322–3.

access to assets so that they can use them or, say, assist us in maintaining them, but it never involves granting them total control. In the case of the house and the repairman, we grant him a mere licence to enter the house and perform the necessary work; we never transfer the legal title to him. But granting him a licence to enter the premises is only the beginning. The key to regulating his behaviour—in addition to mandatory public regulation like health and safety rules—is the contract.

A contract between the house owner and the repairman will usually suffice for a simple repair task. Among other things, it stipulates the scope of work, the finishing standards, and limitations of liability. Although the contract will inevitably be incomplete, together with the licence to enter the premises, it is reasonably sufficient to regulate the repairman's activities inside the house. This is so not only because the contract will cover the essential terms but also because of the limited nature of the licence. The repairman enters the premises on a licence that is terminable at the owner's will and he does not have many rights and powers. Coupled with the contract, what he can and cannot do is reduced to a reasonable and certain scope.

The trust is very different because the trustee starts off with the legal title to the trust asset. This is problematic because the legal title is so broad and powerful, and, as a starting point, to subtract and reduce the trustee's permissible activities to a reasonable and certain scope, there is too much to cover and too many unforeseeable contingencies. Imagine granting the repairman the legal title to the house for the sake of repairing. If he abuses the title, he can sell the house, rent it out, mortgage it, or do anything with it. No simple contract with the repairman can safely prevent him from abusing the title. But here we do want to give the trustee legal title not only because of his special attributes (investment attributes, longevity, tax status, etc.), but also because we want him to deal with the trust assets as part of a fund.

So how does one go about disarming the trustee without actually taking away his legal title? In a world without trusts, the main answer would probably be a contract. But it is obvious by now a contract cannot be complete or cover even a fraction of the contingencies that could occur if a stranger abuses the legal title that he holds. Another idea would be to place a security interest on the trustee's title as this would ensure that all asset dealings would require the consent of the security interest holder (presumably the beneficiary), but not all assets are capable of being attached with a security interest. Even more problematic is that attaching a security interest defeats the very purpose of transferring title to the trustee: to allow him to deal freely with the asset as though it was his. With only the basic tools of property and contracts, the objectives of a trust simply cannot be achieved.

The Legal and Beneficial Title Split and the Resulting Exclusion and Governance Paradox

It is not surprising, therefore, that the basic tools of property and contracts cannot achieve what is required of trusts. This is simply a reflection of the fact that the exclusion and governance strategies sit at opposing ends of the spectrum of resource use regulation. On this, Smith discusses the two strategies when applied to land use and says 'in the case of land, it is easier to monitor a boundary crossing than to evaluate the quality of a use by someone who is permitted *complete* physical access. This avoids the problem of having to separate out the interacting uses but forgoes the benefits of specialization of use by multiple parties'.[20] Clearly, Smith is not saying that exclusion and specialization are mutually exclusive. It is just that specialization often requires the governance strategy, and, surely, it is not possible to adopt both strategies concurrently and yield their full benefits. The exclusion strategy applies to a resource in its entirety but is all-or-nothing in nature; the governance strategy offers more precision but often only on specific uses of a resource and only at high costs.

As a specialized and separate legal institution, the trust employs primarily the governance strategy to achieve the results of the exclusion strategy, and it does this at a relatively low cost. The trust achieves this with the legal and beneficial title split. As will be seen, the dual existence of legal and beneficial titles underscores the paradoxical features of the trust but at the same time provides the solution to them. One paradox relates to the trustee's holding legal title to the trust asset. He apparently has complete and unfettered control over the asset yet he is effectively excluded from it. To restate, the settlor does not intend the trustee to benefit from the trust asset but, for various reasons, it is best that the trustee holds the legal title. So to the extent that the settlor had a choice of not transferring title to the trustee and thereby excluding him from the asset, the settlor refrains from exercising his right to exclude and grants access to the trustee—completely and permanently—by way of transferring legal title to him.

At the same time, the trust instrument and trust law generally impose on the trustee a tremendous amount of duties and obligations. These include the duties of loyalty, care, investment, and to be ready with accounts. These duties form the core of the trust's governance strategy but, ironically, their net effect is to exclude the trustee from the benefits of the asset. In this sense, the

[20] H. E. Smith, *supra* note 15, 469; author's emphasis.

trust is adopting a strategy of governance-based exclusion. The duties of loyalty and care are specific enough for trustees to comply with but broad enough to cover every aspect of trusteeship over the asset.

Trust rules and the courts that enforce them are overwhelmingly against the trustee. As Alastair Hudson observes, 'traditional trust theory always posits the trustee as the defendant.'[21] Trust law employs a good mix of rules and standards to achieve this healthy bias against the trustee.[22] The duty of loyalty, which consists of the no-profit and no-self-dealing rules, is an example of employing simple and over-inclusive rules to catch all possible breaches and to deter them in the first place. The no-self-dealing rule stipulates that where a trustee self-deals (for example, where he buys trust assets from the trust or sells his personal assets to the trust), it is voidable at the beneficiary's discretion—no matter how fair or lucrative the transaction price is. The rule is simple because there are no exceptions (unless authorized by the trust instrument or the informed beneficiary) and it is over-inclusive because it has the potential to catch beneficial self-dealings (where the beneficiaries are financially better off). This is good because its application and interpretation are unambiguous and also serves as a deterrent against potential trustee misbehaviour. Similarly, the no-profit rule is structured to be simple and over-inclusive to achieve the same effect as the no-self-dealing rule. The main exception is that even if the courts disgorge the trustee's unauthorized profits, they are ever so slightly more willing to authorize payment for the trustee's misguided but nevertheless useful services.[23]

Apart from the prophylactic duty of loyalty, most of the trustee's other duties are formulated as standards, and despite the vast amount of case law and the precedents they have set, these standards have remained largely as such and have not fossilized into rules. For example, take the trustee's duty of care, duty to consider exercising his powers, and duty to provide beneficiaries and objects with trust information. What these duties have in common is that they are clear enough to guide the trustee towards proper performance but at the same time ambiguous enough to give the courts flexibility to interpret the right result. The modern English duty of care requires the trustee to exercise such care and skill as is reasonable in the circumstances. Not only are

[21] A. Hudson, 'The Regulation of Trustees' in M. Dixon and G. Griffiths. (eds.) *Contemporary Perspectives on Property, Equity and Trusts law* (Oxford University Press, Oxford 2007), 164.

[22] On the economic analysis of rules and standards, see L. Kaplow, 'Rules Versus Standards' 42 *Duke L. J.* 557 (1992).

[23] See generally D. J. Hayton, P. Matthews, and C. Mitchell, (eds.) *Underhill and Hayton The Law Relating to Trusts and Trustees* (17th edn. LexisNexis Butterworths, London 2006), art 59. In the United States, *Boardman v Phipps* type payments to trustees are not explicitly recognized; see Restatement (Third) of Trusts §78, comment a.

professional trustees and trustees who hold out as having special knowledge or experience treated differently, each case's unique facts will be taken into account when this standard is applied.[24] This ensures that a large portion of the content of the duty is only stipulated after the trustee has acted and reinforces the anti-trustee bias.

The trustee's duty to consider exercising his powers is also similarly framed. Not only must he consider exercising his powers from time to time, he must also consider relevant considerations and disregard irrelevant considerations.[25] Again, this provides the trustee with sufficient procedural guidance yet leaves enough room for the courts to decide whether the trustee has acted rightly or wrongly. The current law on the trustee's duty to provide trust information (or, more appropriately, the beneficiary's right to it) is not satisfactory as it has less to do with trustee duties than the nature of a beneficiary's interest.[26] But, in one respect, it is another example of the court's preference for standards-based ambiguity and for preserving the final say on trustee actions.

It should not come as a surprise that trust law is ambiguously draconian and trusteeship is a harsh office to assume. All of this is not limited to trustee duties. The various remedies for breaches of trust are also doctrinally one-sided against the trustee. The elective remedy of falsifying accounts is premised on the idea that the beneficiary can choose to assume that an unauthorized transaction never took place and the trustee must 'undo' the transaction at his own cost.[27] Equally, the beneficiary can choose retrospectively to authorize a transaction in breach of trust—if it is to his advantage. The goal of these rules and remedies is to ensure that whatever happens in a breach of trust, the trustee never wins.[28] Apart from trust rules that are against the trustee, it also takes a like-minded court to give the rules maximum effect. Very few areas of private law give the courts an inherent jurisdiction to supervise the administration of private arrangements and intervene if necessary. And when they do intervene, the courts are not shy about imposing proprietary remedies or stretching logic a bit to achieve the desired results.[29]

[24] Trustee Act 2000, s 1, 2 and sch 1. See also D. Hayton, P. Matthews, and C. Mitchell, *supra* note 23, art 52. Similarly, see Restatement (Third) of Trusts, §77 and Restatement (Second) of Trusts, §174.

[25] *Re Hastings-Bass* [1975] Ch 25; Similarly, see Restatement (Third) of Trusts, §50 (1), comment b.

[26] See Chapter 6.

[27] R. Chambers, 'Liability' in P. Birks and A. Pretto (eds.) *Breach of Trust* (Hart, Oxford 2002), 16–17.

[28] The key exception to this is trustees' exemption clauses, which will be discussed in the next chapter.

[29] In the case of *AG for Hong Kong v Reid*, a former prosecutor took bribes from others in return for not prosecuting them. The government sought to recover the property purchased with the bribe money by seeking a declaration of constructive trust. The court obliged but in doing so defied

What the trust has achieved is that, through title transfer to the trustee and the imposition of trust law, the trustee is given complete physical access to the asset yet is excluded from all possible gains and benefits. This is only possible because, in addition to having specific legal rules and clauses in trust instruments governing the trust relationship, the judiciary is doctrinally predisposed to apply and interpret laws and instruments against the trustee. To borrow Smith's terminology, the trust's strategy is neither exclusion nor governance alone, but governance-based exclusion. No other area of private law is as asymmetrically biased against one particular party. On this count alone, trust law is rightly considered as a body of law separate and distinct from contracts, agencies, or entities.

A second paradox mirrors the first, and is related to the beneficiary and his property interest in the trust fund and its assets. It is a trite fact that the beneficiary's interest in a trust asset is not absolute, at least to the extent that it is not good against a *bona fide* purchaser without notice. For a long time, commentators ranging from Maitland in the past to Nolan in the present have deemed this as the beneficial interest's Achilles' heels. This view is mistaken. The beneficiary is not meant to have an absolute interest in the asset. If this were the intention, the settlor would simply transfer the asset to him outright. To compare the beneficiary with an absolute owner misses the point. Instead, the settlor chooses to settle a trust and transfer title to the asset to the trustee but at the same time, the trust's strategy of governance-based exclusion neutralizes any possible gain or benefit that the trustee may receive by virtue of holding title to the asset. The gains and benefits do not flow to the trustee, but rather accrue to the beneficiary.

However, the one thing that a beneficiary will never have—even if all the gain and benefits accrue to him—is the right to veto a sale of the asset to a *bona fide* purchaser. Why? This exception should not be viewed as a weakness of the beneficial interest or a compromise between beneficiaries and potential purchasers. True, the *bona fide* purchaser exception conserves on information-processing, coordination, and transaction costs insofar as any sale is strictly a matter between the trustee with good title and the *bona fide* purchaser. The latter need not be concerned with everything that lies behind the former. Instead, the *bona fide* purchaser exception is an inherent feature of an interest in a fund. Unless or until assets *in specie* are distributed to a

understandings of fiduciary relationships and constructive trusts generally. This is so because accepting bribes is not a breach of any obligation owed in respect of any property of the government. Instead, the court reasoned that the moment the defendant received the bribe, he held it on trust for the government. The right decision may have been reached, but the court's reasoning leaves something to be desired. [1994] 1 All ER 1.

beneficiary, it is wrong to think of a beneficiary as having an interest in a particular asset.

Instead, the beneficiary has an interest in a fund. What distinguishes an interest in a fund (even if it only has a single asset) from an interest in the asset itself is the trustee's power to sell and the *bona fide* purchaser exception. Until distribution, the beneficiary cannot possibly know what he will receive, be it the original asset, cash, or something else. Absolutely owning an asset entails having the right to realize its value. As Penner argues, value is not something that can be 'owned'; it must be realized through certain acts such as use, enjoyment, or a sale.[30] In a trust, because the trustee holds the legal title, the right to realize the asset's value lies with the trustee and not the beneficiary. Of course, the trustee must realize it in a way that benefits the beneficiary and not himself. Nevertheless, the beneficiary does not have the right to realize the value of trust assets.[31]

Until distribution, the beneficiary cannot be said to have an interest in the fund's specific assets or in their value; he can only be said to have an interest in their potential value. Penner argues that 'at any moment, the interest in the fund is perfectly specifiable, consisting of the property rights it contains, and because of this the interest in the fund, though capturing different items of property through time, does not lose its 'specificity' as a property right itself'.[32] Although this is true, unless the beneficiary exercises his *Saunders v Vautier* rights at that very instance, he cannot be absolutely certain what he will receive if the trust is allowed to run its natural course. The irony is that the beneficiary will always know what is inside the fund but, in theory, will never know what in the fund he will end up owning. This description of the beneficiary's interest in the trust asset may sound very inferior to traditional legal understandings of the beneficial interest, but it is the only description that captures the variability and fungibility of assets in trusts with discretionary investment and distribution powers.

Viewed in this way, the second paradox embodied in the legal and beneficial title split is that there are not two titles to the assets—just one, the trustee's legal title. What gives the impression that there are two competing titles is that the 'beneficial title' consists of rights and powers that are so strong that it appears to be quasi-ownership. And this is so because the beneficial interest is indeed a secondary, derivative form of ownership. Penner and Nolan have separately elaborated on the beneficiary's negative

[30] J. Penner, *supra* note 19, 310.

[31] The key exception is the rule in *Saunders v Vautier*, which will be discussed in the next chapter.

[32] J. Penner, *supra* note 19, 315. This comment resonates with that of Smith, who said that 'if enough uses are bunched together [under an exclusion strategy], we can speak approximately of regulating "access" to the thing or even of having a right to the thing itself'. See text accompanying *supra* note 16.

rights to exclude those 'trespassing' on his interests.[33] If one also accepts that a beneficiary's interest is one in a fund and its assets' potential value—and that the *bona fide* exception is part and parcel to the operation of a fund—then the legal and beneficial title split can be coherently explained: the asset for which legal title is held by the trustee is simply a part of a fund, the 'title' of which is held by the beneficiary.

Note that a fund always consists of assets that may fluctuate from time to time; where there is no asset, there is no fund. Title to an asset is also a prerequisite to 'title' to or interest in a fund. Therefore, a fund is a derivative form of ownership of the underlying assets. Being derivative to the trustee's legal title, the beneficiary's 'title' is never meant to compete with the former and this is why the beneficiary should view his interest as not in the underlying assets but rather in their potential value. The 'beneficial title' is just a convenient judicial shorthand for derivative ownership, the content of which can vary significantly as Penner and Nolan observe.

The legal and beneficial title split can also be related back to the exclusion and governance dichotomy. Just as the trustee is effectively excluded by governance rules from all gains and benefits arising out of the trust asset, the beneficiary through various governance rules (that are predominantly *in personam* in nature) can exclude most strangers from the fund and sometimes the underlying asset itself. As with physical trespassers, the beneficiary can ask the trustee to expel them or if the trustee is unwilling, he can join the trustee in a legal action. As with trespassers in Penner's 'successor version' sense, the beneficial interest will subsist and trust law will operate to exclude all transferees or purchasers except the *bona fide* purchaser.

To extend Merrill and Smith's analysis of the property/contract interface, the beneficiary's interest is 'good against the world' because his interest is quasi-multital in nature; the parties that can be affected are of an indefinite identity but the number of such parties is likely to be small.[34] The beneficiary's rights are not good against *bona fide* purchasers, but are good against all others. It is impossible to know *ex ante* the identity of non-*bona fide* purchasers, but, again, in the normal course of things their number is likely to be small. Maitland and others are correct in arguing that the beneficiary's right is strictly speaking *in personam* in nature, but its quasi-multital nature gives it the *in rem* appearance.

To appreciate the beauty of the beneficial interest, one must consider it from the beneficiary's perspective. As long as the beneficiary accepts the role and powers of the trustee and that his interest is one in a fund and not in the assets *in specie*, everything that the trustee does in accordance with the trust

[33] See Chapter 7.

[34] T. W. Merrill and H. E. Smith, *supra* note 13, 846.

instrument and trust law ought to be within his expectations.[35] On matters that should be of the beneficiary's concern, such as trustee negligence and fraud, the beneficiary has a range of personal (and sometimes proprietary) rights against the trustee and against certain third parties. Viewed in this way, the beneficiary's personal and quasi-multital rights that make up his interest in a fund are essentially reified into what appears to be an *in rem* right in the underlying asset. This strongly resonates with Smith's idea that when enough uses are bunched together and protected by the exclusion strategy, we can speak of having a right to the thing itself.[36] What is so special about trusts is that through the use of *in personam* governance rules, it has achieved exclusion by denying the title holder the benefits of the assets and funnelling them instead to the beneficiary. All of this, of course, is achieved at very low information-processing and transaction costs to third parties.

The Asset-Centric Nature of Trust Law

A third paradox of trust law—which admittedly has less to do with the legal and beneficial title split or the exclusion and governance dichotomy—is that although we talk about the three principal trust parties and the rights and duties applicable to them, trust law is all about trust assets and the wealth they represent. This may be a controversial observation but it is not new. Eighty years ago, the French jurist Pierre Lepaulle held out a more extreme asset-centric view of trusts.[37] Lepaulle argues that a trust is a patrimony by appropriation and the essence of it is only (a) the trust asset and (b) its appropriation for some aim. In this regard, Lepaulle could be credited for being the conceptual forefather of non-charitable purpose trusts. Of course, he has been criticized by many for failing to understand the true nature of trusts.[38]

[35] The beneficiary should accept this because he is either a settlor-beneficiary and personally dictated all the trust terms or a gratuitous beneficiary, in which case he has no choice but to gracefully accept the settlor-dictated trust terms. To illustrate further, an investor in a mutual fund may not be happy with the purchase of a particular stock by the fund manager. But so long as the purchase is in accordance with all fund terms and public regulations, the investor's interest has not been violated and he must only accept the fund's holdings. Where the expectations of the trustee and beneficiary do not match, it is unfortunate but this is the nature of a trust and this is also why trusts must eventually terminate. See Chapter 9.

[36] See text accompanying *supra* note 16.

[37] P. Lepaulle, 'An Outsider's View Point of the Nature of Trusts' 14 *C.L.Q.* 52 (1929), 55.

[38] See K. W. Ryan, 'The Reception of the Trust' 10 *ICLQ* 265 (1961), 271–3; M. Lupoi, *Trusts: A Comparative Study* (Cambridge University Press, Cambridge 2000), 268; and A. Nussbaum, 'Sociological and Comparative Aspects of the Trust' 38 *Colum. L. Rev.* 408 (1938), 408.

Lepaulle did not fail to understand the true nature of trusts, he simply went too far with his proposition. For example, Lepaulle interprets the rule that a trust will not fail for want of trustee as to mean that the trustee (and other human participants) are not crucial to the trust. This is clearly wrong because this equitable rule primarily serves to save imperfect wills or unfortunate situations.[39] In the case of *inter vivos* trusts, equity will still insist that the settlor 'do all he can to vest the trust property in [the trustee].'[40] It is not that trusts do not need human participants: as a practical matter, humans are required to administer, enjoy, and enforce trusts. The asset-centric view espoused here does not play down human participants at all.

Rather, the asset-centric vision comes from a much more interesting observation by Lepaulle. He contrasts trusts with private (absolute) ownership and argues that the latter is the consecration of individualism.[41] With private ownership, owners can do whatever they want with their properties, including neglecting, wasting, or even destroying them. As he says, 'ownership means freedom: even anti-social freedom, it does not involve in itself the idea of effort, of care, of efficiency.'[42] On the other hand, 'in a village where all property would be held in trust, fields must be well ploughed, carefully cultivated, houses must be kept in good repair, and trees must be pruned. Trusts involve the duty of preservation, of good management, of production: it has a social value by which it opposes itself to ownership.'[43]

The economic structure of trust law is premised on the idea of efficiently managing and using trust assets. Efficiency is a key criterion in the economic analysis of law but to its detractors, it is a very dirty word.[44] Rather than debating on the merits of efficiency and utilitarianism in general jurisprudence, a more approachable way of understanding efficient resource use is to take on Lepaulle's observation that trusts involve preservation, good management, and production of assets. On this, Lepaulle observes 'the two legal institutions have back of them two profoundly different and even opposed philosophies. It is indeed significant to see them both flourish side by side in Anglo-Saxon countries where individualism and social spirit are at the same

[39] For example, where a testator's intended executor dies along with the testator. For the equivalent rule in the United States, see Restatement (Third) of Trusts, §16 and Restatement (Second) of Trusts, §32 (2).

[40] See D. Hayton, P. Matthews, and C. Mitchell, *supra* note 23, art 8.8.

[41] P. Lepaulle, *supra* note 37, 58.

[42] Ibid. 58.

[43] Ibid. 58.

[44] See for example J. L. Coleman, 'Efficiency, Utility and Wealth Maximization' 8 *Hofstra L. Rev.* 509 (1980); L. A. Kornhauser, 'A Guide to the Perplexed Claims of Efficiency in the Law' 8 *Hofstra L. Rev.* 591 (1980); and M. J. Rizzo, 'The Mirage of Efficiency' 8 *Hofstra L. Rev.* 641 (1980).

time developed to a high degree. We may therefore conclude on this point in saying that Anglo-Saxon countries have two different regimes for property: individual ownership and trusts.'[45] The doctrine that assets should be well managed and productively used is manifested in the trustee's duties to invest,[46] to sell improper assets,[47] and general duty of care.[48] Less obvious but equally important, the rule against perpetuities, the rule in *Saunders v Vautier*, and even the *bona fide* purchaser exception can also be counted as manifestations of the idea of efficient resource use.

But even before the trust is fully established, trust law already flies its asset-centric colours. As a mandatory rule, the subject-matter of the trust must be certain and segregated. Although this rule can be explained the usual way with the need for certainty and administrative workability, there is another aspect to it. Because trusts and beneficial interests are a secondary, derivative form of ownership, it is crucial that the primary asset is positively identified and segregated so that it can form part of the specific fund. Without proper identification and segregation, trust rules and beneficial interests simply cannot latch onto an asset. Therefore, the certainty of subject-matter requirement and the duty to segregate trust assets are logically ahead of all other requirements and duties.

Once the trust is validly set up, why is trust law concerned with efficient resource use? Demsetz, Posner, and Epstein argue that individuals generally maximize resource utilization when they are left to their own devices. This is because the property system internalizes externalities so that asset owners capture both the positive and negative effects of their own actions. The trust separates ownership and control of assets such that the trustee who exercises control rights is not the same person as the beneficiary who captures the positive (and sometimes negative) effects. Much that trust law seeks to ensure that the positive and negative effects are internalized by the beneficiary and the trustee respectively, it is by no means perfect. In any trust, there will always be a mismatch of incentives and preferences between the trustee and

[45] P. Lepaulle, *supra* note 37, 58. See also the United States trustee duty to make the trust property productive; Restatement (Second) of Trusts, §181.

[46] D. Hayton, P. Matthews, and C. Mitchell, *supra* note 23, art 53.1. See also Restatement (Third) of Trusts, §90.

[47] D. Hayton, P. Matthews, and C. Mitchell, *supra* note 23, art 49.1. This rule is motivated by the need for the trustee to act impartially between various classes of beneficiaries (ie if there is a life tenant and a remainderman, trust assets are improper if their returns disproportionately favour one beneficiary over the other). But equally, where trust assets include 'wasting property', the trustee is under a default duty to sell it. For the equivalent rule in the United States, see also Restatement (Third) of Trusts, §79, comment g (1).

[48] D. Hayton, P. Matthews, and C. Mitchell, *supra* note 23, art 52.1. See also Restatement (Third) of Trusts, §77.

the beneficiary. What the trustee does (or is told to do by the settlor-drafted trust instrument) may not be aligned with the preferences of the beneficiary.

Consider the case of boarding up one's house and denying everyone access to it for twenty years or more. It is perfectly legal to do this if one is the absolute owner of the house, but this cannot be done in the case of trusts.[49] At first sight, there is no valid reason to treat the two cases differently. Both involve not using the house the way it is meant to be used. In the latter case, it is deemed to be contrary to public policy but in the former, it is just a legitimate exercise of one's ownership rights. Why? The difference in treatment can only be explained with the misallocation of ownership and control rights. More specifically, unlike an absolute owner who knows what he wants and will act accordingly, the trustee or the settlor does not necessarily know what the beneficiary wants or even if they know, they may not be able or want to act according to the beneficiary's wishes. The trustee who exercises ownership rights and the settlor who influences such exercise through the trust instrument are not the same person as the beneficiary, who is meant to benefit from it. The law decides that upon settlement, a trust should only benefit the beneficiary and not the settlor or the trustee.

But the law does not know what the beneficiary wants either, so it makes a somewhat paternalistic but nevertheless reasonable presumption that he wants the trust assets to be efficiently utilized. This is why the trustee is imposed with duties to invest, to sell improper assets, and a general duty of care. Without these duties, the asset under the trustee's control may be wasted or have its value erode away. So to the extent that the law is more interested in seeing trust assets being well managed and properly utilized—even if this is contrary to the expectations of the settlor or even the beneficiary—trust law is asset-centric. The deal between trust law and its users can be viewed as follows: people can reallocate ownership and control rights to assets in almost any way they want, but whatever the result, the underlying assets must behave as though they are owned by one person absolutely.

As a casual observation but also a normative argument, the law's insistence on the trustee properly managing and investing trust assets is not and should not be uniform. In the barest of bare trusts, a trustee-nominee is simply carrying out the instructions of the beneficiary who is often also the settlor. In such a case, all of the trustee's actions will be consistent with the beneficiary's wishes, and there is no need for the law to make a presumption of what he wants and does not want. Although no such case is known to exist, if a sole beneficiary of a bare trust asks a trustee to board up a house for twenty years,

[49] See *Brown v Burdett*, [1882] 21 Ch D 667; for the equivalent rule in the United States, see Restatement (Second) of Trusts, §62, comment w.

it is doubtful that the court will strike it down as contrary to public policy. After all, the alternative for the beneficiary is to terminate the trust and then board up the house. On the other hand, in a fully discretionary trust where the trustee has significant investment and distribution powers and where trustee and beneficiary expectations and wishes can diverge significantly, it makes sense for the law to impose more onerous duties on the trustee and insist that he properly manage and invest the trust assets.

The Wealth-Centric Protection of the Beneficiary's Interest

Trust law's asset-centric nature must not be confused with its 'thingness', or relationship with things. The beneficiary's relationship with trust assets cannot be characterized as one that is truly related to things. Smith may be correct when he says that if enough uses are bunched together and protected by some exclusion-based strategy, we start to speak of having a right to the 'thing' itself. But this phenomenon is just a very helpful illusion that reifies the trust and gives it its proprietary qualities.

When it comes to the beneficiary, the law is not primarily concerned with protecting his relationship with the assets. Just as the beneficiary's interest in the trust assets is secondary, or derivative in nature, trust doctrine also takes on a second-order flavour and becomes wealth-centric instead of asset-centric. The certainty of subject-matter requirement and the trustee's duty to segregate trust assets are as much about protecting the assets as protecting the wealth they represent. It is well known that if a settlor declares himself the trustee of ten bottles of wine (out of his collection of twenty bottles) without identifying and segregating them specifically, the trust fails because of uncertainty of the subject-matter. But if the settlor declares himself the trustee of his entire collection for himself and the beneficiary in equal shares, we have a valid trust.[50] Not only is the latter example technically more certain, but it also affords the beneficiary a degree of wealth protection. In the former example, if five bottles of wine were destroyed, we cannot allocate the losses as they could be the settlor's or the settlor-as-trustee's. In the latter example, if five bottles were destroyed, both the settlor and the beneficiary—having equal shares—suffer a 25 per cent loss in the trust fund's value. In both examples, it is not clear which bottle belongs to whom *in specie*, but the latter is recognized as a valid trust. This is because the beneficiary's wealth in the fund and all its

[50] See D. Hayton, P. Matthews, and C. Mitchell, *supra* note 23, art 8.14–8.22. Similarly, see Restatement (Third) of Trusts, §40, comment e.

gains and losses are ascertainable. In other words, trust law considers a beneficiary's interest to be one in a fund and the wealth it represents and enforces this doctrine.

Another example is when the beneficiary sues the trustee for damages. If the trustee is liable, he does not pay the damages directly to the beneficiary. Rather, the trustee restores it to the trust fund, where—despite a breach of trust—the trust instrument continues to dictate the beneficiary's entitlements. To this extent, the beneficiary is suing the trustee for damages—or a decrease in value—to his interest in the trust fund. Trust law largely protects the beneficiary at the wealth level.

But there is no clearer example of the beneficiary's wealth-centric protection than the *bona fide* purchaser exception. This exception has been justified by others on grounds of ensuring marketability of assets and reducing information costs. These reasons may be valid but another important justification is that it protects the beneficiary's interest. Having only an interest in a fund, the beneficiary is never meant to be able to bind or veto normal transactions of specific trust assets, so the law does not provide the beneficiary much ownership protection at the asset level.[51] The law protects the beneficiary at the wealth level by ensuring that trust assets can only be sold to a *bona fide* purchaser for value without notice. The law cannot guarantee—nor should it mandate—that an asset is sold at a profit, or even at fair market value. But by requiring assets be sold to *bona fide* purchasers, there is a high probability that the asset's potential value can be properly realized. In this way, the *bona fide* purchaser exception is a rough but useful proxy that protects the beneficiary's wealth in the trust fund.

For example, a house may be settled into a trust and be worth $1 million at settlement. The beneficiary's interest in the trust fund can be said to be worth $1 million at the time of settlement but this will fluctuate from time to time. If the property market suffers a decline and the house is now worth $750,000, then the beneficiary's wealth in the trust fund declines with its underlying asset. If the house is duly marketed and sold to a *bona fide* purchaser, it is likely that the achieved selling price will be close to the $750,000 fair market value. The law protects the beneficiary's wealth in the trust fund by ensuring that the process most likely to fully realize an asset's value is followed. It does not, however, ensure the realization of an actual value.

Many of the foregoing arguments can be used to support the idea of tracing and claiming misplaced assets. Much has been written about the unjust enrichment origins of tracing and claiming, and just as much ink

[51] Asset-level protection for the beneficiary is provided with the trustee's various duties.

has been spilt to rightfully reject such claims. To the extent that it explains areas of tracing that the restitutionary analysis fails to do so, Penner's idea that tracing is just an extension of the fund concept is conceptually sound.[52] But more can be said of the law's treatment of the beneficiary. Tracing is arguably the flipside of the *bona fide* purchaser exception, which is the only type of transfer that can defeat the beneficial interest. The beneficial interest will usually persist even if the asset in question changes hand or changes form. Penner's fund idea rationalizes the various tracing phenomena such as the election of remedies as being consistent with the fluctuating nature of assets in a fund, but that is arguably only half the story. An additional explanation that complements this fluctuating fund view is that through tracing and the various elective remedies, the law protects the beneficiary's wealth in the trust fund.

In the case where a trustee wrongfully uses trust funds to buy shares for himself, the beneficiary can trace into those shares and either 'take' the shares and treat it as part of the trust fund or he can take a security interest in them. Normally, the beneficiary would choose the former if the shares are making a profit and choose the latter if they are making a loss (the rest of the losses must be made up by the trustee personally). The beneficiary's choice in remedy may be mechanically consistent with the idea of a fund of fluctuating assets, but it also embodies the protection of wealth in the trust fund that the law affords to the beneficiary. Whatever the beneficiary chooses, the law offers him the maximum opportunity to maintain the value of his interest in the fund, even if it involves a different asset.

Why does tracing stop, for example, with the destruction of the traceable asset? It is important to remember that the beneficiary's interest is in the wealth or potential value of the asset and until the asset is realized, its value could change or even dissipate. When an asset is destroyed or its value is reduced to zero, the positions of the absolute owner and the beneficiary are the same: it is just an unfortunate loss.[53] True, there may be an insurance policy against the asset's destruction. But insurance is paid out not as part of the tracing process of a destroyed asset; the insurance is simply a trust asset with a contingent pay-off linked to the loss of another asset.

[52] See generally Chapter 7 and J. E. Penner, 'Duty and Liability in Respect of Funds' in J. Lowry and L. Mistelis (eds.) *Commercial Law: Perspectives and Practice* (Lexis Nexis Butterworths, London, 2006).

[53] Obviously, the beneficiary can still sue the trustee for damages.

The Bridge from Wealth to Things

Although the beneficiary's interest largely consists of wealth and potential value, the trust ultimately offers the beneficiary the transition from wealth to things. The rule against perpetuities and the rule in *Saunders v Vautier* both serve to terminate trusts. The former sets a time limit for the existence of a trust and the latter, among other things, allows the beneficiary to terminate a trust at will. This is a crucial mechanism because, until distribution or trust termination (which involves distribution), all the beneficiary has is an interest in a fund of assets, but not in the assets themselves.

Why does the law provide this bridge from intangible wealth to tangible things?[54] Because as long as the beneficiary's interest is in wealth, he is unable to realize it himself. Trustees have a duty to manage and invest the trust assets because the beneficiary is meant to benefit from them and, short of precisely knowing what the beneficiary wants, the law has to make a presumption of how he would want the assets to be utilized. Trusts only exist because they extend the incentivizing effects, the coordination effects, and information-processing limits of property. However, the trust is still a second-best arrangement because only the beneficiary knows what he wants: as long as the trustee holds the asset, there is a mismatch between exercise of ownership rights and enjoyment of ownership rights. The trust can only ever offer a temporary boost to property. When it comes to aligning preferences and incentives, nothing can better internalize benefits and burdens than property itself.

Conclusion

The trust owes its origins, functions, and structure to property. Just as property serves to incentivize and coordinate economic activities, the trust extends these functions. When it comes to incentivizing economic activities, property is limited by human mortality and time but the trust acts as an intergenerational wealth transmission device. With the screen that it provides, the trust also allows the creation of unconventional interests whilst conserving information-processing costs. But the trust's greatest contribution is in its coordination function because it embodies the best of both the exclusion and governance strategies. Exclusion is a cheap but blunt strategy

[54] Of course trust assets such as shares and bonds are not tangible things. In this respect, the properly phrased question is: why does trust law eventually shift beneficiaries from second-order derivative property to first order property?

to regulate resource use and governance is precise but expensive. In the trust, effective exclusion of the trustee is desired yet he needs to be given complete and unfettered access. Conversely, the beneficiary must be able to exclude unwanted third parties but at the same time cannot unduly interfere with the trustee's job.

The solution that the trust offers is governance-based exclusion. The various duties and liabilities imposed on the trustee excludes him from all the benefits of holding title to the trust asset and the beneficiary through his various rights and powers has derivative ownership in the trust assets. However, the beneficiary is the full-fledged owner of a fund. It is wrong to think of the *bona fide* purchaser exception as a weakness in his ownership rights; he is never meant to be able to exclude such purchasers. As long as one appreciates that the beneficiary's interest is one in a fluctuating fund that is managed by the trustee, then one must conclude that, in the context of a fund, his ownership interest is complete.

But the uniqueness of trusts does not end there; trust law is also asset-centric and wealth-centric. Because of the separation of ownership and control that exists in trusts, the law does its best to ensure that assets are efficiently utilized as though there were no such separation. This largely explains the purpose and non-waivability of certain trustee duties. At the same time, the asset-centric nature of trusts must not be confused with the beneficiary's relationship with trust assets. Because of the beneficiary's interest in a fund, his relationship with trust assets is an indirect, derivative one, and the protection that the law affords the beneficiary is wealth-centric. The *bona fide* purchaser exception, the law of tracing, the rule against perpetuities, and the rule in *Saunders v Vautier* all seek to protect the beneficiary's wealth in the trust fund or help him make the transition from wealth to things.

9

The Boundaries of the Trust Concept

Introduction

Innovations such as non-charitable purpose (NCP) trusts, perpetual trusts, generous trustee exemption clauses, or settlor retention of significant powers are critically questioned by scholars on the basis of whether they violate the trust concept. What does it mean to violate the trust concept? In each example, it means something slightly different. In the case of NCP trusts, the lack of beneficiaries is deemed fatal because trust property becomes 'ownerless'. Perpetual trusts are obviously incompatible with the rule against perpetuities and potentially tie up assets forever. Exemption clauses that relieve trustees of most duties seem to render trusteeship meaningless. And settlors' retention of significant powers is frowned upon because it raises the question of whether such trusts are shams or whether the settlor has really parted with his beneficial interest. These innovations, apart from being at the forefront of modern trust developments, also have another thing in common: they prompt us to think about what constitutes the boundaries of the trust concept.

Obligational accounts of trusts do not have much to offer in way of the boundaries of trusts. According to John Langbein, apart from the unwaivable duty of good faith, trust law must give effect to what the settlor and the trustee have agreed to in their trust deal. Robert Sitkoff's account is mainly concerned with agency costs and how trust law reduces them, but it never states what constitutes too much agency costs. The entity account of trusts—which follows the contractarian tradition when it comes to trustee duties—does not properly demarcate trusts as entities, let alone defend their boundaries. Most novel trust developments would be valid under the obligational or entity accounts. For example, the contractarian account can agree to NCP trusts because the trust deal is between the settlor and the trustee, who agrees to apply the trust assets to a purpose. With trustee exemption clauses and the settlor's retention of significant powers, the law should just give effect to what has been agreed upon. Finally, because trusts are *de facto* entities and entities typically have perpetual life, perpetual trusts should be legally valid.

The proprietary approach, however, takes issue on all of these developments. It does so not only because it has an underlying rationale and doctrines—unlike other accounts of trusts—but also because these developments are contrary to our understandings of property. This chapter further develops the ideas introduced by the proprietary approach and applies them to these current trust issues. Crucial to this exercise is to understand the nature of the beneficial interest and what it means to have a residual claim. Once this is understood, and taking into account the asset- and wealth-centric nature of trust law, it becomes apparent why these offshore novelties are bad.

This chapter is organized as follows. First, it rationalizes the nature of the beneficial interest and explains why beneficiaries are residual claimants both jointly and individually. Second, it argues why the triad of exit strategies for beneficiaries must exist and why perpetual trusts are not good even if trustees have the power to sell assets. Drawing on some of the reasons why beneficiaries must have an exit strategy, it argues why NCP trusts are antisocial and wasteful. Third, it applies the asset-centric nature of trust law and argues that *Armitage v Nurse* is bad law unless someone picks up the trustee's slack and performs the duties from which he has been exempted. Fourth, it explores the contentious idea of the settlor's reservation of significant powers and devises a test, based on the beneficiaries' residual claim to the trust fund, to distinguish trusts from non-trusts.

Rationalizing the Nature of the Beneficial Interest

The previous chapter shows that the beneficiary's interest is properly understood as being one in a fund, and that he does not have a direct ownership interest in the underlying assets. But many questions remain: is the beneficiary's interest a right *in rem* or *in personam*? In a discretionary trust, what exactly does an interest in a fund mean? Equally important, what is the beneficial interest in economic parlance? If strict definition is followed, the beneficial interest is not a right *in rem* in the asset simply because it does not bind the whole world. As far as the beneficiary's interest in a specific trust asset is concerned, Maitland is right. But, again, the beneficiary's interest should not be pitched against specific assets, as his is an interest in the fund. In the context of a fund, the beneficiary's ownership interest is full and complete.

Consider first the position of external third parties. The trustee who holds the legal title owes a duty to the beneficiary to exclude unwanted trespassers and interlopers. As for transferees of trust assets, the beneficial interest binds all of them except the *bona fide* purchaser. This, as explained, is essential to the fungible nature of the trust fund. To allow the beneficial interest to bind *bona fide* purchasers is to frustrate the trustee's power to sell, which, if the trustee is indeed granted such a power, should be seen as an inherent limitation of the beneficiary's interest. Where an asset is sold to a *bona fide* purchaser but in breach of trust, the beneficial interest in that asset is nevertheless extinguished because, in addition to enhancing marketability of trust assets generally, the law protects the beneficiary at the wealth level: a sale to a *bona fide* purchaser is likely to have realized the asset's value. Therefore, the *bona fide* purchaser exception should not even be considered when testing the beneficial interest against the definition of an *in rem* right. It is precisely where the beneficial interest fails the *in rem* test—when faced with the *bona fide* purchaser—that it exemplifies an interest in a fund.

The beneficiary's relationship with 'internal' parties is more interesting. The beneficiary is owed a plethora of duties from the trustee and they vary from trust to trust. Apart from earning his remuneration that is authorized by the trust instrument or by law, the trustee cannot profit from his trusteeship. The duty of loyalty exists for a simple yet fundamental reason, to exclude the trustee from benefiting from the trust in any way. So to do away with this duty prospectively or retrospectively opens the floodgate to trustee profiteering opportunities. It is better to have the trustee focus his mind on trusteeship rather than seeking profits. The duty of care is as much about protecting the beneficiary's interest as ensuring that trust assets are well managed. The net result of the duties of loyalty and care is that trust assets are put to productive use and all the benefits flow to the beneficiary, or, if there are many of them, the beneficiary class as a whole.

That there may be multiple beneficiaries is one of the most interesting aspects of the beneficial interest in a discretionary trust. These trusts pose significant conceptual challenges to lawyers and academics. For too long, we have clung to the belief that equitable title to trust assets must always be vested in somebody. This may work for bare trusts or trusts with a life tenant and a remainderman, but it does not in discretionary trusts. In a trust where the trustee has full discretion to choose among objects for distribution, it is extremely difficult to argue—even under the most charitable interpretation of what ownership means—that any particular object has property rights over the trust fund, let alone assets *in specie*. As long as the trustee considers relevant factors and ignores irrelevant ones and makes a well-informed decision, objects are almost at the complete mercy of the trustee. What does a beneficial interest in a discretionary trust mean?

Collectively as a class, objects can exercise their *Saunders v Vautier* rights and terminate the trust. This has led to the mistaken belief that the group as a whole has some kind of identity. As Ungoed-Thomas J. in *Sainsbury* reminds us, the label of the 'objects class' is just a convenient way to describe those eligible to benefit from the trust; there is no collective persona. He says 'to treat separate unquantifiable interests as quantifiable seems to me to fuse and confuse the conception of group persona with the separate rights of individuals'.[1] Although useless as a legal concept, the object class is useful in understanding the nature of beneficial interests in all kinds of trusts. Beneficiaries as a class take trust assets after all non-beneficiaries' claims are satisfied, including those of the trustee and trust creditors. Therefore, a beneficiary or the object class as a whole can be considered residual claimants—just like shareholders of corporations who take their share of assets after all other claims have been satisfied.

Crucially, there is a second aspect to the residual claim nature of beneficial interests. In *Gartside v IRC*,[2] Lord Reid said that objects are in competition with each other, as far as trustee distributions are concerned; if at all, objects enjoy the trust assets competitively and not jointly. The second aspect of the residual claim is that each object personally holds the residual claim to all the trust assets—subject to the claims of all non-beneficiaries and all other objects. What are the claims of other objects? As Penner and Nolan suggest, they are whatever the trust instrument provides. In the case of a typical discretionary trust, each object would hold a claim against the trustee for due consideration for distribution.

This is how each object's residual claim works: after all creditors and non-beneficiaries have been paid off, the trustee would have to consider the claim of each object. If the trustee selects a particular object for some distribution, that object's claim is satisfied. Ideally, every object would receive some distribution; but that hardly ever happens. If a trustee chooses to distribute to three out of five objects, then what is the position of the two unfortunate ones? The two un-chosen objects are in a position similar to shareholders of an insolvent corporation—trust assets have been exhausted and their claims cannot be satisfied. The claims of both objects have been duly considered by the trustee, who has ultimately decided against the objects: they walk away with nothing. In short, the first aspect of the residual claim deals with 'external' non-beneficiaries. Beneficiaries and objects collectively possess this residual claim because they as a class take after 'external' non-beneficiaries. The second aspect deals 'internally' with the various beneficiaries and objects competing for the trust asset, as dictated by the trust instrument.

It is this simple and shoestring-like idea of the residual claim that ties discretionary objects with trust assets. What is more, the residual claim is

[1] *Sainsbury v IRC* [1970] 1 Ch 712, 770.
[2] [1968] AC 553, 605.

merely a chose in equity but from it an object can asymmetrically project his rights and powers to bind other objects, the trustees, and third parties. This is also testament to trusts and equity: simple *in personam* rights can appear and actually have quasi-*in rem* reach. The benefit of this is obvious: such property rights significantly conserves on information-processing costs for all the parties involved. Because any form of beneficial interest can originate from a simple *in personam* right, the variability of beneficial interests is just a mirror image of the fluctuating nature of the assets in a trust fund. Within a trust in which the trustee has full discretionary authority with respect to investment and distribution, it is safe to say that until assets are fully distributed, one cannot know what specific assets will be distributed to which specific objects. This dual uncertainty is bearable because, from an information-processing costs point of view, it affects very few people. Both insiders and outsiders dealing with the trustee are doing so on simplified terms, only the trustee is required to process all of the complex information.

Alienation of Beneficial Interests

By understanding that the beneficial interest is an interest in a fund, it becomes clearer why beneficiaries must retain the right to alienate their interests. There are many ways that they can do so. Beneficiaries can (a) wait for the trust to run its natural course and eventually receive distribution; (b) terminate the trust and have assets distributed to them *in specie*; or (c) sell or assign their interests to third parties. Conversely, there are many ways that settlors can frustrate beneficiaries' ability to alienate their interests. Settlors can (a) create a perpetual trust so that the trust has an infinite life; (b) tie the trust to a material purpose such that the *Claflin* rule operates and beneficiaries cannot terminate prematurely;[3] or (c) add a spendthrift clause in the trust instrument so that beneficiaries cannot sell or assign their interests to others (nor can their creditors claim the trust fund to satisfy debts).[4] The settlor can also employ concurrently all three methods to create a virtually indestructible trust.

[3] Briefly stated, the rule holds that a trust cannot be prematurely terminated unless settlor consent is obtained or termination would not frustrate a material purpose of the trust. This distinctly American rule is the antithesis of the rule in *Saunders v Vautier*. For a detailed discussion, see P. Matthews, 'The Comparative Importance of the Rule in *Saunders v Vautier*' 122 *LQR* 266 (2006).

[4] This is another phenomenon unique to the United States. If the terms of a trust provide that a beneficial interest shall not be transferable by the beneficiary or subject to claims of the beneficiary's creditors, the restraint on voluntary and involuntary alienation is valid. The main exception to this rule is where the settlor of such a trust retains a beneficial interest. See Restatement (Third) of Trusts §58.

Interestingly, these anti-alienation techniques are not valid in England but are valid in parts of the United States and in many offshore jurisdictions. In England, there are rules against remote vesting of interests and excessive accumulation of income. But the rule that embodies beneficial ownership the most is the well-known rule in *Saunders v Vautier*. The rule states that where a beneficiary (or a group of beneficiaries) is absolutely entitled to the trust property and is of full capacity, he can terminate the trust by demanding the trustee to convey the trust property to him. The rule arguably represents the essential difference between English trusts and United States trusts. It has often been said that the rule illustrates and exemplifies the idea of beneficial (or 'equitable') ownership or property.[5] Paul Matthews observes that the rule exemplifies beneficiaries' exclusive decision-making and says 'if I give something to you, then the "property" idea should mean that it is yours to deal with as you please. Property means—indeed, etymologically, has to mean—that you decide. I should not be able, consistently with the idea of property, to make something your "property", and then tell you how to deal with it'.[6]

The same argument can be made about the rule against perpetuities and beneficiaries' right to sell or assign their equitable interest. In both cases, beneficiaries should be able to assert their property rights and decide what to do with their interests. But like Blackstone's vision of property, Matthews' observation unnecessarily exalts the proprietary nature of the rule in *Saunders v Vautier* when it cannot feasibly be exercised in many modern trusts. Matthews is absolutely right regarding bare trusts or trusts with just a few living beneficiaries; in these instances, the right can be taken for granted and exercised at will. In discretionary trusts, however, objects cannot exercise the rule individually but must unanimously band together to do so. Therefore, in modern trusts with numerous and disparate objects, the rule exists only in contemplation and can almost never be exercised. Equally, the rule against perpetuities and beneficiaries' right to sell or assign their equitable interests do not mean much to objects of a discretionary trust because even if they have such rules and rights, they do not have readily cashable interests and are at the mercy of the trustee.

A better explanation for these rules—which share the common theme of ridding beneficiaries of the trustee's shackles—is that they are not just about equitable ownership, but are exit strategies for beneficiaries to transition from purely intangible wealth to more tangible things. Trust law provides this not only because it protects beneficiaries' wealth in the trust fund, but it ensures that they can realize this wealth. Beneficiaries of a trust fund do not have an interest in specific trust assets; they have an interest in the fund. As long as the

[5] P. Matthews, *supra* note 3, 273.
[6] Ibid. 274.

assets are in a trust fund managed by a trustee, beneficiaries cannot realize the value of the assets themselves. Why is it important that beneficiaries should be able to determine for themselves how to best realize trust assets? Because even though assets are managed by the trustee exclusively for their benefit, the trustee cannot possibly know their true preferences and desires.

That trust law allows settlors and trustees to be paternalistic and dictate what is good for beneficiaries is an important aspect of the incentivizing function of trusts. Trusts would be a lot less popular among settlors if beneficiaries could veto or change trustee decisions just because they did not like them. But this licence to be paternalistic cannot last forever. No matter how great the differences in opinion between settlors and beneficiaries about what is 'good', settlors ultimately settle trusts for beneficiaries and with that comes the eventuality that beneficiaries will determine how to realize the value of trust assets for themselves.

This argument can be extended against perpetual trusts and spendthrift trusts. Apologists of perpetual trusts argue that they are acceptable so long as they come with the trustee's mandatory power to sell trust assets. This way, they say, will ensure that assets—in particular, land and other finite resources—do not become tied up forever in trusts. Mandating a power to sell will indeed satisfy the need to ensure marketability of assets in the economy: farms, houses, and diamonds will not be locked up in perpetual trusts and never see the light of day again. In fact, trust assets in a perpetual trust may be as productively used or invested as assets in a non-perpetual trust. But this misses the point. In the context of alienating beneficial interests, perpetual trusts are simply trusts with no *Saunders v Vautier* rights for beneficiaries; this part of their wealth is forever locked up in the trust and it is not dissimilar to having a bank account with a big balance but never being able to withdraw substantial amounts from it. Only by eventually giving beneficiaries the right to determine how they want to realize their wealth in the trust fund can we ensure that resources are best allocated within the economy.

With spendthrift trusts, beneficiaries are not able to sell or assign their interests to third parties and creditors cannot use their trust interests to satisfy outstanding debts. This, again, defeats the purpose of settlors transmitting wealth to beneficiaries.[7] If a beneficiary wants to risk his wealth and start a business because he has a great idea, it is no good that his wealth is forever

[7] The other frequently cited argument against spendthrift trusts is that they defeat creditors' rights and expectations. Where the beneficiary of a spendthrift trust enjoys the trust assets or receives periodic distribution, it gives creditors the false impression that he has abundant assets to satisfy their claims. This argument, however, is as weak as that against the limited liability of corporate shareholders. Creditors of both the beneficiary and the company have themselves to blame if they transact without conducting due diligence and understanding their counterparties' true assets and liabilities.

locked up in government bonds held by the trustee, who pays him a fixed annual income. Market-oriented capitalist economies depend on entrepreneurs whose ventures may succeed spectacularly or fail miserably. Spendthrift trusts lock up wealth and, for those affected by them, substantially inhibit risk-taking activities. Trusts must eventually transmit wealth, not just hold them in suspension.

But apart from ensuring that beneficiaries can determine for themselves how to realize their wealth, there is an overriding reason why they must have an exit strategy. Trusts may be a functional extension of property but they are a temporary, second-best solution that must come to an end. Even if trusts are not contracts, agencies, or entities, the problems that other scholars identify in trusts are real. Much that trustees are supposed to act in the best interest of beneficiaries, they are very much capable of opportunistic behaviour and shirking. Therefore, even if trust rules do their best to exclude the trustee from trust assets, it is not perfect and trustees are never fully excluded. Whatever benefits the settlor and beneficiary cannot monitor or enforce, the trustee can and will indeed capture. This misalignment of interests and preferences can only last for a temporary period of time. Only when trust assets are distributed and beneficiaries properly own them can all the benefits and burdens be internalized to them.

For all the above reasons on why trusts must terminate, it is clear that non-charitable purpose (NCP) trusts are bad. Supporters of NCP trusts tend to borrow the charitable trust model and argue that a private, non-beneficiary enforcer can fulfil the role played by the attorney-general and if we add rules on administrative workability and rules against perpetuities, we have a workable NCP trust.[8] Such a trust may be workable, but it turns a second-best property concept into a third-best, if not least-best, one. In an ideal world, private enforcers would faithfully discharge their duties and keep trustees on a tight leash. But because they do not have a vested interest in the trust fund, what effectively happens is one agent monitors another; and the principal is missing.

Apart from enjoying and receiving trust assets, beneficiaries are also good for something else: they are the world's best enforcers of trusts. In an NCP trust, since the trustee only answers to the enforcer and because the enforcer answers to nobody, nothing can stop the two from conspiring together to defraud the trust—especially if it is a lesser known one.[9] Equally, one can say, nothing stops beneficiaries from conspiring with the trustee to frustrate a

[8] See D. J. Hayton, 'Developing the Obligation Characteristic of the Trust' 117 *LQR* 96 (2001).

[9] See J. E. Penner, *The Law of Trusts* (6th edn. Oxford University Press, Oxford 2008), para 9.27.

settlor's material purpose and prematurely terminate the trust, in violation of the spirit of the *Claflin* rule. The big difference, however, is that beneficiaries are the ultimate and eventual owners of the trust assets. The settlor may be unhappy about such a conspiracy, but at least his intended beneficiaries get to benefit from the trust, albeit prematurely. The same cannot be said about trustees and enforcers, who are never meant to benefit from the trust assets. When it comes to aligning incentives and realizing value, trusts with residual claimants already are second-best compared to property. NCP trusts do not have residual claimants[10] and their proliferation will just lead to more unproductive and wasteful uses of resources.

The Limits of Trustee Duties and Exemption Clauses

If trustee duties—especially those related to care and investments—exist to ensure the trustee will properly and productively manage trust assets, theoretically, should they not all be mandatory and non-waivable? In stark contrast to this notion is the leading case of *Armitage v Nurse*, which held that trustee exemption clauses are valid even if a trustee's breach of trust is caused by the trustee's gross negligence.[11] So long as the trustee's actions or omissions do not involve dishonesty or fraud, he can be excused for any losses. Crucially, Lord Millet said 'there is an irreducible core of obligations owed by the trustees to the beneficiaries and enforceable by them which is fundamental to the concept of a trust. If the beneficiaries have no rights enforceable against the trustees there are no trusts. But I do not accept the further submission that these core obligations include the duties of skill and care, prudence and diligence. The duty of the trustees to perform the trusts honestly and in good faith for the benefit of the beneficiaries is the minimum necessary to give substance to the trusts, but in my opinion it is sufficient'.[12]

Can this be reconciled with the asset-centric nature of trust law espoused in this and the previous chapter? Clearly, the more onerous the trustee's duties are, the more likely trust assets will be well managed. This is so for the simple reason that apart from anything else, the trustee faces significant monetary liabilities. On the other hand, lesser trustee duties will not inevitably lead to

[10] Enforcers only enforce; they have no interest whatsoever in the trust fund or its assets.

[11] [1998] Ch 241. Neither Restatement discussed the validity of a clause exempting gross negligence. Both simply stated that clauses permitting bad faith and wilful default will be struck down. See Restatement (Third) of Trusts §87, Reporter's Note on comment d and Restatement (Second) of Trusts, §222.

[12] [1998] Ch 241, 253–4.

worse management of trust assets. In the normal course of things, if the trustee is protected by a generous exemption clause, he will lack the incentives to perform well.[13] But trust assets will not necessarily be mismanaged if someone else picks up the slack. In cases where settlors and beneficiaries play an active role in the management of trust assets, trustees often ask to be excused from liabilities arising out of the settlors and beneficiaries' own actions. Where settlors and beneficiaries seek some kind of an active role in the management of trust assets, there is good justification to lower the standards required of the trustee. This is so for two reasons: first, when some of a trustee's duties are reallocated to another person, the trustee should not be responsible for the consequences; second, if it is decided that this other person is better able to manage the trust assets, then the law should give effect to this, so long as someone is indeed managing the trust assets.

So common is the desire to de-activate the trustee and let settlors and beneficiaries take an active role that there are two principal responses to trustee duties. The first is the anti-*Bartlett* clause, which is inserted in the trust instrument that nullifies a rather peculiar common law position. A trustee who holds a controlling interest in a company and whose duty is dictated by the unmodified prudent investor rule is required to monitor the conduct of company directors and intervene if necessary.[14] He is also under a duty to exploit the shareholding to maximum financial advantage.[15] Clearly, for a trustee who is holding the company operating a family business, it is too much work to monitor and intervene and it may not be the settlors' and beneficiaries' expectations that the trustee sells the company to the highest bidder, just like any other financial investment. An anti-*Bartlett* clause rightfully exempts a trustee from such duties. What is important to appreciate is that such a clause is appropriate not because it selfishly relieves the trustee of liability, but rather because it is neither the settlor's nor the beneficiaries' intention that the trustee should be under such a duty in the first place.

The second response is the increasingly popular VISTA trusts from the British Virgin Islands (BVI). The VISTA trust is a highly specialized kind of trust that only holds shares in BVI companies and the trustee is exempted from intervening in the management of the underlying company. According to its creators, the VISTA trust removes, rather than circumvents, the

[13] In the face of an all-encompassing exemption clause, the only ways a trustee may be incentivized are: (a) his own conscience and (b) his reputation for integrity and competence.

[14] The court in this case held that the trustee breached its duties when the family company, the shares of which were held by the trustee as its sole trust asset, embarked on an aggressive expansion but suffered significant financial losses. *Bartlett v Barclays Bank Trust Co Ltd* [1980] 1 Ch 515.

[15] C. McKenzie and J. Glasson, 'VISTA Trusts' in J. Glasson and G. Thomas (eds.) *The International Trust* (2nd edn. Jordan, Bristol 2006), para 13.4.

problems arising from the prudent investor rule. It does this by validating the idea that the trustee's foremost duty is to simply hold shares in the underlying company and that he is under no duty to intervene in the company's business operations. While some have questioned whether such trusts are valid beyond their home jurisdiction, it is not only consistent with the principle found in *Armitage v Nurse*, it is better. The trustee of a VISTA trust may have his duties and liabilities substantially reduced, but those duties—or at least the actions required by those duties—are performed by others. If the underlying asset of a VISTA trust is a family business and the business is being managed by the settlor and his family, it would appear that the business and its assets are being put to productive use. This arrangement would fulfil the original intent of trustee duties: to ensure that trust assets are well managed and put to productive use.

So *Armitage v Nurse* on its face is bad law because it allows trustees to not perform essential duties without requiring someone else to pick up the slack; this can only be bad for trust assets and beneficiaries.[16] What is argued here is that trustees should be able to gain exemption from most duties, but only if the settlor or beneficiaries consent to it in action by discharging those duties themselves. Letting beneficiaries and, to some extent, settlors help themselves to trust assets is not as controversial as it seems. Allowing beneficiaries to operate a business held by the trustee is entirely consistent with the idea of letting them—in a limited way—realize their wealth in the trust fund. Their wealth may be temporarily locked up in the trust fund and they cannot sell the business at will, but their participation and influence on how the trust asset—the business—is being managed is significantly greater than that of normal beneficiaries.

The Proper Role of the Settlor: When is a Trust not a Trust?

The controversy surrounding any modern trust is really the settlor's role after settlement. From the previous chapters, it is clear that settlors' excessive retention of powers is frowned upon. But if a settlor's retention of control leads to a very well run trust fund (in terms of putting assets to productive use and aligning the preferences of the settlor with trust investment activities),

[16] If *Armitage v Nurse* is bad law, then the Law Commission's response is pathetic. In its recent report on trustee exemption clauses, it avoided the idea of legislating minimum requirements and simply put forward the idea of trust industry best practices. See Law Commission. *Trustee Exemption Clauses* (Law Commission 301, 2006).

then surely there is a case for the settlor's retention of control? To answer this, one must ask why does the settlor want to retain control in the first place.

In the most benign of cases, a settlor may believe that he has superior asset management skills that he can contribute to the trust. If trust assets can be put to better use and generate more returns with the help of the settlor acting as an investment manager or CEO of the underlying business, then allowing him to play this role is only consistent with what has been said about the asset-centric nature of trust law. The next level is the case where a settlor retains the power to remove and appoint trustees. In principle, there is nothing wrong with a settlor retaining this power because all he is doing is replacing one manager with another. In practice, however, it is through his ability to fire trustees that a settlor wields control over the trust. The understanding is that trustees who perform largely in accordance to the wishes of the settlor (and within the four corners of the trust instrument and letter of wishes) will not get fired and lose their fee income. But this is so subjective and difficult to prove that, in cases involving third parties with powers to remove trustees, the courts rely on the fictitious presumption that whoever is appointed as trustee will act in the best interest of the beneficiaries and will not be influenced by his appointor.[17]

There are also settlors who retain powers to direct the distribution of trust assets. Apart from the outright power to revoke the trust, the power to direct distribution is most closely associated with shams and settlors who have not really parted with their beneficial interests. Why would a settlor want to direct trust distributions? Charitably interpreted, it is because he always intends to part with the beneficial interest in the trust assets but at the time of settlement does not know to whom to convey the interest. If the power to direct distribution was given to an uninterested third party, say the beneficiaries' godfather, there would be no argument about sham trusts or settlor retention of control. As widely understood,[18] it is only when settlors retain the power to direct distribution along with other important powers that he may be deemed not to have settled a trust.

What other powers must the settlor retain to make his trust a non-trust? It is much more acceptable if his power to direct distribution is confined to a fixed and immutable beneficiary class. But if this power is coupled with another one that enables to add and remove individuals from the beneficiary

[17] See *Re Skeats' Settlement* [1889] 42 Ch D 522 and *Schroder v IRC* [1983] STC 480. Similarly, in the United States, the holder of a power to control acts of the trustee is normally considered a fiduciary. See Restatement (Third) of Trusts, §75, comment e.

[18] See generally G. Thomas, 'Shams, Revocable Trusts, and Retention of Control' in J. Glasson and G. Thomas (eds.) *The International Trust* (2nd edn. Jordan, Bristol 2006).

class, then his supposedly narrow power to direct distribution becomes a general power of appointment. This is so because he can effectively add anyone in the world to the class and direct distribution to that person. Equally, if the settlor retains the power to revoke the trust, he crosses the thin red line. Given the validity and recognition of revocable trusts in the United States, why should a settlor's ability to revoke a trust nullify his 'trust'? Because in both cases, where the settlor has the power to revoke and where he has the power to direct distribution (and add anyone to the beneficiary class), there is one thing in common: beneficiaries are fundamentally transformed from residual claimants to mere claimants.

Beneficiaries as a class are residual claimants because no one else has a claim to the trust assets after them. As long as the trust fund is solvent, at least one of the beneficiaries is certain to receive a distribution after the claims of creditors and trustees are satisfied. But the same cannot be said about a revocable trust. Beneficiaries of revocable trusts are exposed to three possible outcomes. The first is that the settlor revokes the trust before any distribution has been made. In this case, the settlor becomes the residual claimant as the trust assets revert back to him as absolute owner. The second possible outcome is that the settlor directs the trustee to make some distributions to the beneficiaries before revoking the trust. Here, the beneficiaries may have received something, but they are mere claimants who do not stand last in line; their position is akin to a corporation's creditors or suppliers during the normal course of business. The third possible outcome is that the settlor never revokes the trust during his lifetime and upon his death the trust becomes irrevocable. In this case, only upon the settlor's death do the beneficiaries become residual claimants and stand last in line. In all three scenarios, beneficiaries cannot at the outset say with certainty that they are or will always be residual claimants. For these reasons, revocable 'trusts' are better considered as testamentary dispositions and not as trusts because beneficiaries cannot safely be said to be residual claimants.

What about a settlor's power to direct distribution and to add people to the beneficiary class? At first sight, it may seem harmless because whoever the settlor directs the trustee to distribute to is a member of the beneficiary class and therefore the class as a whole is still the residual claimant of the trust fund. This view is mistaken. With his power to add anyone—including himself—to the beneficiary class, the settlor is in fact the residual claimant. One day the settlor can add the entire world—less himself—to the beneficiary class; the next day he can then add himself to it and direct distribution to himself. The residual claim idea loses its meaning because either everyone in the world is a member of the beneficiary class, which makes nobody a *residual* claimant; or everyone in the world less the settlor is a member but he pulls the rug from under the beneficiaries by adding himself to the class and distributing to himself.

Therefore, the proper role of the settlor includes dictating the terms of the trust and even participating in aspects of investment and distribution. But he overreaches himself as soon as the beneficiaries as a class can no longer be certain that they hold the residual claim; at this point, a trust purportedly for non-settlor beneficiaries is no longer a trust. This could be a useful analytical tool to distinguish so-called 'trusts' from trusts, but tax law may employ tests of a much lower threshold so to catch even proper trusts that unfortunately exhibit too much settlor influence.[19]

Conclusion

Being grounded in ideas of why trusts exist and what trust law is about, the proprietary account can identify the boundaries of the trust concept and critique modern, detrimental trust developments. Obviously, the position the account takes is not new. NCP and perpetual trusts have many critics, so do laws that grossly exempt trustees from their duties and allow settlors to retain too many powers. The difference is that whereas opponents of these developments disparately attack them in a piecemeal fashion, the proprietary approach critiques them consistently with the same philosophy.

Key to the findings in this chapter is the nature of the beneficiary's interest—wealth in the trust fund in the form of a residual claim. This idea explains to a large extent why there is a difference between tying up assets and tying up wealth and why perpetual trusts may address the former but can do nothing about the latter. Equally, there is no hard and fast rule on when does a settlor overreach himself when he reserves significant powers. The residual claim idea of the beneficial interest can serve as the litmus test: if it cannot be certain that the beneficiaries as a class hold the residual claim, then either the settlor or someone else holds it and the 'trust' is not what it appears to be. Equally, being a trustee requires much more than just having good faith and being nice. Trust law is asset-centric in nature because it ensures that assets are well managed and put to productive use, even when ownership and

[19] The tax laws of the United Kingdom and the United States employ similar anti-avoidance strategies. For example, a decedent's estate is liable to inheritance tax on property previously disposed by him if the disposal came with reservations of enjoyment (so long as the property was not enjoyed to the total exclusion of the decedent) or powers (held by the decedent to designate persons who shall possess or enjoy the property); this is so even if the trustee of a valid trust is now holding the property in question. See Finance Act 1986, s 102 (UK) and Internal Revenue Code § 2036(a) and 2038(a) (US).

control have been separated. Exempting a trustee from duties and liabilities is not a bad thing in itself, but there comes a point—especially if no one else performs those duties—when this separation becomes inefficient and unproductive. The arguments made in this chapter are by no means the end of the debate on the limits of the trust concept. But, hopefully, its main contribution to the debate is to provide a coherent, analytical foundation for understanding trusts as property.

Conclusion

The Relationship Between Property and Trusts

If the purpose of trusts is to extend the function of property, what then is the function of property in trusts? The short and simple answer is that property enables trusts to exist in the first place; no property, no trusts. But there is a lot more to it than the mandatory rule requiring trusts to have trust properties. We must remember that in pre-trust times, society functioned just as well with only property, contracts, and other legal and economic institutions. As the Introduction discussed, trusts came into being under the confluence of testators and land transfers. Therefore, historically speaking, the original purpose of trusts is to extend property's incentivizing function by providing a smarter and more flexible wealth transmission system.

Modern trust law has very little to do with the original purpose of trusts. This is because there is not much scope to improve on the trust's incentivizing functions. As long as trustees are under the immutable duty to perform their duties in good faith and trust law provides recourse against unfaithful ones, it is difficult to strengthen further the settlor's security and expectations. In the same way that post-Blackstonian property theories are no longer interested in securing and reifying the property institution because it is already established, modern trust law and theory are not about establishing or strengthening the trust concept but rather focus on resolving specific trust problems.

In modern times, the key contribution of the trust is that it extends property's coordination function. It is the trust's role in enabling fluctuating interests in a fund of fluctuating assets—at relatively low information processing costs—that makes it a unique legal institution. For sure, some of these functions can indeed be fulfilled by contracts, agencies, and entities. But, ultimately, the trust is a derivative form of property and the beneficial interest is a derivative form of ownership. No matter how default or how anti-agency-costs trust rules are or how much asset-partitioning features trusts have, one cannot escape from the fact that trusts are about property and ownership.

By neglecting the trust asset and the beneficial interest, the various accounts by Langbein, Sitkoff, and HKM are simply ignoring the elephant in the room. It is true that some trustee duties are default in nature and some seek to reduce agency costs. Equally, trusts have some asset-partitioning features that contracts and agencies do not. For these reasons, the various accounts are useful for shedding light on the more interesting perspectives of trusts. But they overreach by claiming that the trust is something it is not. If anything, the unique trust features they studied exist to serve the trust assets and the beneficial interest. Any discussion that does not make reference to the trust assets and the beneficial interest simply misses the point.

What is the implication of failing to see the important role of property in trusts? Put simply, by doing so, one ignores the very thing upon which the trust is based, for the trust is intended to extend property. What the trust essentially does is that it takes property in an asset and temporarily divides up control and ownership rights among different parties. This is a very unnatural act that, without trust law, would probably be struck down as against public policy. Ironically, the law allows and encourages trusts because it mimics and extends the effects of property. In addition, despite the separation of ownership and control, trust assets remain well managed and productively used. Trust law allows and encourages the settling of trusts because, when done properly, it extends the incentivizing and coordinating functions of property. It is hazardous to split up ownership and control rights to an asset without appreciating why it is being done. Any approach that does not appreciate the role of property in trusts risks wandering off the wrong path.

Apart from the rhetoric of individual autonomy and consent, the contractarian, agency costs, and entity accounts have nothing substantive to say when it comes to evaluating perpetual trusts, NCP trusts, trustee exemption clauses, and settlors' retention of substantive powers. This is because they missed the heart of the matter: the trust asset and the beneficial interest. Novel trust developments, which also happen to be popular manifestations of the trust deal syndrome, may appeal to practitioners and end-users in the short term. But, for reasons already explained, the real, long-term risk is that they waste assets and resources as they further misalign incentives and preferences.

This is not a trivial or academic concern. That the Cayman Islands prohibit domestic land from becoming assets in their industry-leading STAR trusts is testament to the uncertainty, if not outright toxicity, of their legislative creation.[1] But most STAR trusts will probably not hold domestic land. Instead they will hold assets—tangible or otherwise—in the

[1] P. Matthews, 'Shooting STAR: the new special trusts regime from the Cayman Islands' 11 *TLI* 67 (1997).

onshore world, where most economic wealth is created. This leads to another interesting problem. The offshore world is effectively creating structured legal products that have harmful effects but these effects are only experienced by assets and wealth in the onshore world.[2] To use Demsetz's terminology, the offshore world is creating a harmful externality—just like the polluters found in law and economics textbooks.

Given the current demand for total transparency in offshore jurisdictions when it comes to fighting tax evasion and terrorism, it is surprising that offshore trust law has been subjected to relatively little scrutiny. Although it is now often mandatory to disclose the true identity of beneficial owners when opening bank accounts or conducting financial transactions, the inherent nature of trusts coupled with offshore novelties make them ideal for concealing true ownership and control. If the history of trusts is any guide, it should not come as a surprise if the offshore trust model eventually comes under attack.

But any attempt to roll back such trusts could, for better or worse, suffer from the same fate as the Statute of Uses. Just as the Statute of Uses failed to kill off uses and instead gave birth to trusts, history could easily repeat itself by legitimizing offshore trusts or even creating something completely new. In this respect, the modern trust is extremely versatile and has an enviable track record of evolution. But, arguably, this is the result of its internal inconsistencies and inherent instability, which have been repeatedly criticized here and elsewhere. Much that conistency and stability are essential attributes of good laws and institutions, perhaps the trust deliberately thrives on being highly unstable and full of contradictions.

[2] J. C. Dobris, 'The Death of the Rule Against Perpetuities, or the RAP Has No Friends: An Essay' 35 *Real Prop., Probate & Trust J.* 601 (2000), 605.

Bibliography

Alchian, Armen A, 'Some Economics of Property Rights', 30 *Il Politico* 816 (1965)

Alchian, Armen A. and Harold Demsetz, 'Production, Information Costs, and Economic Organization', 62 *Am. Econ. Rev.* 777 (1972)

——'The Property Right Paradigm', 33 *J. Econ. Hist.* 16 (1973)

Alexander, Gregory S., 'The Dead Hand and the Law of Trusts in the Nineteenth Century', 37 *Stan. L. Rev.* 1189 (1985)

——'Property as Propriety', 77 *Neb. L. Rev.* 667 (1999)

——'A Cognitive Theory of Fiduciary Relationships', 85 *Cornell L. Rev.* 767 (2000)

Ambrose, Mary, 'Disclosure to Beneficiaries – Whither Confidentiality', *PCB* 236 (2006)

American Law Institute, *Restatement (Second) of Trusts* (American Law Institute Publishers, St Paul 1959)

——*Restatement (Second) of Contracts* (American Law Institute Publishers, St Paul 1979)

——*Restatement (Third) of Trusts* (American Law Institute Publishers, St Paul 2003)

Anderson, Terry L. and Fred S. McChesney (eds.), *Property Rights: Cooperation, Conflict, and Law* (Princeton University Press, Princeton 2003)

Argyres, Nicholas, 'Evidence on the Role of Firm Capabilities in Vertical Integration Decisions', 17 *Strategic Manage. J.* 129 (1996)

Armour, John and Michael J. Whincop, 'The Proprietary Foundations of Corporate Law', Cambridge University Centre for Business Research – Working Paper 299, 2004, <http://papers.ssrn.com/sol3/papers.cfm?abstract_id=665186>, last accessed 7 January 2010

Atkinson, Rob, 'Altruism in Nonprofit Organizations', 31 *B. C. L. Rev.* 502 (1990)

——'Reforming Cy Pres Reform', 44 *Hastings L. J.* 1112 (1993)

——'Obedience as the Foundation of Fiduciary Duty', 34 *J. Corp. L.* 43 (2008)

Austin, R. P, 'Moulding the Content of Fiduciary Duties' in A. J. Oakley (ed.) *Trends in Contemporary Trust Law* (Oxford University Press, Oxford 1996)

Ayotte, Kenneth and Henry Hansmann, 'Legal Entities as Transferable Bundles of Contracts', 2009, <http://www.kernbureau.uva.nl/template/downloadAsset.cfm?objectid=7BA63183-AE57-4DE0-A8EEA2AB9673374E>, last accessed 16 September 2010

Ayres, Ian, *Optional Law: The Structure of Legal Entitlements* (University of Chicago Press, Chicago 2005)

Ayres, Ian and Robert Gertner, 'Filling Gaps in Incomplete Contracts: An Economic Theory of Default Rules', 99 *Yale L. J.* 87 (1989)

Bainbridge, Stephen M., 'Abolishing LLC Veil Piercing', *U. Ill. L. Rev.* 77 (2005)

Baird, Douglas G., Robert H. Gertner, and Randal C. Picker, *Game Theory and the Law* (Harvard University Press, Cambridge 1994)

Baird, Douglas and Thomas Jackson, 'Information, Uncertainty, and the Transfer of Property', 13 *J. Leg. Stud.* 299 (1984)

Bajt, Alexander, 'The Property Rights School: Is Economic Ownership the Missing Link?', 13 *Int'l Rev. L. & Econ.* 85 (1993)

Ballard, Megan J., 'The Shortsightedness of Blind Trusts', 56 *Kan. L. Rev.* 43 (2007)

Baron, Charles Bryan, 'Self-Dealing Trustees and The Exoneration Clause: Can Trustees Ever Profit From Transactions Involving Trust Property?', 72 *St. John's L. Rev.* 43 (1998)

Baron, Jane B., 'The Trust *Res* and Donative Intent', 61 *Tul. L. Rev.* 45 (1986)

Barzel, Yoram, *Economic Analysis of Property Rights* (2nd edn. Cambridge University Press, Cambridge 1997)

Baxendale-Walker, Paul, *Purpose Trusts* (Butterworths, London 1999)

Bell, Abraham and Gideon Parchomovsky, 'A Theory of Property', 90 *Cornell L. Rev.* 531 (2005)

Ben-Ner, Avner, 'A Theory of Nonprofit Organizations', PONPO Working Paper 51, 1982, <http://ponpo.som.yale.edu/paper.php?ArticleID=-1410>, last accessed 15 June 2010

Ben-Shahar, Omri and John A. E. Pottow, 'On the Stickiness of Default Rules', 33 *Fla. St. U. L. Rev.* 651 (2006)

Benson, Bruce L., 'Rent Seeking from a Property Rights Perspective', 51 *Southern Econ. J.* 388 (1984)

Bentham, Jeremy, *The Limits of Jurisprudence Defined* (Columbia University Press, New York 1945)

Bergemann, Dirk and Juuso Valimaki, 'Dynamic Common Agency', 111 *J. Econ. Theory* 23 (2003)

Berle, Adolph A. and Gardiner C. Means, *The Modern Corporation and Private Property* (Macmillan, New York 1933)

Bernheim, B. Douglas and Michael D. Whinston, 'Common Agency', 54 *Econometrica* 923 (1986)

Biancalana, Joseph, 'Medieval Uses' in Richard Helmholz and Reinhard Zimmermann (eds.) *Itinera Fiduciae: Trust and Treuhand in Historical Perspective* (Duncker & Humblot, Berlin 1998)

Bines, Harvey E., 'Modern Portfolio Theory and Investment Management Law: Refinement of Legal Doctrine', 76 *Colum. L. Rev.* 721 (1976)

Birks, Peter, 'The Content of Fiduciary Obligation', 16 *TLI* 34 (2002)

Birks, Peter and Arianna Pretto (eds.), *Breach of Trust* (Hart, Oxford 2002)

Black, Fischer and Myron Scholes, 'The Pricing of Options and Corporate Liabilities', 81 *J. Polit. Economy* 637 (1973)

Blackstone, William, *Commentaries on the Laws of England* (Clarendon Press, Oxford 1765)

Blair, Margaret A. and Lynn A. Stout, 'A Team Production Theory of Corporate Law', 85 *Va. L. Rev.* 247 (1999)

Blumberg, Philip I., *The Multinational Challenge to Corporation Law* (Oxford University Press, Oxford 1993)

Borrie, Gordon, 'Law and Morality in the Market Place', *JBL* 433 (1987)

Brody, Evelyn, 'Agents without Principals: The Economic Convergence of the Nonprofit and For-Profit Organizational Forms', 40 *N. Y. L. Sch. L. Rev.* 457 (1996)

Brownbill, David, 'When is a sham not a sham?', 2 *JITCP* 13 (1993)

——'The Role of Offshore Jurisdictions in the Development of the International Trust', 32 *Vand. J. Transnat'l L.* 953 (1999)

Brudney, Victor, 'Contract and Fiduciary Duty in Corporate Law', 38 *B. C. L. Rev.* 595 (1997)

Buchanan, James M., 'Rent Seeking, Noncompensated Transfers, and Laws of Succession', 26 *J. L. & Econ.* 71 (1983)

Burns, Robert P., 'Blackstone's Theory of the "Absolute" Rights of Property', 54 *U. Cin. L. Rev.* 67 (1985)

Butler, Henry N. and Larry E. Ribstein, 'Opting Out of Fiduciary Duties: A Response to the Anti-Contractarians', 65 *Wash. L. Rev.* 1 (1990)

Butler, Keith L.,'Long Live the Dead Hand: A Case for Repeal of the Rule Against Perpetuities in Washington', 75 *Wash. L. Rev.* 1237 (2000)

Cai, Hongbin, 'A Theory of Joint Asset Ownership', 34 *RAND J. Econ.* 63 (2003)

Calabresi, Guido and A. Douglas Melamed, 'Property Rules, Liability Rules, and Inalienability: One View of the Cathedral', 85 *Harv. L. Rev.* 1089 (1972)

Campbell, Kenneth, 'On the General Nature of Property Rights', 3 *KCLJ* 79 (1992)

Campbell, Rutherford B., Jr, 'Corporate Fiduciary Principles for the Post-Contractarian Era', 23 *Fla. St. U. L. Rev.* 561 (1996)

Chambers, Robert, 'Liability' in Peter Birks and Arianna Pretto (eds.) *Breach of Trust* (Hart, Oxford 2002)

Chambers, Robert, 'Integrating Property and Obigations' in Michael Bryan and Andrew Robertson (eds.) *Law of Obligations: Connections and Boundaries* (UCL, London 2004)

——'Two Kinds of Enrichment' in Robert Chambers, Charles Mitchell,and James Penner (eds.) *Philosophical Foundations of the Law of Unjust Enrichment* (Oxford University Press, Oxford 2009)

Chapman, Bruce, 'Trust, Economic Rationality, and the Corporate Fiduciary Obligation', 43 *U. Toronto L. J.* 547 (1993)

Chesterman, Michael R., 'Family Settlements on Trust: Landowners and the Rising Bourgeoisie' in G. R. Rubin and David Sugarman (eds.) *Law, Economy and Society, 1750–1914: Essays in the History of English Law* (Professional Books, Abingdon 1984)

Cheung, Steven N. S., 'Transaction Costs, Risk Aversion, and the Choice of Contractual Arrangements', 12 *J. L. & Econ.* 23 (1969)

——'The Structure of a Contract and the Theory of a Non-Exclusive Resource', 13 *J. L. & Econ.* 49 (1970)

——'The Transaction Costs Paradigm', 36 *Econ. Enquiry* 514 (1998)

'Choses in Action' in 6(1) *Halsbury's Laws of England* (4th edn. Butterworths, London 2003)

Clark, Robert C., 'Agency Costs Versus Fiduciary Duties' in John W. Pratt and Richard J. Zeckhauser (eds.) *Principals and Agents: The Structure of Business* (Harvard Business School Press, Cambridge 1991)

Coase, Ronald H., 'The Nature of the Firm', 4 *Economica* 386 (1937)

——'The Federal Communications Commission', 2 *J. L. & Econ.* 1 (1959)

——'The Problem of Social Cost', 3 *J. L. & Econ.* 1 (1960)

—— *The Firm, the Market, and the Law* (University of Chicago Press, Chicago 1988)

——'The Conduct of Economics: The Example of Fisher Body and General Motors', 15 *J. Econ. Manage. Strategy* 255 (2006)

Coffee, John C., 'The Rise of Dispersed Ownership: The Roles of Law and the State in the Separation of Ownership and Control', 111 *Yale L. J.* 1 (2001)

Cole, Daniel H. and Peter Z. Grossman, 'The Meaning of Property "Rights:" Law vs. Economics?', 2000, <http://papers.ssrn.com/sol3/papers.cfm?abstract_id=219408>, last accessed 7 January 2010

Coleman, Jules L., 'Efficiency, Utility and Wealth Maximization', 8 *Hofstra L. Rev.*

—— *The Practice of Principle: In Defence of a Pragmatist Approach to Legal Theory* (Oxford University Press, Oxford 2001)

Conner, Kathleen R. and C. K. Prahalad, 'A Resource-Based Theory of the Firm: Knowledge versus Opportunism', 7 *Organization Science* 477 (1996)

'Contracts' in 9(1) *Halsbury's Laws of England* (4th edn. Butterworths, London 1998)

Cook, Walter Wheeler, 'The Powers of Courts of Equity - I', 15 *Colum. L. Rev.* 37 (1915)

——'The Powers of Courts of Equity - II', 15 *Colum. L. Rev.* 106 (1915)

——'The Powers of Courts of Equity - III', 15 *Colum. L. Rev.* 228 (1915)

Cooter, Robert and Bradley J. Freedman, 'The Fiduciary Relationship: Its Economic Character and Legal Consequences', 66 *N. Y. U. L. Rev.* 1045 (1991)

Coricelli, Giorgio, Luis Gonzalez Morales, and Amelie Mahlstedt, 'Trust and Reciprocity under Asymmetric Information', University of Siena, Economics Working Paper No. 367, 2002, <http://papers.ssrn.com/sol3/papers.cfm?abstract_id=366162>, last accessed 7 January 2010

Cotterrell, Roger, 'Trusting In Law: Legal and Moral Concepts of Trust', 46 *Current Legal Problems* 75 (1993)

Council of Economic Advisors, 'Economic Report of the President', 2003, <http://www.gpoaccess.gov/usbudget/fy04/pdf/2003_erp.pdf,> last accessed 15 June 2010

Craswell, Richard, 'On the Uses of "Trust": Comment on Williamson, "Calculativeness, Trust and Economic Organization"', 36 *J. L. & Econ.* 487 (1993)

Curtis, Jerome J., Jr, 'The Transmogrification of the American Trust', 31 *Real Prop., Probate & Trust J.* 251 (1996)

Dagan, Hanoch and Michael A. Heller, 'Conflicts in Property', 2004, <http://papers.ssrn.com/sol3/papers.cfm?abstract_id=556261>, last accessed 24 July 2006

Dagan, Hanoch, 'The Craft of Property', 91 *Cal. L. R.* 1517 (2003)

Dan-Cohen, Meir, 'The Value of Ownership', 9 *J. Polit. Phil.* 404 (2001)

Danforth, Robert T, 'Rethinking the Law of Creditors' Rights in Trusts', 53 *Hastings L. J.* 287 (2002)
Davidson, Nestor M, 'Standardization and Pluralism in Property Law', 61 *Vand. L. Rev.* 1597 (2008)
Davies, J. D.,'Integrity of Trusteeship', 120 *LQR* 1 (2004)
Davies, James B., 'Uncertain Lifetime, Consumption, and Dissaving in Retirement', 89 *J. Polit. Economy* 561 (1981)
Deakin, Simon and Alan Hughes, 'Economics and Company Law Reform: A Fruitful Partnership', 20 *Co Law* 212 (1999)
Delany, Hilary, 'Unconscionability: A Unifying Theme in Equity', *Conv.* 401 (2008)
DeMott, Deborah A, 'Beyond Metaphor: An Analysis of Fiduciary Obligation', *Duke L. J.* 878 (1988)
Demsetz, Harold, 'The Exchange and Enforcement of Property Rights', 7 *J. L. & Econ.* 11 (1964)
——'Some Aspects of Property Rights', 9 *J. L. & Econ.* 61 (1966)
——'Towards a Theory of Property Rights', 57 *Am. Econ. Rev.* 347 (1967)
——'The Structure of Ownership and the Theory of the Firm', 26 *J. L. & Econ.* 375 (1983)
——'The Firm in Economic Theory: A Quiet Revolution', 87 *Am. Econ. Rev.* 426 (1997)
——'Towards a Theory of Property Rights II: The Competition between Private and Collective Ownership', 31 *J. Leg. Stud.* 653 (2002)
Demsetz, Harold and Kenneth Lehn, 'The Structure of Corporate Ownership: Causes and Consequences', 93 *J. Polit. Economy* 1155 (1985)
Depoorter, Ben, Francesco Parisi, and Nobert Schultz, 'Fragmentation in Property: Towards a General Model', 158 *J. Inst. Theoretical Econ.* 594 (2002)
Dewey, John, 'The Historic Background of Corporate Legal Personality', 35 *Yale L. J.* 655 (1925)
Dignam, Alan and John Lowry, *Company Law* (5th edn. Oxford University Press, Oxford 2009)
Dine, Janet, 'Fiduciary Duties as Default Rules, European Influences and the Need for Caution in the Use of Economic Analysis', 20 *Co Law* 190 (1999)
Dixit, Avinash, Gene M. Grossman, and Elhanan Helpman, 'Common Agency and Coordination: General Theory and Application to Government Policy Making', 105 *J. Polit. Economy* 752 (1997)
Dobris, Joel C., 'Changes in the Role and the Form of the Trust at the New Millennium, or, We Don't Have to Think of England Anymore', 62 *Alb. L. Rev.* 543 (1998)
——'Undoing Repeal of the Rule Against Perpetuities: Federal and State Tools for Breaking Dynasty Trusts', 27 *Cardozo L. Rev.* 2537 (2006)
Duckworth, Antony G. D., 'Protectors - Fish or Fowl? Part 1', *PCB* 169 (1996)
——'Protectors - Fish or Fowl? Part 2', *PCB* 245 (1996)
——'Protectors - Fish or Fowl? Part 3', *PCB* 328 (1996)

Duckworth, Antony G. D., 'STAR WARS: The colony strikes back', 12 *TLI* 16 (1998)
——'STAR WARS: Smiting the bull', 13 *TLI* 158 (1999)
Duggan, Anthony J., 'Is Equity Efficient?', 113 *LQR* 601 (1997)
——'Constructive Trusts From a Law and Economics Perspective', 55 *U. Toronto L. J.* 217 (2005)
Dukeminier, Jesse and James E. Krier, 'The Rise of the Perpetual Trust', 50 *UCLA L. Rev.* 1303 (2003)
Dwyer, John P. and Peter S. Menell, 'Reunifying Property', 46 *St. Louis U. L. J.* 599 (2002)
Easterbrook, Frank H. and Daniel R. Fischel, 'The Corporate Contract', 89 *Colum. L. Rev.* 1416 (1989)
—— *The Economic Structure of Corporate Law* (Harvard University Press, Cambridge 1991)
——'Contract and Fiduciary Duty', 36 *J. L. & Econ.* 425 (1993)
Eisenberg, Melvin Aron, 'Donative Promises', 47 *U. Chi. L. Rev.* 1 (1979)
Eleftheriadis, Pavlos, 'The Analysis of Property Rights', 16 *OJLS* 31 (1996)
Elkin-Koren, Niva and Eli M. Salzberger, 'Towards an Economic Theory of Unjust Enrichment Law', 20 *Int'l Rev. L. & Econ.* 551 (2000)
Ellickson, Robert C., 'Property in Land', 102 *Yale L. J.* 1315 (1993)
Ellman, Ira Mark, 'Another Theory of Nonprofit Corporations', 80 *Mich. L. Rev.* 999 (1981)
Emery, Carl, 'Do We Need A Rule Against Perpetuities?', 57 *MLR* 602 (1994)
Epstein, Richard A., 'Notice and Freedom of Contract in the Law of Servitudes', 55 *S. Cal. L. Rev.* 1353 (1982)
——'Past and Future: The Temporal Dimension in the Law of Property', 64 *Wash. U. L. Q.* 667 (1986)
——'Inducement of Breach of Contract as a Problem of Ostensible Ownership', 16 *J. Leg. Stud.* 2 (1987)
——'How to Create-or Destroy-Wealth in Real Property', 58 *Ala. L. Rev.* 741 (2007)
Fama, Eugene F., 'Agency Problems and the Theory of the Firm', 88 *J. Polit. Economy* 288 (1980)
Fama, Eugene F. and Michael C. Jensen, 'Agency Problems and Residual Claims', 26 *J. L. & Econ.* 327 (1983)
'Separation of Ownership and Control', 26 *J. L. & Econ.* 301 (1983)
——'Organizational Forms and Investment Decisions', 14 *J. Finan. Econ.* 101 (1985)
Farber, Daniel A., 'Contract Law and Modern Economic Theory', 78 *Nw. U. L. Rev.* 303 (1983)
Feenstra, Robert, 'Foundations in Continental Law since the 12th Century: The Legal Person Concept and Trust-like Devices' in Richard Helmholz and Reinhard Zimmermann (eds.) *Itinera Fiduciae: Trust and Treuhand in Historical Perspective* (Duncker & Humblot, Berlin 1998)

Financial Services and the Treasury Bureau (Hong Kong), 'Review of the Trustee Ordinance and Related Matters - Consultation Paper', 2009, <http://www.fstb.gov.hk/fsb/ppr/consult/doc/to_review_consultation_e.pdf>, last accessed 15 June 2010

Finn, Paul, 'The Fiduciary Principle' in T. G. Youdan (ed.) *Equity, Fiduciaries and Trusts* (Carswell, Toronto 1989)

Finnegan, Thomas J. and Joseph P. Garner, 'The Separate Account as an Investment Company: Structural Problems of the "Ectoplasmic Theory"', 3 *Conn. L. Rev.* 106 (1970)

Fischel, Daniel and John H. Langbein, 'ERISA's Fundamental Contradiction: The Exclusive Benefit Rule ', 55 *U. Chi. L. Rev.* 1105 (1988)

Fitzgerald, Brian, 'Tracing at Law, the Exchange Product Theory and Ignorance as an Unjust Factor in the Law of Unjust Enrichment', 13 *U Tas LR* 116 (1994)

FitzGibbon, Scott, 'Fiduciary Relationships are Not Contracts', 82 *Marq. L. Rev.* 303 (1999)

Flannigan, Robert, 'The Fiduciary Obligation', 9 *OJLS* 285 (1989)

——'Business Applications of the Express Trust', 36 *Alberta. L. Rev.* 630 (1998)

——'The Economics of Fiduciary Accountability', 32 *Del. J. Corp. L.* 393 (2007)

——'The (Fiduciary) Duty of Fidelity', 124 *LQR* 274 (2008)

Ford, Emma, 'Rights of Creditors against Trustees and Trust Funds', 124 *NLJ* 28 (1997)

Fox, David, 'Overreaching' in Peter Birks and Arianna Pretto (eds.) *Breach of Trust* (Hart, Oxford 2002)

Frankel, Tamar, 'Fiduciary Law', 71 *Cal. L. R.* 795 (1983)

——'The Legal Infrastructure of Markets: The Role of Contract and Property Law', 73 *B. U. L. Rev.* 389 (1993)

——'Fiduciary Duties as Default Rules', 74 *Or. L. Rev.* 1209 (1995)

——'Trusting and Non-Trusting: Comparing Benefits, Cost and Risk', Boston University School of Law Working Paper 99–12, 1999, <http://papers.ssrn.com/sol3/papers.cfm?abstract_id=214588>, last accessed 7 January 2010

——'The Delaware Business Trust Act Failure as the New Corporate Law', 23 *Cardozo L. Rev.* 325 (2002)

——'What Default Rules Teach Us About Corporations; What Understanding Corporations Teaches Us About Default Rules', 33 *Fla. St. U. L. Rev.* 697 (2006)

French, Susan F., 'Perpetual Trusts, Conservation Servitudes, and the Problem of the Future', 27 *Cardozo L. Rev.* 2523 (2006)

Fulda, Carl H. and Walter Pond, 'Tort Liability of Trust Estates', 41 *Colum. L. Rev.* 1332 (1941)

Furubotn, Eirik G. and Svetozar Pejovich, 'Property Rights and Economic Theory: A Survey of Recent Literature', 10 *J. Econ. Lit.* 1137 (1972)

Gallanis, T. P., 'The Future of Future Interests', 60 *Wash. & Lee L. Rev.* 513 (2003)

——'The Trustee's Duty to Inform', 85 *N. C. L. Rev.* 1595 (2007)

Gambetta, Diego, 'Can We Trust Trust?' in Diego Gambetta (ed.) *Trust: Making and Breaking Co-operative Relations* (Basil Blackwell, New York 1988)

Gardner, Simon, *An Introduction to the Law of Trusts* (2nd edn. Clarendon Law Series, Oxford University Press, Oxford 2003)
Garrouste, Pierre and Stephane Saussier, 'Looking for a Theory of the Firm: Future Challenges', 58 *J. Econ. Behav. Organ.* 178 (2005)
Garton, Jonathan, 'Trustee Act 2000', 15 *TLI* 34 (2001)
Gatti, Roberta, 'Family Altruism and Incentives', 107 *Scand. J. Econ.* 67 (2005)
Geis, George S., 'The Space Between Markets and Hierarchies', 95 *Va. L. Rev.* 99 (2009)
Getzler, Joshua (ed.), *Rationalizing Property, Equity and Trusts: Essays in Honour of Edward Burns* (Oxford University Press, Oxford 2003)
——'Am I My Beneficiary's Keeper? Fusion and Loss-Based Fiduciary Remedies' in Simone Degeling and James Edelman (ed.) *Equity in Commercial Law* (Lawbook Co., Sydney 2005)
——'Plural Ownership, Funds, and the Aggregation of Wills', 10 *Theo Inq L* 241 (2009)
Getzler, Joshua and Mike Macnair, 'The Firm as an Entity Before the Companies Act', University of Oxford Faculty of Law Legal Studies Research Paper Series - Working Paper No 47/2006, 2006, <http://papers.ssrn.com/sol3/papers.cfm?abstract_id=941231>, last accessed 7 January 2010
Geus, Arie De, *The Living Company: Habits for Survival in a Turbulent Business Environment* (Harvard Business School Press, Cambridge 2002)
Glasson, John and Geraint W. Thomas (eds.), *The International Trust* (Jordans, Bristol 2006)
Goetz, Charles J. and Robert E. Scott, 'Enforcing Promises: An Examination of the Basis of Contract', 89 *Yale L. J.* 1261 (1980)
——'Principles of Relational Contracting', 67 *Va. L. Rev.* 1089 (1981)
Gordon, Jeffrey N., 'The Puzzling Persistence of the Constrained Prudent Man Rule', 62 *N. Y. U. L. Rev.* 52 (1987)
——'The Mandatory Structure of Corporate Law', 89 *Colum. L. Rev.* 1649 (1989)
Gray, Kevin, 'Equitable property', *Current Legal Problems* 157 Vol 47 (1994)
Grbich, Yuri F, *Selected Problems in Discretionary Trusts* (PhD Thesis, London School of Economics 1971)
Green, Brian, 'Grey, Oughtred and Vandervell – A Contextual Reappraisal', 47 *MLR* 385 (1984)
Gregory, William A, 'The Fiduciary Duty of Care: A Perversion of Words', 38 *Akron L. Rev.* 181 (2005)
Gretton, George L., 'Trust and Patrimony' in Hector L. Macqueen (ed.) *Scots Law into the 21st Century: Essays in Honour of W.A. Wilson* (Sweet and Maxwell, Edinburgh 1996)
——'The Evolution of the Trust in a Semi-Civilian System' in R. H. Helmholz and Reinhard Zimmermann (eds.) *Itinera Fiduciae: Trust and Treuhand in Historical Perspective* (Duncker & Humblot, Berlin 1998)
——'Trusts Without Equity', 49 *ICLQ* 599 (2000)

Grey, Thomas C., 'The Disintegration of Property' in J. Roland Pennock and John W. Chapman (eds.) *Property* (New York University Press, New York 1980)

Grossman, Sanford J. and Oliver D. Hart, 'The Costs and Benefits of Ownership: A Theory of Vertical and Lateral Integration', 94 *J. Polit. Economy* 691 (1986)

Grundmann, Stefan, 'The Evolution of Trust and *Treuhand* in the 20th Century' in Richard Helmholz and Reinhard Zimmermann (eds.) *Itinera Fiduciae: Trust and Treuhand in Historical Perspective* (Duncker & Humblot, Berlin 1998)

Hadfield, Gillian K., 'An Incomplete Contracting Perspective on Fiduciary Duty', 28 *C.B.L.J.* 141 (1997)

The Hague Convention on the Law Applicable to Trusts and on their Recognition 1984

Halbach, Edward C., Jr, 'Standing to Enforce: Renewing and Expanding Professor Gaubatz's 1984 Discussion of Settlor Enforcement', 62 *U. Miami L. Rev.* 713 (2008)

Haliwell, Margaret,. *Equity and Good Conscience in a Contemporary Context* (Old Bailey Press, London 1997)

Hanbury, Harold, 'A Periodical Menace to Equitable Principles', 44 *LQR* 468 (1928)

Hanbury, Harold Greville and Jill Martin, *Hanbury and Martin Modern Equity* (16th edn. Sweet and Maxwell, London 2001)

Hansmann, Henry, 'The Role of Nonprofit Enterprise', 89 *Yale L. J.* 835 (1980)

——'Reforming Nonprofit Corporation Law', 129 *U. Pa. L. Rev.* 498 (1981)

——'What is the Appropriate Structure for Non-Profit Corporation Law? A Response to Ellman', PONPO Working Paper 100, 1985, <http://ponpo.som.yale.edu/paper.php?ArticleID=-1203>, last accessed 7 January 2010

——'Ownership of the Firm', 4 *J. L. Econ. & Org.* 267 (1988)

—— 'Organization of Production in Human Services', PONPO Working Paper 200, 1994, <http://ponpo.som.yale.edu/paper.php?ArticleID=-1314>, last accessed 7 January 2010

Hansmann, Henry and Reinier Kraakman, 'The Essential Role of Organizational Law', 110 *Yale L. J.* 387 (2000)

——'Property, Contract, and Verification: The Numerus Clausus Problem and the Divisibility of Rights', 31 *J. Leg. Stud.* 373 (2002)

Hansmann, Henry and Ugo Mattei, 'The Functions of Trust Law: A Comparative Legal and Economic Analysis', 73 *N. Y. U. L. Rev.* 434 (1998)

——'Trust Law in the United States. A Basic Study of Its Special Contributions', 46 *Am. J. Comp. L.* 133 (1998)

Hansmann, Henry, Reinier Kraakman, and Richard Squire, 'The New Business Entities in Evolutionary Perspective', *U. Ill. L. Rev.* 5 (2005)

——'Law and the Rise of the Firm', 119 *Harv. L. Rev.* 1135 (2006)

Hardin, Garrett, 'The Tragedy of the Commons', 162 *Science* 1243 (1968)

Hardingham, I. J. and R. Baxt, *Discretionary Trusts* (Butterworths, Sydney 1984)

Harpum, Charles, 'Overreaching, Trustee's Powers and the Reform of the 1925 Legislation', 49 *CLJ* 277 (1990)

Harris, David, 'No Such Thing as a Sham Trust?', *PCB* 95 (2004)
Harris, James W., *Property and Justice* (Oxford University Press, Oxford 1996)
Hart, Oliver, 'An Economist's Perspective on the Theory of the Firm', 89 *Colum. L. Rev.* 1757 (1989)
——'Is 'Bounded Rationality' an Important Element of a Theory of Institutions?', 146 *J. Inst. Theoretical Econ.* 696 (1990)
——'An Economist's View of Fiduciary Duty', 43 *U. Toronto L. J.* 299 (1993)
——*Firms, Contracts, and Financial Structure* (Oxford University Press, Oxford 1995)
——'Norms and the Theory of the Firm', 149 *U. Pa. L. Rev.* 1701 (2001)
Hart, Oliver and Sanford J. Grossman, 'Implicit Contracts, Moral Hazard, and Unemployment', 71 *Am. Econ. Rev.* 301 (1981)
Hart, Oliver and John Moore, 'Property Rights and the Nature of the Firm', 98 *J. Polit. Economy* 1119 (1990)
Haskell, Paul G., 'Justifying the Principle of Distributive Deviation in the Law of Trusts', 18 *Hastings L. J.* 267 (1967)
——'The Prudent Person Rule for Trust Investment and Modern Portfolio Theory', 69 *N. C. L. Rev.* 87 (1990)
Hayton, David J., 'Time to overhaul trust laws', 141 *NLJ* 210 (1991)
——'When is a trust not a trust?', 1 *JITCP* 3 (1992)
——'Uncertainty of Subject-Matter of Trusts', 110 *LQR* 335 (1994)
——'Rights of Creditors Against Trustees and Trust Funds', 11 *TLI* 58 (1997)
——'English Fiduciary Standards and Trust Law', 32 *Vand. J. Transnat'l L.* 555 (1999)
——'Exploiting the Inherent Flexibility of Trusts', 7 *JITCP* 69 (1999)
——(ed.), *Modern International Developments in Trust Law* (Kluwer Law International, London 1999)
——'The Development of the Trust Concept in Civil Law Jurisdictions', 8 *J. Int. P.* 159 (2000)
——'Trustee Liability: Exculpations and Indemnities', 8 *J. Int. P.* 71 (2000)
——'Whither Trusts in the Twenty-First Century? Part 1', *PCB* 94 (2000)
——'Whither Trusts in the Twenty-First Century? Part 2', *PCB* 163 (2000)
——'Whither Trusts in the Twenty-First Century? Part 3', *PCB* 244 (2000)
——'Developing the Obligation Characteristic of the Trust', 117 *LQR* 96 (2001)
——(ed.) *Extending the Boundaries of Trusts and Similar Ring-Fenced Funds* (Kluwer Law International, London 2002)
——'Overview' in Peter Birks and Arianna Pretto (eds.) *Breach of Trust* (Hart Publishing, Oxford 2002)
——'Beneficiaries' and Objects' Right To Information', 10 *JITCP* 139 (2003)
——'The Distinctive Characteristics of the Trust in Anglo-Saxon Law', 2003, Copy with Author
——'The Future of the "Trust": An Introductory Overview', 2003, Copy with Author
——*The Law of Trusts* (4th edn. Sweet and Maxwell, London 2003)
——'The Trust Concept', 2003, Copy with Author

——'Unique Rules for the Unique Institution, the Trust' in Simone Degeling and James Edelman (ed.) *Equity in Commercial Law* (Lawbook Co., Sydney 2005)
——'Future Trends in International Trust Planning', 13 *JITCP* 55 (2006)
——'The Trust in European Commercial Life' in J. Lowry and L. Mistelis (eds.) *Commercial Law: Perspectives and Practice* (LexisNexis Butterworths, London 2006)
——'Trading Trusts, Trustee's Liabilities and Creditors' in John Glasson and Geraint Thomas (ed.) *The International Trust* (Jordan, Bristol 2006)
——'Major Trends in the Trust World: Part 1', *PCB* 39 (2007)
——'Major Trends in the Trust World: Part 2', *PCB* 122 (2007)
——'A Review of Current Trust Law Issues', 22 *TLI* 81 (2008)
Hayton, David J., Sebastian C. J. J. Kortmann, and H. L. E. Verhagen (eds.), *Principles of European Trust Law* (Kluwer Law International, The Hague 1999)
Hayton, David J., Paul Matthews, and Charles Mitchell (eds.), *Underhill and Hayton The Law Relating to Trusts and Trustees* (17th edn. LexisNexis Butterworths, London 2006)
Helfman, Tara, 'Land Ownership and the Origins of Fiduciary Duties', 41 *Real Prop., Probate & Trust J.* 651 (2006)
Heller, Michael A., 'The Tragedy of the Anticommons: Property in the Transition From Marx to Markets', 111 *Harv. L. Rev.* 622 (1998)
——'The Boundaries of Private Property', 108 *Yale L. J.* 1164 (1999)
——'Critical Approaches to Property Institutions: Three Faces of Private Property', 79 *Or. L. Rev.* 417 (2000)
——'Three Faces of Private Property', 79 *Or. L. Rev.* 417 (2000)
——'The Dynamic Analytics of Property Law', 2 *Theo Inq L* 79 (2001)
Helmholz, Richard, 'Trusts in the English Ecclesiastical Court 1300–1640' in Richard Helmholz and Reinhard Zimmermann (eds.), *Itinera Fiduciae: Trust and Treuhand in Historical Perspective* (Duncker & Humblot, Berlin 1998)
Helmholz, Richard and Reinhard Zimmermann (eds.), *Itinera Fiduciae: Trust and Treuhand in Historical Perspective* (Duncker & Humblot, Berlin 1998)
Hildebrand, Ira P., 'Liability of the Trustees, Property, and Shareholders of a Massachusetts Trust', 59 *A. L. Rev.* 17 (1925)
Hilliard, Jonathan, 'Re Hastings-Bass: too good to be true?', 16 *TLI* 202 (2002)
——'On the irreducible core content of trusteeship – a reply to Professors Matthews and Parkinson', 17 *TLI* 144 (2003)
—— 'The Rights to Information of an Object of a Fiduciary Mere Power', 10 *JITCP* 209 (2003)
—— 'The Flexibility of Fiduciary Doctrine in Trust Law: How Far Does It Stretch in Practice?', 23 *TLI* 119 (2009)
Hillman, Robert W., 'The Bargain in the Firm: Partnership Law, Corporate Law, and Private Ordering Within Closely-Held Business Associations', *U. Ill. L. Rev.* 171 (2005)
Hirsch, Adam J, 'Bequests for Purposes: A Unified Theory', 56 *Wash. & Lee L. Rev.* 33 (1999)

Hirsch, Adam J, 'Trusts for Purposes: Policy, Ambiguity, and Anomaly in the Uniform Laws', 26 *Fla. St. U. L. Rev.* 913 (1999)

——'Default Rules in Inheritance Law: A Problem in Search of Its Context', 73 *Fordham L. Rev.* 1031 (2004)

Hirsch, Adam J. and William K. S. Wang, 'A Qualitative Theory of the Dead Hand', 68 *Ind. L. J.* 1 (1992)

Hirschman, Albert O., *Exit, Voice, and Loyalty: Responses to Decline in Firms, Organizations, and States* (Harvard University Press, Cambridge 1972)

Ho, Lusina, *Trust Law in China* (Sweet & Maxwell Asia, Hong Kong 2003)

Hohfeld, Wesley Newcomb, 'The Relation Between Law and Equity', 11 *Mich. L. Rev.* 537 (1913)

——'Some Fundamental Legal Conceptions as Applied in Judicial Reasoning', 23 *Yale L. J.* 16 (1913)

——'Fundamental Legal Conceptions as Applied in Judicial Reasoning', 26 *Yale L. J.* 710 (1917)

Holderness, Clifford G., 'A Legal Foundation for Exchange', 14 *J. Leg. Stud.* 321 (1985)

——'Joint Ownership and Inalienability', 23 *Int'l Rev. L. & Econ.* 75 (2003)

Holmes, Jane and Patricia Milner, 'Trust Law Reforms: Are We Nearly There Yet?', *PCB* 114 (2000)

Holmstrom, Bengt, 'The Firm as a Subeconomy', 15 *J. L. Econ. & Org.* 74 (1999)

Honoré, Tony, 'Ownership' in Anthony Guest (ed.) *Oxford Essays in Jurisprudence: First Series* (Clarendon Press, Oxford 1961)

——'Trusts: The Inessentials' in Joshua Getzler (ed.) *Rationalizing Property, Equity and Trusts: Essays in Honour of Edward Burn* (Oxford University Press, Oxford 2003)

——'On Fitting Trusts Into Civil Law Jurisdictions', Oxford Legal Studies Research Paper No. 27/2008, 2008, <http://papers.ssrn.com/sol3/papers.cfm?abstract_id =1270179>, last accessed 7 January 2010

Horton, David, 'Unconscionability in the Law of Trusts', 84 *Notre Dame L. Rev.* 1675 (2009)

Hudson, Alastair *Equity & Trusts* (Cavendish, London 2003)

——(ed.), *New Perspectives on Property Law, Human Rights and the Home* (Cavendish, London 2003)

——(ed.), *New Perspectives on Property Law, Obligations and Restitution* (Cavendish, London 2004)

——'The Regulation of Trustees' in Martin Dixon and Gerwyn Griffiths (eds.) *Contemporary Perspectives on Property, Equity and Trusts law* (Oxford University Press, Oxford 2007)

Hurd, Michael D.,'Mortality Risk and Bequests', 57 *Econometrica* 779 (1989)

Iacobucci, Edward M. and George G. Triantis, 'Economic and Legal Boundaries of Firms', 93 *Va. L. Rev.* 515 (2007)

International Swaps and Derivatives Association, 'ISDA Publishes Year-End 2008 Market Survey Results – Press Release – April 22 2009', (2009)

Ireland, Paddy, 'Property and Contract in Contemporary Corporate Theory', 23 *Legal Studies* 453 (2003)
Jackson, Nicola, 'Overreaching and Unauthorised Disposition of Registered Land', *Conv.* 120 (2007)
——'Overreaching and the Rationale of the Law of Property Act 1925', 15 *Nott. LJ* 1 (2006)
Jaconelli, Joseph, 'Privity: The Trust Exception Examined', *Conv.* 88 (1998)
Jarman, Chris, 'Killing Off Royal Lives', *PCB* 23 (2006)
Jensen, Michael C. and William H. Meckling, 'Theory of the Firm: Managerial Behavior, Agency Costs and Ownership Structure', 3 *J. Finan. Econ.* 305 (1976)
Johnson, Lyman P. Q., 'Corporate Officers and the Business Judgment Rule', 60 *Bus. Law* 439 (2005)
Johnston, Jason Scott, 'Strategic Bargaining and the Economic Theory of Contract Default Rules', 100 *Yale L. J.* 615 (1990)
Jones, Neil, 'Trusts in England after the Statute of Uses: A View from the 16th Century' in Richard Helmholz and Reinhard Zimmermann (eds.) *Itinera Fiduciae: Trust and Treuhand in Historical Perspective* (Duncker & Humblot, Berlin 1998)
——'The Use Upon a Use in Equity Revisited', 33 *Cambrian LR* 67 (2002)
Jones, Sheldon A., Laura M. Moret and James M. Storey, 'The Massachusetts Business Trust and Registered Investment Companies', 13 *Del. J. Corp. L.* 421 (1988)
Kaplow, Louis, 'Rules Versus Standards', 42 *Duke L. J.* 557 (1992)
Kaplow, Louis and Steven Shavell, 'Property Rules versus Liability Rules: An Economic Analysis', 109 *Harv. L. Rev.* 713 (1996)
——'Economic Analysis of Law' in A.J. Auerbach and M. Feldstein (eds.) 3 *Handbook of Public Economics* (Elsevier Science, Amsterdam 1999)
——'Fairness versus Welfare', 114 *Harv. L. Rev.* 961 (2000)
Katz, Robert A., 'Can Principal-Agent Models Help Explain Charitable Gifts and Organizations?', *Wis. L. Rev.* 1 (2000)
Katz, Robert S. and Harvey S. Rosen, *Microeconomics* (3rd (International) edn. McGraw-Hill Education, New York 1997)
Keynes, John Maynard, *A Tract on Monetary Reform* (Macmillan, London 1923)
Klein, Peter G., 'New Institutional Economics', 1998, <http://papers.ssrn.com/sol3/papers.cfm?abstract_id=115811>, last accessed 24 July 2006
Klick, Jonathan and Robert H. Sitkoff, 'Agency Costs, Charitable Trusts, and Corporate Control: Evidence from Hershey's Kiss-Off', 108 *Colum. L. Rev.* 749 (2008)
Klinck, Dennis R., 'The Nebulous Equitable Duty of Conscience', 31 *Q.L.J.* 206 (2005)
Kohler, Paul, 'The Death of Ownership and the Demise of Property', 53 *Current Legal Problems* 237 (2000)
Koltikoff, Laurence J. and Avia Spivak, 'The Family as an Incomplete Annuities Market', 89 *J. Polit. Economy* 372 (1981)
Kornhauser, Lewis A., 'A Guide to the Perplexed Claims of Efficiency in the Law', 8 *Hofstra L. Rev.* 591 (1980)

Kraus, Jody S., 'Transparency and Determinancy in Common Law Adjudication: A Philosophical Defense of Explanatory Economic Analysis', 93 *Va. L. Rev.* 287 (2007)

Kydland, Finn E. and Edward C. Prescott, 'Rules Rather than Discretion: The Inconsistency of Optimal Plans', 85 *J. Polit. Economy* 473 (1977)

Lametti, David, 'The Concept of Property: Relations Through Objects of Social Wealth', 53 *U. Toronto L. J.* 325 (2003)

Landes, William M. and Richard A. Posner, 'Altruism in Law and Economics', 68 *Am. Econ. Rev.* 417 (1978)

—— *The Economic Structure of Intellectual Property Law* (Harvard University Press, Cambridge 2002)

Langbein, John H., 'The Twentieth-Century Revolution in Family Wealth Transmission', 86 *Mich. L. Rev.* 722 (1988)

——'Reversing the Nondelegation Rule of Trust-Investment Law', 59 *Mo. L. Rev.* 105 (1994)

——'The Contractarian Basis of the Law of Trusts', 105 *Yale L. J.* 625 (1995)

——'The Uniform Prudent Investor Act and the Future of Trust Investing', 81 *Iowa L. Rev.* 641 (1996)

——'The Secret Life of the Trust: The Trust as an Instrument of Commerce', 107 *Yale L. J.* 165 (1997)

——'Mandatory Rules in the Law of Trusts', 98 *Nw. U. L. Rev.* 1105 (2004)

——'Questioning the Trust Law Duty of Loyalty: Sole Interest or Best Interest?', 114 *Yale L. J.* 929 (2005)

——'Trust Law as Regulatory Law: The Unum/Provident Scandal and Judicial Review of Benefit Denials under ERISA', 101 *Nw. U. L. Rev.* 1315 (2007)

——'Why Did Trust Law Become Statute Law in the United States?', 58 *Ala. L. Rev.* 1069 (2007)

Langbein, John H. and Richard A. Posner, 'Market Funds and Trust-Investment Law', *American Bar Foundation Research Journal* 1 (1976)

——'Market Funds and Trust-Investment Law II', (1977) *American Bar Foundation Research Journal* 1

——'Social Investing and the Law of Trusts', 79 *Mich. L. Rev.* 72 (1980)

Latham, V., 'The Right of the Beneficiary to Specific Items of the Trust Fund', 32 *Can B.R.* 520 (1954)

Law Commission, *Fiduciary Duties and Regulatory Rules* (Consultation Paper 124, 1992)

Law Commission, *Restitution: Mistakes of Law and Ultra Vires Public Authority Receipts and Payments* (Law Commission 227, 1994)

Law Commission, *Fiduciary Duties and Regulatory Rules* (Law Commission 236, 1995)

Law Commission, *Company Directors: Regulating Conflicts of Interests and Formulating a Statement of Duties* (Law Commission 261, 1999)

Law Commission, *Trustees' Powers and Duties* (Law Commission 260, 1999)

Law Commission, *Trustee Exemption Clauses* (Consultation Paper 171, 2003)

Law Commission, *Capital and Income in Trusts: Classification and Apportionment* (Consultation Paper 175, 2004)
Law Commission, *Trustee Exemption Clauses* (Law Commission 301, 2006)
Lawson, F. H. and Bernard Rudden, *The Law of Property* (Clarendon Law Series, Oxford University Press, Oxford 2002)
Legair, Issac N., 'Modern Portfolio Theory: a primer', 14 *TLI* 75 (2000)
Lepaulle, Pierre, 'Civil Law Substitutes for Trusts', 36 *Yale L. J.* 1126 (1927)
——'An Outsider's View Point of the Nature of Trusts', 14 *C.L.Q.* 52 (1929)
—— *Traité Théorique et Pratique des Trusts en Droit Interne, en Droit Fiscal et en Droit International* (Rousseau & Cie, Paris 1932)
——'Book Review', 4 *Revue Internationale de Droit Comparé* 377 (1952)
——'Reflexions sur l'expansion des trusts', 7 *Revue Internationale de Droit Comparé* 318 (1955)
——'The Strange Destiny of Trusts' in Erwin N. Griswold and Arthur E. Sutherland Roscoe Pound (ed.) *Perspectives of Law – Essays for Austin Wakeman Scott* (Little, Brown and Company, Boston 1964)
Leslie, Melanie B., 'In Defense of the No Further Inquiry Rule: A Response to Professor Langbein', 47 *Wm. & Mary L. Rev.* 541 (2005)
——'Trusting Trustees: Fiduciary Duties and the Limits of Default Rules', 94 *Geo. L. J.* 67 (2005)
Levmore, Saul, 'Two Stories About the Evolution of Property Rights', 31 *J. Leg. Stud.* 421 (2002)
Levmore, Saul, 'Uncorporations and the Delaware Strategy', *U. Ill. L. Rev.* 195 (2005)
Levy, Jennifer E., 'Idaho's Noncharitable Purpose Trust Statute: Leaping Over Age-Old Trust Laws in a Single Bound', 44 *Idaho L. Rev.* 801 (2008)
Lueck, Dean, 'Yoram Barzel and the New Institutional Economics', 2005, <http://papers.ssrn.com/sol3/papers.cfm?abstract_id=744224>, last accessed 7 January 2010
Lupoi, Maurizio, *Trusts: A Comparative Study* (Cambridge University Press, Cambridge 2000)
——'Trust and Confidence', 125 *LQR* 253 (2009)
Luxton, Peter, 'Variation of Trusts: Settlors' Intentions and the Consent Principle in *Saunders v Vautier*', 60 *MLR* 719 (1997)
Lyons, Timothy and Richard Frimston, 'The Contemporary Usufruct', *PCB* 33 (2009)
Macnair, Michael, 'The Conceptual Basis of Trusts in the Later 17th and Early 18th Centuries' in Richard Helmholz and Reinhard Zimmermann (eds.) *Itinera Fiduciae: Trust and Treuhand in Historical Perspective* (Duncker & Humblot, Berlin 1998)
Madison, Michael, 'The Real Properties of Contract Law', 82 *B. U. L. Rev.* 405 (2002)
Mahoney, Paul G., 'Mandatory Disclosure as a Solution to Agency Problems', 62 *U. Chi. L. Rev.* 1047 (1995)

Mahoney, Paul G., 'Contract or Concession? An Essay on the History of Corporate Law', 34 *Ga. L. Rev.* 874 (2000)

Maitland, Frederic W., *The Collected Papers of Frederic William Maitland* (Cambridge University Press, Cambridge 1911)

——'Trust and Corporation' in H.A.L. Fisher (ed.) *The Collected Papers of Frederic William Maitland* (Cambridge University Press, Cambridge 1911)

——*Equity: a course of lectures* (2nd edn. Cambridge University Press, London 1936)

Manne, Geoffrey A., 'Agency Costs and the Oversight of Charitable Organizations', *Wis. L. Rev.* 227 (1999)

Manne, Henry G. 'Our Two Corporation Systems: Law and Economics', 53 *Va. L. Rev.* 259 (1967)

Martimort, David and Lars Stole, 'The Revelation and Delegation Principles in Common Agency Games', 70 *Econometrica* 1659 (2002)

Martimort, David, 'Exclusive Dealing, Common Agency, and Multiprincipals Incentive Theory', 27 *RAND J. Econ.* 1 (1996)

Martin, Jill E, *Hanbury & Martin: Modern Equity* (17th edn. Sweet & Maxwell, London 2005)

Mason, Anthony, 'Equity's Role in the Twentieth Century', 8 *KCLJ* 1 (1997)

Matthews, Paul, 'The Efficacy of Trustee Exemption Clauses in English Law', 53 *Conv.* 42 (1989)

——'Protectors: two cases, twenty questions', 9 *TLI* 108 (1995)

——'The New Trust: Obligations without Rights' in A. J. Oakley (ed.) *Trends in Contemporary Trust Law* (Oxford University Press, Oxford 1996)

——'Shooting STAR: the new special trusts regime from the Cayman Islands', 11 *TLI* 67 (1997)

——'STAR WARS: Big Bang or Red Dwarf?', 12 *TLI* 98 (1998)

——'Untitled', 13 *TLI* 168 (1999)

——'Trustee exoneration clauses and comparative law', 14 *TLI* 103 (2000)

——'From Obligations to Property, and Back Again? The Future of the Non-Charitable Purpose Trust' in David J. Hayton (ed.) *Extending the Boundaries of Trusts and Similar Ring-Fenced Funds* (Kluwer Law International, London 2002)

——'All About Bare Trusts: Part 1', *PCB* 266 (2005)

——'All About Bare Trusts: Part 2', *PCB* 336 (2005)

——'The Comparative Importance of the Rule in *Saunders v Vautier*', 122 *LQR* 266 (2006)

——'The Doctrine of Fraud on a Power: Part 1', *PCB* 131 (2007)

——'The Doctrine of Fraud on a Power: Part 2', *PCB* 191 (2007)

——'The Sham Trust Argument, and How to Avoid It', 21 *TLI* 191 (2007)

McAdams, Richard H, 'Signaling Discount Rates: Law, Norms, and Economic Methodology', 110 *Yale L. J.* 625 (2000)

McChesney, Fred S., 'What'd I Say?: Coase, Demsetz and the Unending Externality Debate', Northwestern University School of Law, Law & Economics Research

Paper Series, Research Paper No. 04–01, 2004, <http://papers.ssrn.com/sol3/papers.cfm?abstract_id=491182>, last accessed 7 January 2010

McCormack, Gerard, 'Debts and Non-Assignment Clauses', *JBL* 422 (2000)

McKendrick, Ewan (ed.), *Commercial Aspects of Trusts and Fiduciary Obligations* (Clarendon, Oxford 1992)

McKenzie, Christopher and John Glasson, 'VISTA Trusts' in John Glasson and Geraint Thomas (eds.) *The International Trust* (2nd edn. Jordan, Bristol 2006)

McKenzie, Christopher, 'Having and Eating the Cake: A Global Survey of Settlor Reserved Power Trusts: Part 1', *PCB* 336 (2007)

——'Having and Eating the Cake: A Global Survey of Settlor Reserved Power Trusts: Part 2', *PCB* 428 (2007)

Meek, Alison, 'Reducing the "Irreducible Core of Obligations"', 9 *Trusts & Estates Law Journal* 16 (1999)

Menell, Peter S. and John P. Dwyer, 'Reunifying Property', 46 *St. Louis U. L. J.* 599 (2002)

Merges, Robert P., 'A Transactional View of Property Rights', 20 *Berkeley Tech. L. J.* 1477 (2005)

Merrill, Thomas W., 'Property Rules, Liability Rules, and Adverse Possession', 79 *Nw. U. L. Rev.* 1122 (1985)

——'Time, Property Rights, and the Common Law', 64 *Wash. U. L. Q.* 661 (1986)

——'Wealth and Property', 38 *UCLA L. Rev.* 489 (1990)

——'Property and the Right to Exclude', 77 *Neb. L. Rev.* 730 (1998)

——'Introduction: The Demsetz Thesis and The Evolution of Property Rights', 31 *J. Leg. Stud.* 331 (2002)

Merrill, Thomas W. and Henry E. Smith, 'Optimal Standardization in the Law of Property: The Numerus Clausus Principle', 110 *Yale L. J.* 1 (2000)

——'The Property/Contract Interface', 101 *Colum. L. Rev.* 773 (2001)

——'What Happened to Property in Law and Economics?', 111 *Yale L. J.* 357 (2001)

Meurer, Michael J., 'Law, Economics, and the Theory of the Firm', 52 *Buff. L. Rev.* 727 (2004)

Milgrom, Paul and John Roberts, *Economics, Organization, and Management* (Prentice Hall, Englewood Cliffs 1992)

Milhaupt, Curtis J., 'Property Rights in Firms', 84 *Va. L. Rev.* 1145 (1998)

Millett, Peter J., 'Equity's Place in the Law of Commerce', 114 *LQR* 214 (1998)

Mossoff, Adam, 'What Is Property? Putting The Pieces Back Together', 45 *Ariz. L. Rev.* 371 (2003)

Nelson, J. Alan, 'The Prudent Person Rule: A Shield for the Professional Trustee', 45 *Baylor L. Rev.* 933 (1993)

Newman, Alan, 'The Intention of the Settlor Under the Uniform Trust Code: Whose Property is It, Anyway?', 38 *Akron L. Rev.* 649 (2005)

—— 'Spendthrift and Discretionary Trusts: Alive and Well Under the Uniform Trust Code', 40 *Real Prop., Probate & Trust J.* 567 (2005)

Nolan, Richard, 'Property in a Fund', 120 *LQR* 108 (2004)

——'Equitable Property', 122 *LQR* 232 (2006)

Nolan, Richard, 'Understanding the Limits of Equitable Property', 1 *J. Eq.* 18 (2006)

Norman, A. W., *A digest of the death duties: with numerous examples illustrating their incidence, a copious index, and an appendix of the Customs and Inland Revenue Acts, 1880, 1881, 1888, 1889, the Mortmain and Charitable Uses Acts, 1888, 1891, and the Intestates' Estates Act, 1890* (W. Clowes, London 1892)

North, Douglass C., *Institutions, Institutional Change and Economic Performance* (Political Economy of Institutions and Decisions, Cambridge University Press, Cambridge 1990)

Noseda, Filippo, 'Switzerland's Consultation Paper on Hague Trust Convention: Benefits and Missed Opportunities of the Current Proposals', 19 *TLI* 37 (2005)

——'The Trusts (Guernsey) Law 2007 and Other Modern Trust Laws: A Civilian Perspective', 22 *TLI* 117 (2008)

——'The International Foundation Scene in Trepidation – Opportunities and Pitfalls for Newcomers', *PCB* 109 (2009)

Nussbaum, Arthur, 'Sociological and Comparative Aspects of the Trust', 38 *Colum. L. Rev.* 408 (1938)

O'Hagan, Patrick and Alec Anderson, 'Purpose Trusts and Charitable Trusts in Securitisation and Other Structured Finance Transactions' in David J. Hayton (ed.) *Extending the Boundaries of Trusts and Similar Ring-Fenced Funds* (Kluwer Law International, London 2002)

Oakley, A. J., 'Towards A Law of Trusts for the Twenty-First Century', 60 *Conv.* 401 (1996)

Ogus, A. I., 'The Trust as Governance Structure', 36 *U. Toronto L. J.* 186 (1986)

Oliphant, Ken, 'Book Review', 62 *MLR* 320 (1999)

Oosterhoff, A.H., 'Indemnification of Trustees: The Rule in *Hardoon v. Belilios*', 4 *Estates and Trusts Quarterly* 180 (1977)

Otsuka, Keijiro, Hiroyuki Chuma, and Yujiro Hayami. 'Land and Labor Contracts in Agrarian Economies: Theories and Facts', 30 *J. Econ. Lit.* 1965 (1992)

Papandreou, Andreas, 'Externality, Convexity and Institutions', FEEM Working Paper No. 48.00, 2000, <http://papers.ssrn.com/sol3/papers.cfm?abstract_id=235469>, last accessed 7 January 2010

Parkinson, Patrick, 'Chaos in the Law of Trusts', 13 *Syd LR* 227 (1991)

——'Reconceptualising the Express Trust', 61 *CLJ* 657 (2002)

Pawlowski, Mark and Jo Summers, 'Private Purpose Trusts – A Reform Proposal', *Conv.* 440 (2007)

Penner, James E., 'The "Bundle of Rights" Picture of Property', 43 *UCLA L. Rev.* 711 (1996)

——*The Idea of Property in Law* (Oxford University Press, Oxford 1997)

——'Book Review', 14 *TLI* 118 (2000)

——'Exemptions' in Peter Birks and Arianna Pretto (eds.) *Breach of Trust* (Hart, Oxford 2002)

——'The Common Law Controversy over the Nature of the Trust', 2005, Copy with Author

——'Duty and Liability in Respect of Funds' in J. Lowry and L. Mistelis (eds.) *Commercial Law: Perspectives and Practice* (LexisNexis Butterworths, London 2006)

——'Misled by Property', 18 *Can. J. Law & Jur.* 75 (2005)

——'Ownership, Co-ownership, and the Justification of Property Rights' in Timothy Endicott, Joshua Getzler, and Edwin Peel (eds.) *Properties of Law: Essays in Honour of Jim Harris* (Oxford University Press, Oxford 2005)

——(Personal Email Correspondence. 19 July 2006)

—— *The Law of Trusts* (6th edn. Oxford University Press, Oxford 2008)

——(Personal Email Correspondence. 17 September 2009)

——'Value, Property, and Unjust Enrichment: Trusts of Traceable Proceeds' in Robert Chambers, Charles Mitchell, and James Penner (eds.) *Philosophical Foundations of the Law of Unjust Enrichment* (Oxford University Press, Oxford 2009)

——'Property, Community, and the Problem of Distributive Justice', 10 *Theo Inq L* 194 (2009)

Perell, Paul M., 'Covenants as Contracts and as Interests in Land', 29 *Advocates' Quarterly* 476 (2005)

Pettit, Philip H., *Equity and the Law of Trusts* (Butterworths, London 2001)

Polinsky, A. Mitchell, 'Economic Analysis as a Potentially Defective Product: A Buyer's Guide to Posner's Economic Analysis of Law', 87 *Harv. L. Rev.* 1655 (1974)

Posner, Eric A., 'Altruism, Status, and Trust in the Law of Gifts and Gratuitous Promises', *Wis. L. Rev.* 567 (1997)

——'Agency Models in Law and Economics' in Eric A. Posner (ed.) *Chicago Lectures in Law and Economics* (Foundation Press, New York 2000)

——(ed.), *Chicago Lectures in Law and Economics* (Foundation Press, New York 2000)

——*Law and Social Norms* (Harvard University Press, Cambridge 2000)

Posner, Richard A., 'Gratuitous Promises in Economics and Law', 6 *J. Leg. Stud.* 411 (1977)

——'The Ethical and Political Basis of the Efficiency Norm in Common Law Adjudication', 8 *Hofstra L. Rev.* 487 (1980)

——'A Reply to Some Recent Criticisms of the Efficiency Theory of the Common Law', 9 *Hofstra L. Rev.* 775 (1981)

——*Economic Analysis of Law* (6th edn. Aspen Publishers, New York 2003)

Pound, Roscoe, *Jurisprudence* (West Publishing, St. Paul 1959)

Prat, Andrea and Aldo Rustichini, 'Games Played Through Agents', 71 *Econometrica* 989 (2003)

Qu, Charles Zhen, 'The Doctrinal Basis of the Trust Principles in China's Trust Law', 38 *Real Prop., Probate & Trust J.* 345 (2003)

Quint, Francesca, 'The Perpetuities and Accumulations Bill: Clarity or Confusion', *PCB* 126 (2009)

Radin, Max, 'The Endless Problem of Corporate Personality', 32 *Colum. L. Rev.* 643 (1932)

Radner, Roy, 'Bounded Rationality, Indeterminacy, and the Theory of the Firm', 106 *Econ. J.* 1360 (1996)

Rasmusen, Eric, 'Moral Hazard in Risk-Averse Teams', 18 *RAND J. Econ.* 324 (1987)

——'A Theory of Trustees, and Other Thoughts', Indiana University - Center for Econometric Model Research - 98–007, 1998, <http://papers.ssrn.com/sol3/papers.cfm?abstract_id=84388>, last accessed 7 January 2010

Reed, Edward, 'Trustee Exemption Clauses: The Law Commission Pronounces', *PCB* 196 (2007)

Reich, Charles A., 'The New Property', 73 *Yale L. J.* 733 (1964)

Reichman, Uriel, 'Towards a Unified Concept of Servitudes', 55 *S. Cal. L. Rev.* 1180 (1982)

Reid, Kenneth G., 'Patrimony Not Equity: The Trust in Scotland', 8 *E.R.P.L.* 427 (2000)

Ribstein, Larry E., 'Fiduciary Duty Contracts in Unincorporated Firms', 54 *Wash. & Lee L. Rev.* 537 (1997)

——'Law v. Trust', 81 *B. U. L. Rev.* 553 (2001)

——'The Structure of the Fiduciary Relationship', U Illinois Law & Economics Research Paper No. LE03–003, 2003, <http://preprodpapers.ssrn.com/sol3/papers.cfm?abstract_id=397641&rec=1&srcabs=401680>, last accessed 7 January 2010

——'Why Corporations?', 1 *Berkeley Bus. L. J.* 1 (2004)

——'Are Partners Fiduciaries?', *U. Ill. L. Rev.* 209 (2005)

——'Introduction to the "Uncorporation"', *U. Ill. L. Rev.* 1 (2005)

Rickett, Charles, 'Old and New in the Law of Tracing' in Simone Degeling and James Edelman. (ed.) *Equity in Commercial Law* (Lawbook Co., Sydney 2005)

Rizzo, Mario J., 'The Mirage of Efficiency', 8 *Hofstra L. Rev.* 641 (1980)

Robinson, Glen O., 'Personal Property Servitudes', 71 *U. Chi. L. Rev.* 1449 (2004)

Rock, Edward B., 'Saints and Sinners: How Does Delaware Corporate Law Work?', 44 *UCLA L. Rev.* 1009 (1997)

Rock, Edward B. and Michael Wachter, 'Dangerous Liaisons: Corporate Law, Trust Law, and Interdoctrinal Legal Transplants', 96 *Nw. U. L. Rev.* 651 (2002)

Romans, J. T., 'Moral Suasion as an Instrument of Economic Policy', 56 *Am. Econ. Rev.* 1220 (1966)

Rose-Ackerman, Susan, 'Altruisms, Nonprofits, and Economic Theory', 34 *J. Econ. Lit.* 701 (1996)

Rose, Carol M., 'The Shadow of the Cathedral', 106 *Yale L. J.* 2175 (1997)

——'Canons of Property Talk, or, Blackstone's Anxiety', 108 *Yale L. J.* 601 (1998)

——'Servitudes', Arizona Legal Studies – Discussion Paper No.09–13, 2009, <http://ssrn.com/abstract=1371251>, last accessed 7 January 2010

Rosin, Gary S., 'The Entity-Aggregate Dispute: Conceptualism and Functionalism in Partnership Law', 42 *Ark. L. Rev.* 395 (1989)

Rubin, G. R. and David Sugarman (eds.), *Law, Economy and Society, 1750–1914 Essays in the History of English Law* (Professional Books, Abingdon 1984)

Rudden, Bernard, 'Book Review', 44 *MLR* 610 (1981)

——'Things as Thing and Things as Wealth', 14 *OJLS* 81 (1994)
Ryan, K. W., 'The Reception of the Trust', 10 *ICLQ* 265 (1961)
Samet, Irit, 'Guarding the Fiduciary's Conscience – A Justification of a Stringent Profit-Stripping Rule', 28 *OJLS* 763 (2008)
Scallen, Eileen A., 'Promises Broken vs. Promises Betrayed: Metaphor, Analogy, and the New Fiduciary Principle', *U. Ill. L. Rev.* 897 (1993)
Schenkel, Kent D., 'Trust Law and the Title-Split: A Beneficial Perspective', 78 *UMKC L. Rev.* 181 (2009)
Schmitz, Patrick W., 'The Coase Theorem, Private Information, and the Benefits of Not Assigning Property Rights', 11 *Eur. J. L. & Econ.* 23 (2001)
Schonfeld, Victoria E. and Thomas M. J. Kerwin, 'Organization of a Mutual Fund', 49 *Bus. Law* 107 (1993)
Schwarcz, Steven L., 'Commercial Trusts as Business Organizations: An Invitation to Comparatists', 13 *Duke J. Comp. & Int'l L.* 321 (2003)
——'Commercial Trusts as Business Organizations: Unraveling the Mystery', 58 *Bus. Law* 559 (2003)
Schwartz, Alan and Robert E. Scott, 'The Political Economy of Private Legislatures', 143 *U. Pa. L. Rev.* 595 (1995)
——'Contract Theory and the Limits of Contract Law', 113 *Yale L. J.* 541 (2003)
Scott, Austin W., 'Liabilities Incurred in the Administration of Trusts', 28 *Harv. L. Rev.* 725 (1915)
——'The Nature of the Rights of the Cestui Que Trust', 17 *Colum. L. Rev.* 269 (1917)
——'Book Review', 31 *Yale L. J.* 455 (1922)
Scott, Elizabeth S. and Robert E. Scott, 'Marriage as Relational Contract', 84 *Va. L. Rev.* 1225 (1998)
Scottish Law Commission, *Discussion Paper 138 – Liability of Trustees to Third Parties* (2008)
Sealy, L.S., 'Fiduciary Relationships', 20 *CLJ* 69 (1962)
Sears, John H., *Trust Estates as Business Companies* (Vernon Law Book Company, Kansas City 1921)
Shavell, Steven, 'An Economic Analysis of Altruism and Deferred Gifts', 20 *J. Leg. Stud.* 401 (1991)
——'Economic Analysis of Property Law', Harvard Law and Economics Discussion Paper No. 399, 2002, <http://papers.ssrn.com/sol3/papers.cfm?abstract_id=370029>, last accessed 7 January 2010
——'Law versus Morality as Regulators of Conduct', 4 *Am. L. Econ. Rev.* 227 (2002)
Shepherd, J.C., 'Towards a Unified Concept of Fiduciary Relationships', 97 *LQR* 51 (1981)
Sheridan, Lionel A. and George W. Keeton, *Law of Trusts* (Rose, Chichester 1983)
Sicilian, Paul and Paul Thorsnes, 'A Property-Rights Approach for Unifying the Teaching of Externalities, Moral Hazard, and Market Power', 2004, <http://

papers.ssrn.com/sol3/papers.cfm?abstract_id=610724>, last accessed 7 January 2010

Siegel, Stephen A.,'John Chipman Gray, Legal Formalism, and the Transformation of Perpetuities Law', 36 *U. Miami L. Rev.* 439 (1982)

Sin, Kam Fan, *The Legal Nature of the Unit Trust* (Clarendon, Oxford 1997)

Sitkoff, Robert H.,'Trust Law, Corporate Law, and Capital Market Efficiency', 28 *J. Corp. L.* 565 (2003)

——'An Agency Costs Theory of Trust Law', 89 *Cornell L. Rev.* 621 (2004)

——'The Lurking Rule Against Accumulation of Income', 100 *Nw. U. L. Rev.* 501 (2006)

Sitkoff, Robert H. and Max Schanzenbach, 'Jurisdictional Competition for Trust Funds: An Empirical Analysis of Perpetuities and Taxes', 115 *Yale L. J.* 356 (2005)

Skeel, David A., 'Shaming in Corporate Law', 149 *U. Pa. L. Rev.* 1811 (2001)

Smith, Adam, *Lectures on Jurisprudence* (Clarendon Press, Oxford 1978)

Smith, Bryant, 'Legal Personality', 37 *Yale L. J.* 283 (1928)

Smith, D. Gordon, 'The Critical Resource Theory of Fiduciary Duty', 55 *Vand. L. Rev.* 1399 (2002)

Smith, Henry E., 'Exclusion Versus Governance: Two Strategies for Delineating Property Rights', 31 *J. Leg. Stud.* 453 (2002)

——'The Language of Property: Form, Context and Audience', 55 *Stan. L. Rev.* 1105 (2003)

——'Exclusion and Property Rules in the Law of Nuisance', 90 *Va. L. Rev.* 965 (2004)

——'Property and Property Rules', 79 *N. Y. U. L. Rev.* 1719 (2004)

——'Intellectual Property as Property: Delineating Entitlements in Information', 116 *Yale L. J.* 1742 (2007)

——'Mind the Gap: The Indirect Relation between Ends and Means in American Property Law', 94 *Cornell L. Rev.* 959 (2009)

Smith, J. C., 'Stealing Tickets', *Crim. LR* 723 (1998)

Smith, Lionel, 'Transfers' in Peter Birks and Arianna Pretto (eds.) *Breach of Trust* (Hart, Oxford 2002)

——'Philosophical Foundations of Proprietary Remedies' in Robert Chambers, Charles Mitchell, and James Penner (eds.) *Philosophical Foundations of the Law of Unjust Enrichment* (Oxford University Press, Oxford 2009)

Smith, Stephen A., *Contract Theory* (Oxford University Press, Oxford 2004)

Society of Trust and Estate Practitioners, 'STEP Survey 2004', 2004, Copy with Author

Stake, Jeffrey E., 'Darwin, Donations, and the Illusion of Dead Hand Control', 64 *Tul. L. Rev.* 705 (1990)

Stebbings, Chantal, *The Private Trustee in Victorian England* (Cambridge Studies in English Legal History, Cambridge University Press, New York 2001)

Sterk, Stewart E., 'Jurisdictional Competition to Abolish the Rule Against Perpetuities: R.I.P. for the R.A.P.', 24 *Cardozo L. Rev.* 2097 (2003)

Stevens, John, 'Vindicating the Proprietary Nature of Tracing', *Conv.* 94 (2001)

Stevens, Robert S., 'Limited Liability in Business Trusts', 7 *C.L.Q.* 116 (1921)

Stigler, George J., 'The Law and Economics of Public Policy: A Plea to the Scholars', 1 *J. Leg. Stud.* 12 (1972)

Stone, Harlan F., 'The Nature of the Rights of the Cestui Que Trust', 17 *Colum. L. Rev.* 467 (1917)

——'A Theory of Liability of Trust Estates for the Contracts and Torts of the Trustee', 22 *Colum. L. Rev.* 527 (1922)

Stout, Lynn A., 'On the Nature of Corporations', *U. Ill. L. Rev.* 253 (2005)

Strotz, R. H., 'Myopia and Inconsistency in Dynamic Utility Maximization', 23 *Rev. Econ. Stud.* 165 (1956)

Sturges, Wesley A., 'Unincorporated Associations as Parties to Actions', 33 *Yale L. J.* 383 (1924)

Sugarman, David and G. R. Rubin, 'Towards a New History of Law and Material Society in England 1750–1914' in G. R. Rubin and David Sugarman (eds.) *Law, Economy and Society, 1750–1914: Essays in the History of English Law* (Professional Books Abingdon 1984)

Sunstein, Cass R. and others, *Behavioral Law and Economics* (Cambridge University Press, Cambridge 2000)

Swadling, William, 'Property and Conscience', 12 *TLI* 228 (1998)

Swiss Government, 'Arrêté fédéral portant approbation de la Convention de La Haye relative à loi applicable au trust et à sa reconnaissance', 2004, <http://www.bj.admin.ch/etc/medialib/data/wirtschaft/gesetzgebung/trust.Par.0008.File.tmp/vn-ber-f.pdf>, last accessed 15 June 2010

Tepper, Rubin, 'Liability of the Trust Estate Arising Out of Trustee's Contracts with Third Persons', 2 *Hastings L. J.* 53 (1950)

Tettenborn, Andrew, 'Trusts of Unassignable Agreements', *LMCLQ* 498 (1998)

Tey, Tsun Hang, 'Trust Enforcer', 23 *TLI* 151 (2009)

Tham, Chee Ho, 'Trust, not Contract: Restoring Trust in the Contracts (Rights of Third Parties) Act', 21 *JCL* 107 (2005)

Thomas, Geraint, 'Shams, Revocable Trusts, and Retention of Control' in John Glasson and Geraint Thomas (eds.) *The International Trust* (2nd edn. Jordan, Bristol 2006)

Thompson, Robert, 'Agency Law and Asset Partitioning', Vanderbilt University Law School Law and Economics – Working Paper 03–11, 2003, <http://papers.ssrn.com/sol3/papers.cfm?abstract_id=429620>, last accessed 7 January 2010

Tjio, Hans, 'Lending to a Trust', 19 *TLI* 75 (2005)

Triantis, George G., 'Organizations As Internal Capital Markets: The Legal Boundaries of Firms, Collateral, and Trusts in Commercial and Charitable Enterprises', 117 *Harv. L. Rev.* 1102 (2004)

Trukhtanov, Alexander, 'The Irreducible Core of Trust Obligations', 123 *LQR* 342 (2007)

Trust Law Committee, 'Rights of Creditors Against Trustees and Trust Funds – Consultation Paper', 1997, <http://www.kcl.ac.uk/content/1/c6/01/11/89/RightsofCreditorsConsultationPaperApril1997.pdf>, last accessed 15 June 2010

——'Rights of Creditors Against Trustees and Trust Funds – Report', 1999, <http://www.kcl.ac.uk/content/1/c6/01/11/90/TLCCredRightsReport140499_1.pdf>, last accessed 15 June 2010

'Trusts' in 48 *Halsbury's Laws of England* (4th edn. Butterworths, London 2000)

Tullock, Gordon, 'Inheritance Justified', 14 *J. L. & Econ.* 465 (1971)

Turnbull, Shann, 'Should Ownership Last Forever?', 27 *J. Socio-Econ.* 341 (1998)

United States Uniform Statutory Trust Entity Act (Tentative Draft, 2009)

United States Uniform Trust Code (2005)

Vandevelde, Kenneth J., 'The New Property of the Nineteenth Century: The Development of the Modern Concept of Property', 29 *Buff. L. Rev.* 325 (1980)

Wadham, James (ed.), *Willoughby's Misplaced Trust* (2nd edn. Gostick Hall, London 2002)

Waldron, Jeremy, 'What is Private Property?', 5 *OJLS* 313 (1985)

Warburton, A. Joseph, 'Commercial Trusts Versus Corporations: Evidence from the British Mutual Fund Industry', 2009, <http://papers.ssrn.com/sol3/papers.cfm?abstract_id=1290722>, last accessed 7 January 2010

Warnock-Smith, Shan and Morven McMillan, 'One Strike and You Are Out: The Validity of No-Contest Clauses', *PCB* 23 (2008)

Waters, Donovan, 'The Nature of the Trust Beneficiary's Interest', 45 *Can B.R.* 219 (1967)

——'The Future of the Trust Part I', 13 *JITCP* 179 (2006)

——'The Future of the Trust Part II', 14 *JITCP* 1 (2007)

——'Property Management Concepts and The Entity Trust in the Common Law Setting', 14 *JITCP* 73 (2007)

——'The Trust: Continual Evolution of a Centuries-Old Idea', 14 *JITCP* 207 (2007)

——'The Trust in a Changed and Yet Changing World', 15 *JITCP* 205 (2008)

Watkin, Thomas Glyn, 'Changing Concepts of Ownership in English Law During the Nineteenth and Twentieth Centuries' in Martin Dixon and Gerwyn Ll. H. Griffiths (ed.) *Contemporary Perspectives on Property, Equity and Trusts law* (Oxford University Press, Oxford 2007)

Watt, Gary, 'Relational Theory and the Trust Concept', 3 *Nott. LJ* 56 (1995)

——'Unconscionability in Property Law: A Fairy-Tale Ending?' in Martin Dixon and Gerwyn Ll. H. Griffiths (ed.) *Contemporary Perspectives on Property, Equity and Trusts Law* (Oxford University Press, Oxford 2007)

Weber, Pauline, 'Separation of Ownership and Control in an Economic Experiment', 7 *J. Behavioral Econ.* 1 (1978)

Weinrib, Ernest J., 'The Fiduciary Obligation', 25 *U. Toronto L. J.* 1 (1975)

Weir, Tony, *Economic Torts* (Clarendon Press, Oxford 1997)

Wendel, Peter T., 'The Evolution of the Law of Trustee's Powers and Third Party Liability for Participating in a Breach of Trust: An Economic Analysis', 35 *Seton Hall L. Rev.* 971 (2005)

Wessman, Mark B., 'Should We Fire the Gatekeeper? An Examination of the Doctrine of Consideration', 48 *U. Miami L. Rev.* 45 (1993)

Wiedenbeck, Peter J., 'Missouri's Repeal of the Claflin Doctrine-New View of the Policy Against Perpetuities?', 50 *Mo. L. Rev.* 805 (1985)

Williams, Joan, 'The Rhetoric of Property', 83 *Iowa L. Rev.* 277 (1998)

Williamson, Oliver E., 'The Vertical Integration of Production: Market Failure Considerations', 61 *Am. Econ. Rev.* 112 (1971)

——*Markets and Hierarchies: Analysis and Antitrust Implications* (Free Press, New York 1975)

——'The Modern Corporation: Origin, Evolution, Attributes', 19 *J. Econ. Lit.* 1537 (1981)

——*The Economic Institutions of Capitalism: Firms, Markets, Relational Contracting* (Free Press, New York 1985)

——'Calculated Trust, A Reply to Craswell's Comment on Williamson', 36 *J. L. & Econ.* 501 (1993)

——'Calculativeness, Trust and Economic Organization', 36 *J. L. & Econ.* 453 (1993)

——'The New Institutional Economics: Taking Stock, Looking Ahead', 38 *J. Econ. Lit.* 595 (2000)

——'Why Law, Economics, and Organization?', UC Berkeley School of Law – Public Law and Legal Theory – Working Paper No. 37, 2000, <http://papers.ssrn.com/sol3/papers.cfm?abstract_id=255624>, last accessed 7 January 2010

Worthington, Sarah, 'The Commercial Utility of the Trust Vehicle' in David J. Hayton (ed.) *Extending the Boundaries of Trusts and Similar Ring Fenced Funds* (Kluwer, New York 2002)

——*Equity* (Clarendon Law Series, Oxford University Press, Oxford 2003)

——'The Disappearing Divide Between Property and Obligation: The Impact of Aligning Legal Analysis and Commerical Expectation' in Simone Degeling and James Edelman (eds.) *Equity in Commercial Law* (Lawbook Co., Sydney 2005)

Young, Dennis R., 'Incentives and the Nonprofit Sector', PONPO Working Paper 53, 1982, <http://ponpo.som.yale.edu/paper.php?ArticleID=-1412>, last accessed 7 January 2010

Index

The manufacturer's authorised representative in the EU for product
safety is Oxford University Press España S.A. of El Parque Empresarial
San Fernando de Henares, Avenida de Castilla, 2 - 28830 Madrid
(www.oup.es/en or product.safety@oup.com). OUP España S.A. also acts
as importer into Spain of products made by the manufacturer.
Printed and bound by CPI Group (UK) Ltd, Croydon, CR0 4YY
14/09/2026
02216304-0019